Hannah Khalil: Plays of Arabic Heritage

Plan D
Scenes from 73* Years
A Negotiation
A Museum in Baghdad
Last of the Pearl Fishers
Hakawatis

Edited and with an introduction by
CHRIS WHITE
and a foreword by Alia Alzougbi

methuen | drama
LONDON · NEW YORK · OXFORD · NEW DELHI · SYDNEY

METHUEN DRAMA
Bloomsbury Publishing Plc
50 Bedford Square, London, WC1B 3DP, UK
1385 Broadway, New York, NY 10018, USA
29 Earlsfort Terrace, Dublin 2, Ireland

BLOOMSBURY, METHUEN DRAMA and the Methuen Drama logo are trademarks of
Bloomsbury Publishing Plc

This collection first published in Great Britain 2022

Introduction copyright © Chris White, 2022

Foreword copyright © Alia Alzougbi, 2022

Plan D first published by Methuen Drama 2022
Copyright © Hannah Khalil, 2022

Scenes From 73 Years* first published by Methuen Drama 2016
Copyright © Hannah Khalil, 2016, 2022

A Negotiation first published by Methuen Drama 2022
Copyright © Hannah Khalil, 2022

A Museum in Baghdad first published by Methuen Drama 2019
Copyright © Hannah Khalil, 2019, 2022

Last of the Pearl Fishers first published by Methuen Drama 2022
Copyright © Hannah Khalil, 2022

Hakawatis first published by Methuen Drama 2022
Copyright © Hannah Khalil, 2022

Hannah Khalil has asserted her right under the Copyright, Designs and Patents Act, 1988,
to be identified as author of this work.

For legal purposes the Acknowledgements on pp. x–xi constitute an extension of this copyright page.

Cover design: Rebecca Heselton
Cover images from *L'elephant et le singe de Jupiter* by Willy Aractingi

All rights reserved. No part of this publication may be reproduced or transmitted in any form or
by any means, electronic or mechanical, including photocopying, recording, or any information
storage or retrieval system, without prior permission in writing from the publishers.

Bloomsbury Publishing Plc does not have any control over, or responsibility for, any third-party
websites referred to or in this book. All internet addresses given in this book were correct at the time
of going to press. The author and publisher regret any inconvenience caused if addresses have
changed or sites have ceased to exist, but can accept no responsibility for any such changes.

No rights in incidental music or songs contained in the work are hereby granted and performance
rights for any performance/presentation whatsoever must be obtained from the
respective copyright owners.

All rights whatsoever in these plays are strictly reserved and application for performance etc.
should be made before rehearsals begin to Curtis Brown Group Ltd
(Haymarket House, 28–29 Haymarket, London SW1Y 4SP).

No performance may be given unless a licence has been obtained. No performance may be given
unless a licence has been obtained.

A catalogue record for this book is available from the British Library.

A catalog record for this book is available from the Library of Congress.

ISBN: PB: 978-1-3502-4219-7
ePDF: 978-1-3502-4220-3
eBook: 978-1-3502-4221-0

Series: Modern Plays

Typeset by RefineCatch Limited, Bungay, Suffolk
Printed and bound in Great Britain

To find out more about our authors and books visit www.bloomsbury.com
and sign up for our newsletters.

Hannah Khalil: Plays of Arabic Heritage

Hannah Khalil's stage plays include *A Museum in Baghdad* (Royal Shakespeare Company) which marked the first play by a woman of Arab heritage on a main stage at the RSC, *The Censor Or How to Put on A Political Play without Getting Arrested* (Central School of Speech and Drama, London), *Interference* (National Theatre of Scotland) and the critically acclaimed *Scenes from 68* Year*s – shortlisted for the James Tait Black Award (Arcola Theatre, London, 2016). *Scenes* has also been mounted in San Francisco by Golden Thread Productions and in Tunisia as *Trouf* in a British Council supported production. Further work includes *The Scar Test* (Soho Theatre, London), *Bitterenders* (Golden Thread Productions) and *Plan D* (Tristan Bates Theatre, Meyer Whitworth Award nominee).

In 2020, Hannah adapted four Greek myths as part of *Myths and Adventures from Ancient Greece* which were rendered as cardboard cut-out puppets online for Waterman Arts. She also adapted Ovid's *Penelope* as part of *15Heroines* at the Jermyn Street Theatre. Her children's plays *Mrs Scrooge* and *Not the Gingerbread Man* were hosted by Fly High Stories online.

Hannah's radio plays include *The Unwelcome*, *Last of the Pearl Fishers* and *The Deportation Room* all for BBC Radio 4. Her first short film *The Record* took the Tommy Vine screenplay award and premiered at the Palestinian Film Festival in London in November 2019.

Hannah was the Bush Theatre's writer on attachment in 2016/17 as part of Project 2036. With Hassan Abdulrazzak she is a founder member and Artistic Associate of Manara Theatre, whose mission is to champion the work of Arab writers. Her awards include the Arab British Centre's Award for Culture in 2017 and she was a contributing artist to their London's Theatre of the East exhibition at Dr Johnson's House in 2019. She was Heimbold Chair for Villanova University, Philadelphia in 2021 and has been named a Creative Fellow of the Samuel Beckett Archive, Reading University for 2021/22.

For all those juggling and struggling with different identities and narratives. If we keep talking and walking along this path together we may – in the end – find home.

Contents

Foreword *Alia Alzougbi* viii
Acknowledgements x
Introduction *Chris White* xii

Plan D 1

Scenes From 73* Years 59

A Negotiation 117

A Museum in Baghdad 129

Last of the Pearl Fishers 197

Hakawatis: The Women of the Arabian Nights 229

Foreword
Alia Alzougbi

On a rare occasion a script lands in your inbox that isn't like anything you have seen before. Here are voices that speak with unusual authenticity, voices that sound like uncle and friend. Here is a piece with a pace and a rhythm of its own, unbound and irreverent to what has come before and to how things are 'done'. A dialogue so light it skips off the page and through an actor's lips. And this same script slams injustice and inequality onto the table with palpable force. It is a script that has legs and a mind of its own. It runs and takes you with it.

I first came across Hannah's work in 2013 when I read *Bitterenders* for an event I was organising. Hannah had pierced through the large-scale catastrophe of the Nakba to extract the story of a family determined to stay put even as their home is moments from being demolished by an Israeli tank. I had never before encountered a version of this tragic historical event told through dark humour, whilst simultaneously maintaining its gravity and the dignity of those who had endured it. The night we staged it, the reaction of the audience confirmed that there was an appetite for some of our most preciously held stories to be told differently.

In 2014, I was delighted to be invited to perform in a rehearsed reading of an early draft of *Scenes from 66* Years* at the Arcola Theatre. Our joy as a company of Arab actors as we filled the stage was palpable. Together we read this script that spoke to us first-hand, our lines twisting, tumbling and transitioning from the comical to the tragic to the absurd, every one of us coming into our own through Hannah's vignettes, because these were stories we were familiar with on a cellular level.

I went on to produce this play, as *Scenes From 68* Years* at the Arcola Theatre. I could not have been more proud to see my womenfolk perform in ways that I know them, hear them, and live with them. These were my mother, my sisters and my aunties, not the abstracted caricatures I grew accustomed to encountering in theatre-in-the-English-language, so often pieced together from sensationalist news items and orientalist fantasies. There was a pride also of seeing my menfolk drawn truthfully with their own complexities, frailties and inherited masculinities, written into life through the fingertips of a woman from the region for a change.

Hannah carries in her bones a dying tradition from the Arab world – a kind of storytelling passed down across generations through maternal lines. And while she is telling stories based on contemporary events, there is no question that she speaks with the same tongue as our maternal ancestors. In between her lines are the very same subversions – the uncertainty over quite where the power lies; the humour that turns an unbearably oppressive situation into a comedic encounter (a real-life skill many of us ordinary citizens of the Arab world have mastered as a survival tool); the anger and resistance that fizzes through the cracks of this very same humour; and the intricate web of ally-ship between women, running through her scripts like underground tunnels rife with resistance, rebellion and outright provocation.

Collaborating with Hannah itself feels like an act of rebellion, be it as a performer, producer or audience member. Every time, it feels as if we are wildly at play as we scheme to re-tell our version of the world. At once fiercely critical and incisively humane, getting under the skin of her work is an indescribably delicious pleasure. Hannah is not only keeping the spirits of our grandmothers alive, she is writing their worlds for the next generations.

Acknowledgements

I'm big on thank yous. Cards. Flowers. But the thought of thank yous for this anthology terrifies me slightly. The plays in this collection span my writing career and as such there are so many people to thank – people who have helped me on the long road to an anthology, to a writing career. I'm going to do my best. I'll start with individuals to whom I am very grateful: Hanna Slättne as one of the first people to really take my work seriously when she brought me to Tinderbox Theatre in Belfast to workshop *Plan D*, she went on to play a really important dramaturgical role in the development of *A Museum in Baghdad*. Michelle Normanly raised vital funds to ensure it was possible to stage *Plan D* and has been an enduring supporter of my work; and two actresses: Houda Echouafni and Taghrid Choucair-Vizoso have inspired me over the years and brought my work mesmerizingly to life time and again. I must also thank Eyal Sivan for his brilliant Towards a Common Archive project which inspired me to write *Plan D*; Lebanese writer Hanan al-Shaykh whose generosity and support gave me confidence at the start of my career; Iraqi playwright Hassan Abdulrazzak whose kindness and support has always given me confidence; my wonderful agent Jess Cooper who is always there with an ear, sage advice and a glass of fizz when I need it most; Liz Hyder for sharing this journey, producer Mary Peate who is the reason I have had any plays produced on radio at all – and who guided an enthusiastic but inexperienced radio writer every step of the way; and my friend and collaborator Alia Alzougbi who decided *Scenes* needed a production and made it look very easy. It wasn't. In addition I am thankful for David Greig's generosity in sharing his expertise with a fellow writer; also Pippa Hill's championing of my play *A Museum in Baghdad* and Erica Whyman's insightful, gorgeous direction that led to the realisation of my dream to have a play at the RSC. Then there's Michelle Terry at the Globe who commissioned *Hakawatis* on the basis of two chats, I floated down the South Bank after that meeting.

There are also many organisations I owe a debt to: The Arab British Centre in Gough Square was an important discovery when I came to London: to find a place that spoke to my mixed heritage at a time when nowhere else did was so reassuring. I use the library and attend many events, one of which directly influenced the creation and development of *A Museum in Baghdad*. Also the Palestinian Society at SOAS which organised an event that served as the inspiration for *Plan D*. Elsewhere Arts Canteen through its founder Aser El Saqqa and Mosaic Rooms have always provided space for me to present readings of my work and supported me in myriad ways. I must also thank Golden Thread Productions' Torange Yeghiazarian and Evren Odcikin for championing my work on the other side of the world in San Francisco.

Then there are the generous souls who have lent me rooms by the sea to write in, namely Anwen Hooson, Matt Charman, Claire Cox and Tom Vaughan-Lawlor. Also all the trusting people who have told me stories over the years and not minded me magpie-ing them for my plays. And, of course, to the team at Methuen for publishing this anthology.

Finally, the people who live with me day in and out: my family. My Mum for believing in me and declaring pride at every little thing, inspiring me through her tenacity and kindness. My Dad for always fascinating me with stories of Palestine, and my brother for sharing the memories. My wonderful in-laws Margaret and Ian who have supported me in every possible way, always giving, never expecting in return. And of course my two soul mates, my husband Chris and my daughter Muna. Although not into double digits at the time of writing Muna has already offered me a great deal of wise advice on my writing and is an excellent maker of scrambled eggs.

I hope everyone I have mentioned here, and everyone I haven't, knows how much I appreciate them and I hope they and you enjoy reading the fruits of many years labour and collaboration in these pages.

Hannah Khalil

Introduction
Chris White

It's hard to be what you cannot see and tricky too to write Arab stories as a young Irish-Palestinian woman growing up in the UK when you are more likely to encounter an alien than an Arab woman on screen. These plays of Arabic heritage respond to that void, born of resistance as well as research, personal and cultural memory, and a vivid imagination. Hannah's writing is instinctive not theoretical. Just like her process, it differs from play to play, but is marked by a curiosity, willingness to change and shift, a desire to refute easy classification. As her mentor Hanan al-Shaykh says, 'each play is a different tune'. These plays abound with kindness and magnanimity, featuring characters who act not according to self-interest, but in the desire to help others; to find kinship or belonging, out of belief in something beyond themselves. They are articulations of hope and purpose; in the act of remembering, of speaking out, of not giving in, of telling stories and forging bonds.

Her relationship to her Arab heritage is neither fixed nor singular and finds many means of expression here. The plays in this anthology were written over the period of about a decade and vary in form, tone, time and place. *Plan D* is about a family facing a crisis, inspired by testimonies given by Palestinian refugees recalling their displacement in 1948, but the play is set in no specific time or place. *Scenes From 73* Years* is a darkly comic panoramic depiction of the lives lived by upwards of thirty characters in Palestine in the years since 1948. *Last of the Pearl Fishers* is a radio play with an Englishwoman at its centre, set in contemporary Dubai, whilst *A Negotiation* is a monologue by an unnamed woman at the site of a threatened antiquity. *A Museum in Baghdad* is set exclusively in one space but stretches across eighty years of history and beyond, and *Hakawatis* draws on an ancient story to create an original tale in an imagined time and space.

The plays speak to each other and we hope you enjoy bouncing between them, for each play was in some respects a response or reaction to what had come before, steered by a determination not to be confined by one form or subject matter.

Two years after 9/11, as the War on Terror was just beginning, when the predominant representation of Arab characters on stage and screen was in the role of terrorist or victim, Hannah wrote her first full-length play, *Leaving Home*. It is a domestic drama in which an (Irish) woman is presented with a plane ticket by her (Arab) husband and told to go home. Home isn't there any longer though, but it isn't here either. There are no grand geo-political points being made, and not a terrorist in sight, just a family in jeopardy, caught between where they have been and where to go now. This duality, of being in and from more than one place, would become one of the dominant seams that would run through her work from then until now. A subsequent play, *Stolen or Strayed*, fused her mum's lifetime working as a geriatric nurse and her own unlikely stint teaching maths to a young member of the House of Saud to tell the story of a woman with dementia reliving her memories of nursing an Arab prince. In these early plays, Arab characters are present but not at the centre of the experience. That changed entirely with the imaginative leap she took in writing *Plan D*, which dramatises events undergone by previous generations of her family in Palestine.

In *Plan D*, there is an echo of Ibsen in the threat of a woman's secret being exposed by an unexpected arrival, and a subtle inversion of Maurice Maeterlinck's *Someone is Going to Come*; rather than peering out from their windows, here the family are compelled to keep watch upon their own home from afar. The play has folkier roots, too. All of her previous plays had involved a character telling a story or fairy tale to another character – a legacy of every childhood summer spent in rural Ireland – whereas with *Plan D* the play itself assumes the quality of a fairy tale or fable. The crater caused by an explosion on the family's land is 'like a giant's footprint' and there's even an occasion of a granny meeting a wolf in the woods; only this granny gets the better of the wolf. *Plan D* takes its title from the military operation implemented by the Israeli army that was instrumental in the creation of the State of Israel, but otherwise the play eschews any specifics of language or stage directions that squarely locate it there, or then. At the time of writing, in 2008, Hannah was conscious that a UK audience watching the play would arrive with their pre-existing opinions about Israel/Palestine guided largely through a media lens, and that this would impede their connection to the direct human experience of the characters in question. There is something primal in the way it taps into a series of universal questions: What would you do if you felt threatened in your own home? At what point would you leave? Where would you go? What would you take with you and what would you lose by leaving?

Hannah talks further about the immediate inspiration for *Plan D* in her introduction – which you'll find for each of the plays herein – and it also emerged from a burgeoning interest in her own heritage. Around this time she also absorbed the prose of Mourid Barghouti and the photography of Rula Halawani, whose dual evocation of place and places no longer there can be glimpsed in her own work, and the short stories of Ghassan Kanafani, whose charged use of metaphor left a lasting impression on her. Plenty of playwrights have influenced her too, from Winsome Pinnock to Zinnie Harris, but above all the plays in this anthology have been informed by a spirit of openness and years of theatre-going. Two early reference points were Heather Raffo's *Nine Parts of Desire* for its depiction of the subtle activism of Arab women in a variety of domestic spheres, and Tom Stoppard's *Coast of Utopia*. The scale and boldness with which it traversed time would later find expression in her own *A Museum in Baghdad*, a play with a foot in two centuries that took ten years to write. Several years after repeated viewings of his trilogy, she woke up Sir Tom at 6.30am on a Eurostar pulling into Brussels and offered him a piece of homemade cake. It is exactly this openness and ease in talking to people which has helped yield so many stories, which often find their way into her work. After dinner with close friends one night, during which they confided some family shenanigans, she drew them in close and assured: 'I just want you to know, I will be using this in a play one day'. As Akila says in *Hakawatis*, 'we are magpies of literature, gatherers of meaning, magicians of text. And most of all we are thieves'. It is people that most inspire her plays, and one of her gifts lies in honouring their generosity in sharing stories by creating supple, striking characters.

Scenes From 73* Years is just such a magpie of a play: shining stories from different nests lifted and lovingly woven together with the care and dexterity of a reed warbler. It's a bardic play that finds room for as many people as it can muster. Written briskly in the direct aftermath of the production of *Plan D*, it first had a public reading in 2010 at the wonderful Mosaic Rooms Gallery in London, but it would be six years before it became a full production. Part of the reason for this is that she encountered the same reservations from prospective producers: 'but whose story is it?', 'there are too many characters in it', 'it's not balanced enough', 'it would benefit from a clearer beginning, middle and end'. She has long attested that there is little point in UK theatre's soliciting 'diverse' voices unless they are open to diverse forms of telling those stories. Luckily she held her nerve and did it her way. *Scenes From 73* Years* is an inventive response to Samuel Beckett's dictum that it is the job of the artist 'to find a form that accommodates the mess'. Its subject again is Palestine, no longer receded as in *Plan D*, but now in clear view from multiple perspectives across a plethora of dates between 1948 and 2016, the year of the first production. Every scene contributes to a unique patchwork; many have roots in the lived experience of Palestinians, passed on to Hannah by oral storytelling. These range from her friend Haitham telling her about protestors in his hometown of Bil'in dressing up as the blue characters from Avatar to draw attention to their cause; to a musician friend relating a trip to Jerusalem while on tour with the West-Eastern Divan Orchestra and having the courage to knock on the front door of what once was his family home.

This lattice of stories builds to a final scene which, as the stage directions indicate, takes place in '2002 and now'. It is a great example of how Hannah realises a quality of liveness in her work, making her indubitably a theatre writer above all else. It is an occasion of collective storytelling, a yearly ritual that is as raw and real as it is theatrical; the one day a year that Israeli law permits Palestinians to return to the places that were once their villages, in order to 'retain every sight, smell and detail of our home'. The oldest member of the community recalls the events of 1948 and it is incumbent upon the youngest speaking member of the community to repeat as closely as possible what they have heard 'so we know you remember – so you don't forget – so you can tell everyone'. It is this activism and belief in storytelling above all else that the play propounds. Like all the best plays, as soon as it finishes it continues to ripple.

Separation underpins both *Plan D* and *Scenes From 73* Years* on an epic scale, and in *Last of the Pearl Fishers*, it is also one of the starting points, now explored from a new angle. Celeste is a Filipina maid, working in Dubai for an ex-pat English couple, distanced from her children in Manila. Written in 2013, it is possibly telling that this is the first play in this anthology that Hannah wrote after becoming a mother. Justice is the motivating dramatic principle. A place Hannah has known as a child and adult, Dubai itself is so present as to function like a character in the play, 'Pearls. Oil. Money breeds money'. When Celeste vanishes, her 'owner' Lily, who considers herself a friend, is wracked with concern and determined to find her, but her conscience and instinctive concern come into conflict with the acquisitional culture she is privileged to live within: 'you must report it to the police, pay the fine and get another one'.

In *A Negotiation*, a young woman feels compelled to embark on a quest too, but here she knows exactly why and where she must go. A short monologue, written while Hannah was redrafting *A Museum in Baghdad*, it is informed by her research and thinking on the history, nature and purpose of museums. Like the cylinder seal in the story, it is a rare and beautiful miniature. The character springs to life through her need to speak rather than any biographical information yielded to us. She exists urgently in the present, while tugging at the past and committing to a future. In some respects she is like the younger self of Ghalia from *A Museum in Baghdad*. *A Negotiation* is also inflected with personal experience. 'No cheeks pinched. No hair gently tugged. No one *sees* me' speaks to Hannah's recollections of life in England as a young girl having moved from the Middle East. 'I know my skin is pale but we're the same – I'm from here' resonates with the all-too-frequent snipes she has encountered as an adult about where she is 'really from'. The questions the play explores, of where artefacts belong; if, when and how they should be returned to their source of origin, are developed on a larger canvas in the next play in this collection, *A Museum in Baghdad*, a play with deep roots and some killer lines.

Just as precious objects lead contested lives and have disputed origins and destinations, so too this play has no single source. Perhaps the earliest seed lies in a visit to The Museum of Cairo in 2005, where the accessibility of the displays and light curatorial imprint confounded expectations formed since teenage years by trips to European museums. Everything in this museum originated in the country where it had been found and where the museum itself stood – a far cry from the British Museum. She was also extremely taken by an Ancient Egyptian practice whereby people tried to stimulate certain dreams to resolve issues in their waking lives with the help of a Dream Guide. It was believed these trained dreamers could cross time and space, and perhaps this laid the path for her creation of Abu Zaman, 'a character who straddles time and space, trying to affect the future'. Hannah elaborates on further key influences in her Introduction, and what has been fascinating to observe over the ten years she has been writing it is how it has acquired new ones. The British Museum's Babylon exhibition in 2013 prompted new ideas as to how the play could address the consequences of the US-led invasion, and in 2015 the destruction of objects and people in Palmyra had an emotional and artistic impact upon her. Khaled al-Asaad, Head of Antiquities in the ancient city, who sacrificed his life in the attempt to preserve antiquities, is paid homage to in the text: 'I was born in this city and I will die in this city'.

The play acknowledges that heritage is political and explores this through two overlapping time periods: 1926 when Gertrude Bell was trying to open the inaugural Museum of Iraq in Baghdad, and 2006 when the Iraqi team are trying to re-open post looting and the 2003 invasion. When the two are brought together, as Hannah says, 'we see the layers of history refracted'. Along with 'Then' and 'Now', there is also a third time period, 'Later', which encourages us to become complicit with Abu Zaman's question, 'what if you could change the future?' while simultaneously contemplating his lament, 'what's the point in seeing the future if no one will listen to you?'. The play resists easy binaries: while reflecting the colossal impact of the US-led invasion, American soldier Sam York is an implicated yet sympathetic character; Gertrude is a product of Colonial Britain and also 'truly an Arab'; the female characters are leaders, innovators even, but the play charts how they must come to terms with their limitations within male-dominated power structures. And yet they persist. It is a play in which disaster is 'always pounding on the doors – trying to get in' yet hope never dissipates: 'They'll remake the world anew. Inspired by the past'. Continually, it asks probing questions surrounding nationhood and accountability, genuinely wondering whether the efforts to preserve artefacts can be justified while bodies build up in the streets. This play is a fine example of how she pitches her tent along the fault-lines of interweaving arguments, rather than settling for the duller promontories of complaint, explanation or polemic.

Museum offers a lasting image of an archaeological discovery by Woolley of a burial pit in Ur. Just as he starts to romanticise the ritual of the women who 'composed themselves for death', Gertrude puts his find into starker relief: '68 nameless, forgotten, dead, burnt women'. *Hakawatis* is also a play in which a group of women have been confined against their will in a small space by men. But in *Hakawatis* the women, although still guarded by men, refuse to die. They work together to keep the men not just at bay, but out of the room; off-stage altogether.

The play is drawn from the folk classic *1001 Nights*, otherwise known as *The Arabian Nights*, in which Scheherazade must tell a new story every night to her husband the King 'lest her lips be sealed forever'. The story has to be so good that he will forego his practice of killing his wife in the morning and taking a new one each evening. Hannah draws on this rich legacy but was determined to find a fresh approach, hence *Hakawatis: Women of the Arabian Nights*. What if, she imagines, Scheherazade is not the fabled storyteller of legend, but simply a good performer dependent upon the ideas and collaborative efforts of the women who are slated to be up next once she gets the chop. It is they who must work together to keep Scheherazade alive and the show on the road – rather like the writer's room process Hannah was beginning to encounter as she started writing for television around this time.

Like *Museum*, the play has choric sequences, but in contrast it was written very quickly, which is perhaps one reason it has such a free, fleeting quality. If *Museum* is a play of earth and water, *Hakawatis* is a play of air and fire. In a brilliant move to ensure form mirrors content, she invited three other playwrights – Hanan al-Shaykh, Suhayla El-Bushra and Sara Shaarawi – to collaborate with her on the text; four women of Arabic heritage weaving their words around one another to keep the story alive. Hannah also incorporates an element of chance directly into the theatrical process, specifying that one of the stories should be improvised every night by the cast rather than being learnt exactly and performed the same way every night.

This basis of belief in the theatrical act, along with her inventive conceit result in a play ripe with longing, courage and transformation that revels in the wonder, wit and subversion of women telling stories the way they want to, 'free as birds'. We hope you enjoy reading, speaking, imagining and staging these plays. All of them have been worked on and chewed over around a busy kitchen table, just like the opening stage direction in *Plan D* describes, with our daughter Muna sat close by, writing stories of her own.

# Plan D

In this drama inspired by testimonies from people who lived through the creation of the State of Israel in 1948, one family has to leave their home when the threat of danger arises. But can they abandon the place where they've always lived? And will the children be safe if they stay?

Seven characters, 4 males and 3 females.

Plan D was first performed at the Tristan Bates Theatre, London, on 26 January 2010. Directed by Chris White and designed by Paul Burgess, it had the following cast:

Father   George Couyas
Mother   Houda Echouafni
Grandmother   Amira Ghazalla
Daughter   Loukia Pierides
Nephew   Kamal Kaan
Cousin   Richard Sumitro
Old Man   Leonard Fenton

Playwright's Intro

Until *Plan D* I had always avoided writing about Palestine. I wrote Arab characters into my plays in an attempt to redress the negative portrayal of Arabs in the media, but Palestine felt like too big, too important a topic for me to address. That was until I went to an Oral Histories Day organised by the Palestinian Society at the School of African and Oriental Studies (SOAS) in London. While there I heard lots of fascinating stories and watched snippets of a project being undertaken by Eyal Sivan, an Israeli filmmaker, called 'Towards a Common Archive'. This film project interviewed Palestinians and Israelis who lived through the creation of the State of Israel in 1948 as a way of documenting the truth about what happened, while the witnesses were still alive. I found the testimonies eye opening and extremely moving and it was these stories that formed the inspiration for *Plan D*.

Production Note

The time and place in which this play is set are intended to be non-specific, but the inspiration for the play comes from oral testimonies by Palestinians and Israelis who lived through 1948.

Part One

Scene: We are in the kitchen/living area of a very small house. It is evening and it is dark outside. There is a large table in the centre; on one side sits the **Daughter** *and the* **Nephew**. *They are doing their homework, writing in exercise books and helping one another. The* **Father** *sits at the other side of the table smoking a cigarette. The* **Mother** *is washing plates from the dinner in a sink. In one corner sits the* **Grandmother**. *She has a photograph in her lap and is cleaning an old-fashioned gun.*

Mother   I tore it up – I just had to. Are you listening to me?

Father   What? No I was looking at those two working away. Remembering my school days.

Mother   Good boy, helping her with her homework.

Daughter   What was your school like?

Father   On the first day I didn't go.

Nephew   Were you sick?

Father   Yes, scared sick.

Daughter   You? Scared?

Father   I had to go with the boy from next door and as we walked he told me that his brother said the headmaster was evil, and had all kinds of torturing contraptions in his study. On the first day new boys had to go and see him one by one, and he'd try out his latest instrument.

Mother   Don't tell them that!

Father   He said there was a thing you had to put your thumbs in, and he would ask you a question, and every time you got it wrong he'd turn the key and it would twist your thumb.

Daughter   But what if you didn't know the answer?

Father   It'd snap off.

Mother   Please!

Father   And another tool was a ruler covered in nails, which he'd use to –

Mother   Enough!

Nephew   It's not true, is it?

Father   No, but we didn't know that – we were terrified.

Daughter   Who made up those awful lies?

Father The older boys to scare us, or maybe the teacher spread the rumour so we'd be too frightened to misbehave; anyway it worked and we decided to hide in the woods. We played all day long and that night went back home and pretended we had gone to school. But the second day we had the same problem.

Nephew What happened?

Father I went in . . .

Daughter How brave.

Father But he didn't – he never went to school

Nephew Never?

Daughter Did you get caned?

Father I don't remember.

Beat.

Mother Get on with your homework or I'll cane you all – and you.

Father Me?

Mother I said I tore it up.

Father What?

Mother The green shirt – it was so threadbare there was no point stitching it again – there was already more thread than material. I hung it on the line and watched it blowing about, and I could see all the way through, no protection at all.

Father But that was my favourite.

Mother I know – it was falling to bits.

Daughter (*quietly to the* **Nephew**) And it smelled.

Father What did you say?

Daughter Nothing.

Father I heard you – share it with the class . . .

She looks bashful.

Father Come on – stand up and share the joke with the class – what did you say?

Daughter I said . . . it smelled.

He puts his cigarette down and gets up and moves towards her.

Beat.

Father I thought that's what you said . . .

Beat.

Father Give me your thumbs

Daughter No, no!

She hides behind her cousin's chair.

Father You dare to tell your father he smells.

*The **Daughter** squeals as he picks her up in a fireman's lift and starts smacking her bottom playfully.*

Daughter Help me! Help me!

Nephew Let her go Sir!

Father Or what?

Nephew I'm warning you – I'm armed (*brandishing his pencil*).

Father You wouldn't!

Nephew Watch me.

A chase ensues around the table and a lot of noise.

Mother Stop it, stop it – you'll break something.

*It continues, and as they run past the **Grandmother** the air blows the photograph from her lap and it is almost trampled in the play fighting.*

Granny Stop! My picture!

She wades in amongst them shouting. They stop and she picks up the picture smoothing it out with care.

Granny Bloody vandals – my poor man – come here.

She kisses the picture.

Daughter Sorry, Granny (*kissing her*). Did we ruin it?

Nephew It's OK – it's not damaged.

Mother No thanks to you monkeys, now get on with your homework.

*They all retake their places and the **Father** picks up his cigarette. **Granny** puts the picture in her lap again, dabs her eyes with her sleeve and resumes cleaning the gun.*

Father It's just a picture.

Mother Shush!

Granny To you it's just a picture, you don't understand, you've never lost anything – to me it's my love, long dead . . .

Father You don't know that.

Granny What?

Mother Leave her alone – she's not another child for you to tease.

Father I'm not teasing, I'm just saying we don't know he's dead.

Granny I do – if he was alive he would be here with us.

Father He was only a prisoner – they might have set him free – he could be living over there, enjoying himself with a new family.

Mother Don't say that.

Granny He knows he's dead – he knows what they do to their prisoners – unarmed.

She gestures the gun she is holding. She is about to cry.

Mother Please (*she signals the children*).

Pause.

There is a scratching noise, like a knock on the door.

Mother It sounds like someone's at the door.

Father That's the wind.

Mother No there was a knock – will you look?

Father There's no one there.

She goes to the door and opens it – a gust of wind blows through the room. A stray piece of paper floats off the table.

Nephew The wind! It's upset everything!

She closes the door and comes back in.

Father I told you.

Mother It was that branch – I've asked you and asked you to cut it –

Father I've been busy.

Mother but you haven't cut it.

Father I haven't got round to it.

Mother I hate that tree, it grows so quickly, one day it was tiny and the next huge with branches pressed up against the window like they are trying to get in

Father I'll cut it

Mother You keep saying that but you don't. By the time you get round to it the saplings underneath will be fully grown too – we'll be overrun.

He goes to her and puts his arms around her.

Mother That won't make up for it.

He moves his hands to her breasts – she gives him a look. Then he moves his hands to her neck and pretends to strangle her.

Mother Wouldn't you like to . . .

He leans round her where she is still washing the plates and puts the cigarette out in the water.

Mother   Why did you do that – it's not hygienic.

Father   Don't want to burn the house down.

Mother   Put the butt outside.

Father   I was going to.

*He goes to the door. The **Nephew** is watching the old woman.*

Nephew   It looks clean.

Granny   It should be – I'm very thorough.

Nephew   Are there bullets in it?

She nods gravely.

Nephew   Can I hold it?

*The **Grandmother** and **Nephew** both look towards the **Mother** who has her back to them as she continues to wash up.*

Granny   Not yet – but soon – when you are old enough.

Father (*from outside the door*)   Come and see this, you two.

The children get up and go to the door.

Daughter   Oh – blood.

Nephew   It's shaking.

Daughter   No, it's dead.

Nephew   It's not.

Father   Shoo! I think she was bringing you a present, darling.

Nephew   What a horrid present.

Daughter   I think he's sweet – poor thing, he's squeaking a bit.

Nephew   Won't he die, Uncle?

Father   I don't know.

Daughter   Can we put him in the shed – with the chickens – make a bed for him.

Father   If you like.

*The children go out and shut the door behind them – **Father** comes in.*

Granny   That's a vicious cat – always killing things.

Mother   She's not been the same since she got locked in the barn.

Father   It was a field mouse – incredible it wasn't dead.

Granny It's bound to die – they better not get too attached.

Father They're so close those two.

Mother Of course – they grew up together.

He sits at the table and toys with another cigarette.

Father I never thought I'd be happy here.

Granny Why not? You chose to live here, no one forced you.

Mother You liked the house, didn't you?

Father I did – and the woman who was born in it.

Granny Do you mean me or her?

Father Her, Mother, her.

Mother There. That's that done.

Granny If you were after her, then why did you insist she sign the house over to you?

Mother Mother, must you? It's been years.

Granny He saw a good house and he wanted it.

She sits down and puts her feet onto her husband's lap. He removes a slipper and begins to rub her foot.

Father No – I saw a good woman. Then I saw the house and I think that land should always belong to the man. It's his family, his home. I wanted to be the one responsible for looking after the house and everyone in it. And now I am. I work those fields, tend the animals, keep the house in order.

*The **Mother** darts a look at him.*

Father I'll cut the tree – and I don't see you complaining when you tuck in at dinner time, Mother.

*The **Grandmother** takes the gun and puts it away in a drawer.*

There is a nice peaceful moment, then a tapping on the door again.

*The **Father** and **Mother** look at one another.*

Father There's no one there.

She tries to get up – he holds onto her foot.

Mother Let go.

He does – she picks up a large knife from the draining board.

Father Are you going to kill me?

Mother No, I'm going to do your job – cut that bloody tree.

She opens the door and lets out a little cry.

There is a man there.

He is very dishevelled and looks exhausted. He has been travelling for a long time. He has not brought much with him – perhaps one small bag.

Father   What is it?

Granny   Who is he?

The **Father** *goes to her at the door and sees the man.*

Father   Can I help you? Oh – is it you? Cousin? Welcome, welcome – (*to* **Mother**, *pointing to the knife*) put that down.

He hugs the man at the door, the **Mother** *enters looking pale. She puts the knife away and a look passes between* **Mother** *and* **Grandmother**.

Father   You look tired, come in, come in, sit, make tea.

She begins to prepare tea and put together some food for the guest.

Cousin   Thank you.

Father   Sit, sit, how was your journey?

Cousin   Long –

Father   Did you come on foot?

Cousin   Not all of the way.

Mother   We weren't expecting you – were we?

Father   Hush now, he's welcome.

Cousin   Auntie –

He greets her by holding her hand to his lips, he smiles broadly.

Granny   Stop it. No wife yet?

Cousin   God hasn't chosen to bless me with one –

The old lady snorts, he smiles at her and sits down.

Cousin   I'm sorry I didn't let you know of my visit – I left in rather a hurry.

Father   Is everything alright?

Cousin   Yes – no – I – couldn't not come and see you.

Father   Has something happened?

Mother   Let the man drink his tea, he looks famished.

He eats some food.

Father   It's so long since we have seen you –

Granny   Let him eat.

Cousin How's your daughter?

Father Beautiful, a good scholar, and a lovely imagination.

Cousin And the boy?

Granny Don't talk with your mouth full – no manners.

Cousin Excuse me. Thank God you were generous enough to take him in.

Father It was nothing –

Granny I suppose you'd like to see them.

She gets up and goes out through the door to call the children.

Cousin (*to* **Father**) I must speak to you.

Mother There's no hurry, rest. How is your mother? Is your sister married yet?

Cousin (*to* **Father**) There's something I need to tell you.

Mother Say hello to the children, meet them, see us all together as a family, Cousin, please . . .

At this moment the **Grandmother** *re-enters with the children who stand sheepishly looking at the man who they have never met.*

Father Say hello.

Daughter and Nephew Hello.

Father You don't know who this is, do you? It's my cousin – he's come all the way from the village where I was born to see you.

Nephew The village where you were born – that's near where I come from, isn't it, Auntie?

Mother Yes, yes it is, my sister, your mother lived in the village next door to this man.

Nephew Did you know my mother? What was she like?

Granny Is it dead then?

Daughter No – it's a bit shaky though.

Nephew Next door's cat brought a field mouse to the door.

Daughter It was bleeding and everything.

Cousin Poor fellow.

Father Did you make it a little bed?

Daughter Yes and we left some water in half an eggshell.

Nephew That was my idea.

Mother Very clever.

Daughter It was mine actually.

Cousin Do you want to take a bit of my cheese to him in case he gets hungry.

Granny Don't waste good cheese on a mouse.

Daughter Yes, please.

He hands her a bit of the cheese from his plate, the children go out the door.

Mother Come straight back – it's bedtime.

Cousin They are so grown up. The time passes so quickly.

Father Doesn't it?

Cousin They look so alike.

Beat.

Granny Where are we going to put him?

Mother Mother!

Cousin I'll sleep anywhere – in here on the floor will be fine.

Father We should put him in your bed, Mother.

Granny What?

Cousin Oh yes – I'd happily share with a lovely woman like you.

Granny Get out of it!

Father It's a while since you've had a man in your bed isn't it, Mother?

Mother Leave her alone! We'll put him on the mattress in the children's room. Is that alright?

Cousin Of course.

There is a banging and ghostly whooooing noise from the door.

Father Stop playing, you two – trying to frighten your mother.

He opens the door and they run in laughing, shouting good night as they run up to their bedroom.

Granny I'll go and make sure they wash their faces.

She exits.

Cousin Ahh, they're wonderful (*he wipes his eyes*).

Father Is everything alright, Cousin?

Cousin It's so good to be around people again.

Father Travelling is a lonely business.

Cousin You don't understand – everyone left the village. It's like a ghost town.

Mother   What do you mean?

Cousin   There were still clothes hanging on the lines – but no one there – everyone left.

Mother   Everyone?

Father   What about your mother and father, and your sister?

Cousin   They went to a safe place – in the North to my father's people.

Mother   You didn't go with them?

Cousin   I promised them I'd warn you.

Mother   It's a long way.

Cousin   Blood – family is important.

Father   I've heard about this – but I never thought – my own village.

Mother   This is your village now.

Father   But I grew up there.

Cousin   They had no choice. We have no choice.

Father   Of course there's a choice.

Mother   You can't judge – thanks to God we don't have to worry about that.

Cousin   I'm not so sure.

Father   What do you mean?

Cousin   I think the same will happen here.

Mother   No – what would they want with us – we're too far East for them to bother about us. We'll be OK. Won't we?

Father   Of course. And despite its oddities this town is full of men of fighting age – no one will go anywhere – they'll stand and fight.

Mother   Don't talk about fighting – please, I can't bear it.

Cousin   You need someone to fight against though.

Mother   Stop! We are fine here.

Cousin (*directly to the* **Mother**)   There are some truths you have to face up to, which you can't hide from.

Mother   Shush, please.

Father   Don't cry, don't get upset – he's on our side, he's just come to warn us.

Mother   He's threatening us.

Father   No, my darling, he's warning us – aren't you?

Cousin Of course and then we can all leave together.

Father We're not going anywhere – this is my home and there's nothing happening in our village – it's fine, we're safe. Stay with us though – please. Just until things return to normal in your place – then you can go back. But you're family – stay with us.

Cousin Thank you.

Mother You should go back to your people.

Father He's just arrived.

Cousin You'll need me.

Father I think we should all go to bed, it's been a long day and there's a lot to be done in the fields tomorrow – you've come at the right time.

Cousin Good – I'll help.

Father Yes (*the men move to the door*).

Father I'll show you where you are sleeping, are you coming?

Mother I'm just getting some water.

The **Mother** *watches the men go anxiously. She stands over the sink trying to control her breathing. The* **Grandmother** *comes in and the two talk in hushed whispers.*

Granny Are you alright – what did he do?

Mother Nothing, shush!

Granny Why is he here?

Mother He said they've all left his village . . .

Granny Did he?

Mother That's what he said.

Beat.

Granny He's dying to say something.

Mother I know.

Granny Those remarks – heavy with meaning – he knows.

Mother Of course he knows . . .

Beat.

Mother Do you think he picked up on it?

Granny No, no – not yet – we need to get rid of him.

Mother It seems like he's staying.

Granny He can't – he might –

Mother I know but what can I do?

Granny Ask him?

Mother What?

Granny If he intends to tell.

Mother I couldn't.

Granny Do you want me to?

Mother NO, shush!

Granny He's a stirrer, like that mother of his . . . It's OK – we'll just have to keep an eye on him. Come on, let's go to bed.

Mother Oh, Mother, I don't want my life, my children, this house to collapse around me – if he finds out . . .

Granny Shush, child, he won't. Come on, bed.

They exit.

We hear the branch scratching on the door.

Lights down.

Part Two

Scene: The lights gradually fade up on the same setting. The table is in front of the door and the old woman sits in a chair in the centre of the room fast asleep with the gun in her lap. It is the morning. The **Daughter** *enters and takes in the scene, she gently wakes her* **Grandmother**.

Daughter Granny – Granny – are you OK?

Granny What! Oh – oh my back.

Daughter Did you sleepwalk?

Granny No, I did not, oh.

Daughter Did you move the table all alone?

Granny Yes.

Daughter But it's so heavy.

The **Nephew** *enters.*

Nephew What happened?

Daughter Help me move this – I need to check the mouse.

Granny No, don't.

Daughter I want to make sure he's OK – something's going on.

Granny Don't go out there!

Nephew I'll go with her, don't worry.

They are out of the door.

Granny Come back, come back!

The **Cousin** *enters.*

Cousin What's all the noise? Gun? Who you shooting now Mrs?

Granny Stop! They've gone outside – get them – something happened in the night.

Cousin What?

Granny Quickly!

He registers her fear.

Cousin (*shouting*) Children!

He rushes out of the door. **Granny** *looks out of it. The* **Mother** *enters.*

Mother What is it? Put that away (*referring to the gun*).

Granny It's OK – everything looks normal I think.

Mother What do you mean?

Granny Didn't you hear it?

Mother No – what?

Granny In the night – the noise – it terrified me, so I came down and put the table in front of the door and kept guard.

The **Father** *enters.*

Father Why is everyone up – it's barely dawn.

Granny I can't believe none of you woke up.

Mother Mother thinks there was a noise in the night.

Father Probably just wolves.

Granny Not that kind of noise.

Father Then what?

Granny Something bad. A bang.

Father A gun?

Granny Bigger.

Father What? Are you sure you weren't dreaming, Mother?

The children and **Cousin** *come back to the door.*

Nephew   There's a huge hole in the field – behind the shed.

Mother   A hole?

Father   Do you think it was a tremor?

Cousin   A tremor doesn't make a crater.

Mother   It could, couldn't it?

Father   Show me.

The two men exit.

Granny   I knew I wasn't dreaming.

Daughter   The mouse is fine – he was snoozing away as if nothing had happened.

Nephew   The hens were a bit funny though.

Daughter   Like when they see Granny with her gun.

Nephew   That's because they know one of them's for it.

Mother   Oh God – what was it?

Granny   Children move the table back to its proper place. I can't believe you all slept through it – well! It woke me right up and I looked at the picture of your grandfather and I said, did you hear that? We'd better go and see what's happened, and it was eerily still. I didn't trust it. So I set up camp down here.

Nephew   Did you move the table all alone, Granny?

Granny   Yes, I did.

Nephew   But it's so heavy.

Granny   I wasn't going to let anything come in here.

Nephew   Who wants to come in here?

Mother   No one, it was a tremor, nature.

The men appear again.

Father   It's huge. It nearly took out the whole field, the bordering trees were uprooted.

Daughter   Like a giant's footprint.

Father   At least that field was just for grazing – it didn't damage any crops.

Cousin   This time.

Father   Children go and collect eggs for breakfast.

Daughter   Do we have to?

Nephew Don't worry – I'll distract the cock, you get the eggs, then you won't get pecked again.

The children go.

Cousin You see – I told you. This is what happened in my home too.

Father Describe the noise exactly – what was it like?

Granny A bang, a rumble.

Mother A rumble is like a tremor.

Granny I can't believe no one else woke up.

Cousin It was no tremor. It just missed the shed.

Mother What missed the shed?

Granny If it just missed the shed, then it just missed –

Cousin – the house, and next time you might not be so lucky. We must leave.

Father We're not going anywhere.

Granny But the children?

Father This is their home.

Cousin Don't be stupid, you don't want them to die in this place.

Father Who's talking about dying? They are just trying to frighten us.

Mother It's working.

Cousin She's sensible – she knows how to look after herself.

A look passes between the two women.

Father I won't leave – it's taken me years to get it to where it is now – this is our home – and there's the livestock, the fields to be tended – we can't go anywhere.

Cousin You need to get your priorities right, Cousin.

Father If you're afraid, go – my family and I are staying.

Cousin I'm not afraid for myself – talk to him, Auntie.

Granny You are both right.

Cousin What?

Granny Well, we can't leave – this is our home.

Cousin Think of the children. If that thing had been any closer . . .

Mother Maybe we shouldn't stay here.

Granny Listen, we can stay and go.

Father We're not splitting up.

Granny No, no, listen – if we go to the woods beyond the last field – we're still on our property – we can set up a camp and come back to look after everything, but know we are safe. Then this man can go.

Mother The woods?

Father With the wolves and wild boars and hyenas?

Mother I don't go into those woods.

Cousin You'd rather take your chances here?

Granny There hasn't been a hyena there since I was a girl – (*to* **Mother**) you can do it.

Father (*to* **Mother**) Listen to them – this is madness!

Mother The woods? But maybe – we don't need to go in too deep – we'll be close enough to come and do things but we'll be safe – just for a couple of days while we see what happens.

Granny Listen to your wife.

Father What about school?

Cousin I shouldn't think that will be an issue.

Mother Their safety comes first.

Cousin It's amazing how a woman always thinks of her children.

Granny We can tell them it's an adventure.

Mother Yes – good idea.

Father Stop, this is crazy – I've work to do.

Cousin Please, look I'll stay, help you with the work. Just humour me – if I'm wrong, well I hope I'm wrong – either way your family will be safe.

Mother Better safe than sorry – just for a few days.

Granny The children.

The **Mother** *goes to the* **Father**.

Mother Please.

Beat.

Father Oh alright then. But this is . . . Come on, Cousin, we've a lot to do – you get the household things together.

Mother Yes, of course.

Granny And we'll have a hearty breakfast with eggs and cheese before we go.

The men exit. The **Mother** *begins to collect together bits and pieces to take with them – not much though – she knows it's only for a few days.*

Granny   What do you think of that?

Mother   Don't, Mother.

Granny   You know what he's up to.

Mother   Of course – what shall I do? What if he says something? Do you think he means to?

Granny   Yes. I do. You know what he's like. Can't keep it shut. Look what happened to his sister.

Mother   Oh God! What shall I do?

Granny   Nothing – we'll just keep an eye on him.

Mother   Do you think we'll need this? (*Referring to some kitchen utensil.*)

Granny   Probably not – leave it – we can always come back for it.

Beat.

Granny (*in a whisper*)   Shall we bring?

Mother   I was just wondering about that – will it be safe here?

Granny   I don't know – shall I get it?

Mother   Yes – quick.

*The **Grandmother** exits and returns with a small pouch.*

Granny   I've slept on this for eleven years – I think I'll miss lying on it. Can I open it?

Mother   No, Mother.

Beat.

Mother   Oh, go on, but quickly.

*The **Grandmother** opens the pouch and removes four or five pieces of gold jewellery.*

Granny   This one is my favourite – poor you never being able to wear it.

Mother   I wouldn't want to wear it.

Granny   If I'd had something like this, I'd never take it off. You put it on.

Mother   No – you know where it came from – I hate it.

Granny   I can't imagine you cleaning in it. But try it on – you'll look pretty.

Mother   No, it makes my skin crawl.

Granny   It's gold, it's yours.

Mother   It's for him for when he's grown up.

Granny   We may need it sooner than that.

She puts it away.

Mother   What shall we do with it?

Granny   We'll worry about that later – for now it'll be safe here.

She puts it down her ample bosom.

Granny   No one will look there, eh?

They both giggle.

Mother   Will you get some bedding?

*The **Grandmother** goes.*

Mother   No need to go too mad – we shouldn't be there long.

*She continues to collect things together. The **Father** comes in.*

Father   Where's my knife?

Mother   In the drawer – I told you, I don't like it left out with the children.

Father (*finding the knife*)   Here it is. Make sure your mother packs the gun.

Mother   What, why?

Father   Just in case.

Mother   What did he say to you?

No answer.

Mother   Tell me. You are making me frightened.

Beat.

Father   Maybe that's good.

Mother   I hate those woods.

Father   I'll be there to protect you, remember what I promised. I haven't let you down yet have I?

Mother   No.

Beat.

Mother   Is it fair to ask him to come? He's done what he wanted to, warned us, he should go back to his people now.

Father   He wants to stay.

Mother   Why?

Father   To help us. What is it?

Beat.

Mother   Some people, like times like this – they find it exciting. Not me. I want everything safe and routine, in our home.

Father Me too. It'll be OK.

Mother You still love me, don't you?

Father Why are you saying that?

Mother You do though?

Father Of course –

Mother You hesitated.

Father No, I didn't.

Mother You did, you did – you oh –

Father No, what is it?

He holds her.

Father Silly hen. What is it? Why are you crying?

Mother I wish he'd never come.

Father You can't blame him – he's just the messenger.

Mother He's going to ruin everything.

Father What? What is it that you are frightened of?

Beat.

The **Daughter** *and* **Nephew** *run in.*

Daughter What is it, Mother? What's the matter?

Nephew Please don't cry.

Father She's not crying, she's –

Mother Excited – I'm excited – your father has just come up with a great idea.

Father Have I?

Mother Yes, remember? The 'adventure'.

Nephew Adventure?

Father Oh yes, we are going on an 'adventure'.

Daughter Really?

The **Grandmother** *walks into the room, her arms full of blankets, which she puts down. She goes to the dresser and takes the gun.*

Mother What are you doing with that?

Granny I'm going to shoot two chickens to take with us.

Nephew Can I watch?

Granny Yes, come on, boy.

Daughter Don't frighten the mouse.

The **Grandmother** *and* **Nephew** *exit.*

Daughter Why doesn't she just ring their necks like you, Dad?

Father She likes to practise her aim.

Beat.

Father Have you got everything together?

Mother It's hard to know what to bring . . .

Daughter Where are we going?

Mother On an adventure, we're going to sleep in the woods.

Daughter That's creepy though.

Mother Not with your Father to look after us.

Daughter Can I bring Mousey?

Mother If you like.

Daughter What about school?

Father You've got a few days' holiday.

Daughter Oh! Today is the best day, first a giant wakes up and walks in our field and now we get to play in the woods.

Mother Get your things ready, go on.

The **Daughter** *goes to the stairs. There is the sound of a gun shot – the* **Mother** *jumps.*

Daughter Don't be scared, Mum, it's just Granny in the hen house.

Lights down.

Part Three

Scene: The **Mother**, **Grandmother** *and children are in a small clearing in the woods. They are unpacking a few bags of things, making up beds and setting up camp.*

Daughter So if your bed is here, and my bed is here, where shall we put this fellow's bed?

Nephew You could put him in between us.

Daughter No way – what if you roll over in the night and squash him – that would definitely be the end of him.

Nephew   OK, how about here – on this tree trunk, that way he's raised up a bit too so when the wolves come they won't get him.

Daughter   Wolves?

Nephew   Yes – everyone knows there are wolves in this forest – and wild boar too.

Daughter   Is that true?

Granny   Yes.

Mother   No.

Granny   Come, we must tell the child the truth, she's old enough to hear it now – she can't be protected forever.

Mother   She's just a child.

Nephew   She's the smallest here.

Daughter   No I'm not – Mousey is.

Granny   Listen – there are horrid things that live in the forest – once when I was a little girl your great grandfather – he was a tyrant – he sent me to this very wood to collect branches for the fire. It was the middle of winter and freezing and I could hardly see my hand in front of my face . . . I walked in through a path on the other side and began gathering different twigs. But I kept thinking I heard things behind me – it was terrifying. Then, just as I had enough wood, I looked up to find myself nose-to-nose with a wolf.

Nephew   You didn't?

Granny   I'd been so busy looking over my shoulder I hadn't seen him walk right up to me bold as you like and start salivating.

Daughter   It's awful.

Mother   Mother, enough.

Nephew   What did you do?

Granny   I saw in those big yellow eyes of his that he liked the look of me, so I threw the wood at him and jumped up the nearest tree. He was down below looking up at me, and I clung on up there . . . He was prepared to wait for dinner, so he sat himself down.

Mother   I thought wolves could climb trees.

Granny   Not this one. Well there I am getting colder and colder and I know if I stay up there too long, I'll drift off and fall out and that'll be the end of me, or I'll freeze to death.

Nephew   What did you do?

Granny   It was him or me. So I very quietly manoeuvred myself so I was above him and jumped down hard so I landed on his back.

Nephew   Didn't he bite you?

Granny   No – I broke him – he just lay there, sprawled in the snow with blood coming out of his mouth, moaning . . . I ran back to the house.

Daughter   Gosh – what did your father say?

Granny   Nothing, he was too busy knocking me black and blue for forgetting the firewood . . . So you see the forest is like the world, there are horrid things out there too, but look – you've your cousin and your mother and me and here's Grandad's gun – and he'd never let any harm come to us.

Daughter   And Father.

Granny   Yes, of course.

Daughter   Where is he?

Mother   Don't fret, he'll join us in a while – he wanted to check on the animals.

Daughter   And the man – he's coming too, isn't he?

Mother   Yes.

Daughter   I like him, don't you, Mother? He's handsome. Is he going to stay with us?

Granny   Not for long, so don't get too attached to him.

Beat.

Granny   You two help me find wood – we are going to build a pyre in the middle here and that'll keep all the nasties away in the night.

The three begin collecting pieces of wood together from the vicinity of the camp.

*The **Mother** continues to sort things out. She stops and watches the children and **Grandmother** collecting the wood.*

Mother (*to the **Nephew***)   Come here my, boy.

Nephew   Yes, Auntie.

Mother   Give me a kiss.

He does so.

Nephew   Are you alright?

Mother   Yes.

Nephew   We aren't just here on an adventure are we?

Mother   Yes, of course we are – it's a game and I've a task for you. Will you do it?

Nephew   Anything, Auntie.

Mother   I want you to climb that tree over there and keep watch.

Nephew   What for?

Mother   For when our men come back – when they do, you call down to me – OK, can you do that?

Nephew   Of course.

Mother   Go on then.

He climbs up the tree stealthily.

Daughter   Shall I go too?

Mother   No – you help me by finding a good place to dig a hole. Mother, come here.

*The **Grandmother** goes to her.*

Nephew *(from the tree)*   I can see the whole village from up here.

Mother   What do you see?

Nephew   It's dead – there's no one about – but there's smoke coming from a few chimneys – people must be inside having their lunches.

Granny   At 10 in the morning?

Mother   Shush!

Beat.

Mother   Good boy – you keep watch for me and tell me if anything changes – alright?

Nephew   Aye, aye, Captain!

Daughter   How about here, Mother?

Mother   Somewhere further away – but don't go anywhere we can't see you.

Beat.

Mother   Give it to me, Mother – we are going to bury it.

Granny   What about the boars?

Mother   We'll bury it deep – no one will find it.

Daughter   How about here?

Mother   Clever girl, that's perfect now, here we are.

*She gives the **Daughter** and **Grandmother** a spoon and takes one herself.*

Mother   Right, let's dig a hole.

Daughter   What for?

Mother   Treasure – it's part of the game – but this is a girls' secret – you can never tell your father.

Daughter   Or the man?

Granny Definitely not him.

Daughter Or him? (*Pointing to the* **Nephew**.)

Mother Boys aren't good at secrets like us.

The three females begin to dig a hole with their spoons.

Granny Good girl – deeper, deeper.

Nephew What are you doing down there?

Mother Never you mind – you just keep watching and tell me what you see.

Nephew Nothing yet.

Daughter It's getting hard.

They keep going.

Mother Darling, I want you to go and find a special stone – one we will recognise to mark the place – yes?

Daughter OK . . . (*She gets up.*) This is fun.

She goes to look for a stone. The women continue to dig.

Beat.

Mother That should be enough do you think?

Granny I'd say so – a couple more for luck.

They continue.

Daughter What about this?

Granny That's a pebble – it's far too small

Daughter Oh, OK.

The **Mother** *and* **Grandmother** *check the children aren't watching.*

Mother Quick, Mother – put it in.

The **Grandmother** *fishes the pouch from her cleavage, kisses it and drops it into the hole.*

Nephew I think I see something – yes – it's them, they are walking across the fields, Auntie.

Mother Both of them?

Nephew Yes.

Mother Alone?

Nephew Yes. Shall I come down then?

Mother No, stay there a while longer.

Granny Quickly – fill it.

*They both begin to refill the hole. The **Daughter** comes over with a large white stone – she is struggling under its weight.*

Daughter This?

Mother Perfect – put it down, sweetie.

Granny Help us.

*They all fill the hole and then put some leaves over it and place the stone on top. They are brushing off their hands as the men come through the clearing. The **Mother** studies the **Father**'s face anxiously.*

Daughter Daddy, Daddy, look – we made camp and built a pyre and everything – and I made up the bed for you and Mummy over here away from everyone else's – see – under a canopy – isn't it lovely – like a fairy bower.

Father Good girl.

Cousin Where's the boy?

Nephew I'm up here – keeping look out.

Cousin In the crow's nest.

Nephew No, we're not on a boat.

Father Like a monkey in a tree.

Granny Come on, child, let's clean these spoons.

She gets a cloth and wipes them.

Daughter Shouldn't we wash them, they're dirty.

Granny They have the soil of your homeland on – they are not dirty.

Mother What happened?

Cousin Nothing – no houses were hit, this time.

Mother And the animals?

Cousin Restless.

Father They were fine. This is nonsense – I vote we go back to the house.

Mother I hate this place.

Cousin Don't be stupid – at least leave it a day or two to see if anything happens.

Father Everyone's gone – for nothing – nothing has happened. Running from ghosts – things that aren't there.

Nephew Can I come down now?

Mother Come down darling – come down.

*The **Nephew** comes down and instinctively goes to the **Mother** and puts his arms around her waist.*

Nephew Did I do it right?

Mother You did it perfectly.

Beat.

Cousin Well look at you two.

Nephew What?

Cousin There's a striking family resemblance.

Granny Make yourself useful, boy, and fill the pitcher with water, there's a well that way.

Mother He can't go alone.

Cousin I'll come with you.

Nephew No.

Mother Please, darling.

*The **Nephew** sighs in assent.*

Cousin Thank you.

*The **Cousin** puts his hand under the **Nephew**'s chin and looks into his face, then looks pointedly at the **Mother**.*

Cousin Remarkable.

Granny Go on!

*They move away through the woods. **Granny** and **Daughter** take things out of the bags to make a kitchen area.*

Father Look at the bed she made us – isn't it sweet . . .

Mother Does he have to stay?

Father My cousin? He's a good worker and I don't mind having another man around with these things in the air.

Mother But you think this is all nonsense – let him go home – you're probably right.

Father Why don't you like him?

Mother He wants to make trouble – turning everything upside down.

Father It's harmless enough.

Mother I want him gone now.

Father What's this?

Mother   I ask very little of you as a wife, I've been good to you and ministered to all your needs, I just want you to do this one thing for me. This one thing. I'll never ask more of you as long as I live.

Father   But –

Mother   He means to do us harm, I know it.

Father   There is more to this.

Mother   Don't ask me, if you love me don't ask me, just do what I say.

Father   You look so anxious, my darling, undo your frown, come here.

They embrace.

Father   You sense something, don't you?

She nods.

Father   You feel something coming that's bigger than both of us.

Mother   I do, I do.

Father   I have always trusted your intuition.

Mother   Trust me again – do as I ask, please.

The **Cousin** *and* **Nephew** *return with the water.*

Cousin   Are you sure you can carry it alone, it's heavy.

Nephew   Let go – I can, I can – everyone, watch me.

They all watch as the boy tentatively lifts the heavy pitcher slopping a bit of water at first, but then with growing confidence he carries it the final steps to the kitchen area. **Granny** *and* **Daughter** *receive him with a round of applause and then the three of them busy themselves with preparing the food.*

Cousin (*seeing the two embracing*)   Are you OK?

Father   She's an intuitive woman my wife, she's apprehensive.

Cousin   She should be.

Beat.

Father   Maybe it's time you went back.

Cousin   I can't – I made a promise.

Father   You've done your bit, go, I can take care of my own.

Cousin (*directly to* **Mother**)   This is a dangerous time – you are at great risk, your husband, your family, your children, it's all in the balance.

The **Mother** *breaks from* **Father** *and turns to glare at the* **Cousin**.

Mother This is too much, to my face . . . to my very face . . . why are you here? What do you want? I can't take any more of your insinuations, your comments – just go will you, you are not wanted here – leave us alone.

Father Hey, hey, enough.

The **Grandmother** *has noticed this and leads the children into the woods out of earshot.*

Father What's this about, eh?

Mother You allow him to threaten me before my face.

Cousin Not threaten, warn – I've come here to warn you.

Mother It's all the same, I won't allow you to do this – go – just go – I know what this is – well I won't allow it.

Cousin I understand you are afraid of what will come next, but you have to face it.

Mother What? That you want to destroy my home?

Cousin If you don't listen to me, your family will be destroyed. It seems like an impossible situation but really you have no choice in the end – you knew this was coming.

Beat.

Cousin Didn't you?

Mother Yes.

Beat.

Mother I knew.

Beat.

Mother Fine. I'll tell him. But you go.

Cousin What?

Father Tell me what?

Mother You go.

Father Hold on – tell me what?

Mother You've heard him, all his comments.

Cousin My what?

Mother Be quiet, I'm doing it.

Cousin Wait!

Father What's going on?

Mother You must know, don't you? You must . . .

Cousin Stop!

Father What?

Mother The boy. My boy. He's mine.

Father Your nephew?

Mother No.

*The **Mother** shakes her head.*

Beat.

Mother Mine.

*The **Father** grabs her by the throat at arms-length; he doesn't squeeze, just stares at her.*

*The **Cousin** approaches.*

Cousin Don't do anything you'll regret.

Father You knew . . .

Cousin None of this is important now – these are dangerous /

Father / you knew!

*The **Father** punches the **Cousin** and walks into the woods at a pace. He sees the children and **Grandmother** and turns away from them with his head in his hands.*

*The **Nephew** runs into the clearing.*

Nephew What happened?

Cousin Just another game.

Granny No game.

Mother Climb that tree again for me, look out will you?

Nephew Yes.

*He does so. The **Grandmother** hands the **Cousin** a wet cloth for his face.*

Granny You deserved that.

Cousin What for?

Mother You can go now.

Cousin I'm going nowhere.

Mother Your work is done. He knows. Now leave us.

Cousin I had no intention of telling him anything.

Mother You liar.

Beat.

Cousin I thought he knew.

Mother What? But you have been insinuating since you came.

Granny You have, I heard.

Cousin You misunderstood, I . . . I thought he knew.

Beat.

Granny You kept saying how they look alike.

Cousin Well they do . . . why didn't you warn me?

Beat.

Cousin I wouldn't have said – I heard how it happened – it wasn't your fault /

Mother DON'T!

Beat.

Cousin He didn't know?

Mother No.

Beat.

Cousin These things don't matter in times like this, there's more at stake.

Mother They matter to me, and him.

Beat.

Mother What have I done?

Cousin Told him, for no reason.

Mother It's your fault.

Cousin Pointless.

Mother I wish you'd never come here.

Cousin I came to help you.

Daughter Stop arguing, you are upsetting Mousey, he's hiding in the straw.

Nephew Someone's coming.

Granny What?

Cousin Who is it?

Nephew I can't see.

Cousin Look harder.

Daughter I'm scared.

Nephew It's . . . it's . . . a man.

They all move together into a group – the **Cousin** *stands in front and takes* **Granny**'s *gun, while the* **Nephew** *remains in the tree.*

Daughter I don't like this game, I'm scared . . .

Granny Shush!

Cousin What else?

Mother What else do you see?

Nephew He's tall.

Beat.

Nephew – dark –

Cousin What else?

Nephew He's – he's wearing a uniform.

Mother Oh my God.

Granny What else?

Daughter Mum.

Mother Shush!

Cousin What else?

Nephew He's coming this way – he's – he's.

He turns and looks at them and starts to laugh.

Nephew Not really!

Mother You stupid, stupid boy, get down here.

Cousin This is real – can't any of you understand that!

Mother *goes to the foot of the tree, grabs his legs and pulls him down, then hits him around the head.*

Mother Never, ever, ever do that again you stupid, stupid boy, do you hear me? Never.

Nephew I'm sorry – I was only playing – please! Stop! You're hurting me –

Suddenly she stops and holds him hard, uncomfortably hard and then kisses him.

Mother I love you, you're a good boy, I love you.

He pulls away from her and runs to his **Granny**.

Granny Come, boy – come with me – it's time you learned to shoot this thing.

Mother He's too young.

Granny No, he's not.

Cousin He needs to be a man now – go with your granny.

They start to walk.

Cousin Make sure you walk far into the woods.

Daughter Can I come?

Mother No – you stay here with me.

Cousin I'll come with you – in case.

The three set off into the woods.

Mother Don't be too long – we'll need to start the fire.

Daughter Are you OK, Mummy?

Mother Why don't you go and see if you can find any mushrooms, then your father and I can teach you which ones are good to eat when he gets back.

She reluctantly gets up and starts hunting.

Mother Don't put anything in your mouth though.

*The **Mother** leans on the tree and looks into the wood in the direction her husband went. She talks into the tree.*

Mother Where have you gone?

Pause.

Mother I'm worried.

Pause.

Mother I'm sorry.

Pause.

Mother Come back.

Suddenly he appears in front of her like a ghost.

Mother Oh! Please, we can't be arguing at a time like this, we need to be strong and together.

Father I thought we were together – solid.

Mother We are – we are.

Father But you lied to me. What else have you lied to me about – is she even my daughter?

She goes to him.

Mother You know she is.

Father I don't anymore.

Mother   Look at her – she's you through and through, more you than me.

Beat.

She tries to touch his hand – he pulls away.

Father   Why didn't you tell me? Who else knows? Your mother of course – oh – does everyone know?

Mother   No one – no one – he just guessed.

Father   So when we were married you had already had – I don't understand.

Mother   It wasn't something I wanted – it wasn't out of love, the opposite.

Beat.

He looks at her.

Father   And?

Beat.

Father   Do you want me to ask him?

Beat.

Father   How could this happen?

Mother   You were away.

Beat.

Mother   When I found out I was afraid. I thought you'd change your mind . . . I went to visit my sister, had him and left him there.

Beat.

Mother   And then when she died suddenly . . . Mother came, and brought him back.

Father   And like a blind fool I agreed.

Beat.

Father   You didn't tell me.

Beat.

Father   How can you look at him?

Mother   He's mine. Yours too now – really /

Father   NO!

Beat.

Mother   This is his fault – if he hadn't come.

Father   I'd still be ignorant.

Mother   Things would be as they were, we'd be in our house, together, a family . . . send him away, we don't need him, you can protect us, we don't need anyone –

Father No . . . I can't. I don't want to hear anymore. I will stand by you but we don't speak.

Mother What?

Father Only to communicate practical things. We don't sleep in the same bed and what I say goes – no challenging me, right?

Mother But please – I.

Father No challenging me – that's it. He stays. We may need him.

He gets up and goes to the **Daughter**.

Father What did you find?

Daughter All of these – look aren't these ones ugly – they must be dangerous.

Father No – they are fine, but these you have to be careful of.

Daughter But they are so pretty. Mother these can't be bad.

Father Your mother doesn't know which ones are poisonous.

A shot is heard from deep inside the forest.

They all look around.

Daughter What was that?

Beat.

Daughter How long are we going to stay here, Daddy?

He looks at her deeply.

Daughter What is it? What's the matter?

Beat.

She hugs him.

Daughter Don't worry – this is just a little adventure. We'll be back home in a few days and everything will be back to normal – the giant will have gone back to sleep and all that will be left are his footprints as a reminder that he was awake at all. Isn't that right, Mother?

Mother Yes, darling. That's exactly right.

Lights down.

Part Four

Scene: The clearing – early morning. There is a new bed made up further from the others. The **Daughter** *is in her bed –* **Grandmother** *is sitting cleaning the gun with the photo of grandfather not far away.*

Granny   At least he took the boy with him this morning – that's progress.

Mother   As long as he doesn't throw him in the stream – oh look at this – it's ruined – black and it's my favourite pot.

Granny   Don't worry they can bring another one from the house later.

Beat.

Granny   Did he sleep over there?

No answer.

Mother   Are you awake? Darling?

The **Daughter** *turns over in the bed.*

Granny   Let her rest, the little mite – God knows her dreams will be more appealing than this.

Beat.

Mother   No – she should get up and do things – she can't sleep all the time.

Granny   She was up in the night – the noises frightened her – she got in with me.

Mother   Did she? I didn't hear her, with you?

Granny   Were you awake too?

Mother   I'm not sure – half awake – I heard them but they were incorporated in my dreams you know?

Granny   It's the whistle I hate. Makes me hold my breath.

Beat.

Granny   I thought I could hear a baby crying in the night.

Mother   Yes I heard that too – you don't think / someone.

Granny   / A fox – it was just a fox.

Beat.

Mother   I wonder what was hit this time.

Beat.

Mother   Darling – wake up – it's time to get up – look Granny will pour you some nice tea.

Daughter   No – leave me be – I'm cold – I don't want to wake up.

Mother   Granny will give you tea – then you'll be warm.

Granny   Leave her.

Daughter   It's too late, I'm awake now.

Mother Don't be grumpy.

Daughter I'm cold.

Mother Well get up and put some clothes on and then you can have something to eat – that will help.

Daughter Where are they?

Granny Gone to get water.

Daughter All of them? Together?

Granny Yes.

*Slowly the **Daughter** gets up and dresses herself, her **Grandmother** pours her some tea and takes it to her. She begins to brush her granddaughter's hair with her fingers and ties it in a knot on her head.*

Granny There is no law, but the law of the wind, the law of the grass, the law of the earth.

Daughter There is no law, but the law of the earth, the law of the land.

Granny and Daughter the land of our birth.

Granny There – now it won't get in your way.

Daughter Thanks, Granny.

She kisses her.

Mother What was that you said?

Daughter A skipping song – from school.

Mother How do you know it?

Daughter I taught her.

Granny I don't skip though.

Daughter It goes on, there's four verses – shall I say it?

Mother Later.

They all sit and stare.

Mother Where are they? They're taking such a long time.

Granny I can't see the sky – what time is it?

Daughter It's morning of course.

The men return.

Cousin Looking for us?

Mother What took you so long – I was getting worried.

Nephew   We saw the butcher – his family are down by the stream.

Granny   Really?

Nephew   They said everyone else in their street left but he didn't want to leave his stock – and the shop.

Mother   Did you ask them to come and see us – it would be nice to see someone else.

Father   Of course not – look at this place.

Granny   We've done our best.

Cousin   Maybe we should all set up together – there's safety in numbers.

Father   What are you talking about – safety? I am sick of all this talk.

Cousin (*in a whisper*)   Don't start this again – you heard what they said.

Mother   What's that?

Cousin   They said they had seen people in the village – from There.

Mother   Soldiers?

Cousin   No – they weren't sure. Probably just people taking advantage of the fact no one is about.

Nephew   Do you want me to climb the tree and look again? I can.

Mother   Yes /

Father   No.

Cousin   Go on.

The **Nephew** *climbs the tree. They all look up at him except the* **Daughter**, *who is collecting together a few things.*

Granny   What do you see?

Nephew   Nothing different – quiet . . .

Father   You see?

Cousin   What else?

Nephew   There's some smoke coming from the other side of the woods.

Mother   That'll be other families who've done the same as us.

Nephew   There's nothing else to report – I can't see a living soul.

Granny   Come down again.

He does, and the **Daughter** *takes advantage of their attention on him to walk out of the clearing into the woods, in the direction of their house.*

Cousin   Hey, where are you going?

She starts to run.

Cousin   Come back here.

Father   Hey!

Mother   Darling, come back!

The men pursue her – it is the **Father** *who catches her and carries her back screaming. He dumps her in the middle of the clearing. Her* **Mother** *grabs her by the hair, bends her over and smacks her bottom hard with a wooden spoon, over and over. Both* **Mother** *and* **Daughter** *are crying. The* **Nephew**, **Father** *and* **Cousin** *look away. They say the following simultaneously:*

Mother   You stupid, little, girl, what the hell do you think?

Daughter   Stop it – stop it – you can't do that anymore – I'm not a child.

Mother   Well stop behaving like one, you little madam.

Daughter   Let me go – I hate you – I hate you.

Granny   Enough – darling – that's enough.

The **Daughter** *runs to her* **Granny** *holding her bottom, the* **Mother** *sits crying – surprised at herself. The* **Nephew** *comes forward and gently takes the wooden spoon from her hand.*

Granny   What were you doing, huh? Where were you going?

Mother   Stupid child.

Granny   What is it? Why?

Daughter   (*sobbing*)   I just want to go to back.

Nephew   You can't just run away!

Daughter   – I want my teacher –

Pause.

Daughter   My friends . . . where are they?

Granny   We're here.

Daughter   I miss school.

Beat.

Father   Of course you do. It's natural.

Pause.

Father   Come on – we're going to go to your school – I'll take you there.

Cousin   Are you mad?

Granny   No one will be there.

Father She hasn't left these woods since we came here – she misses her home, the house, the school.

Nephew We all do.

Father Well let's go then.

Mother You can't.

Father Yes I can – we need to collect more things from the house anyway – get some eggs, some more clothes – the weather is turning.

Cousin It's not safe.

Father She won't go inside – she can hide – but just see from outside – would you like that my dove?

*The **Daughter** nods and goes and puts her arms around her **Father**'s neck, sniffling.*

Father There we are then.

Mother I'm against this.

Father I don't care.

Beat.

Cousin I'll come with you – in case. Is there anything you want from the house?

Mother I just want you to all come back.

Father Stop being so dramatic.

Granny Bring a new pot.

Cousin You stay here with your auntie and keep watch. You keep guard.

Nephew Yes sir (*he does a salute*).

Mother Don't do that.

*The **Father**, **Daughter** and **Cousin** start to go.*

Mother Wait – come here.

*The girl is holding her **Father**'s hand, she doesn't move. The **Mother** moves to her, kneels down in front of her and whispers something in her ear. She tucks her **Daughter**'s hair behind her ear, then gets up and the group walk away. The boy goes to the **Mother**.*

Nephew We'll be OK – I'll protect us. I'm going to take up post.

No answer.

Granny Good boy. Better take this with you (*she hands him the gun*).

Nephew Really?

She nods.

Granny Your grandfather gave that to me you know?

Nephew I know.

Granny He used to give it to me every time he went out, so if anything happened I'd be able to protect myself in his absence. But then one day he went out and he needed it, but I had it . . . and he didn't come back.

Beat.

Granny Take it.

He does. She goes to the **Mother**, *brings her to the bed and sits her on it. She then lights the fire. The* **Nephew** *meantime has climbed the tree.*

Long pause . . .

The **Mother** *shivers.*

Pause.

Granny Come in closer to the fire.

Beat.

Granny Are you warm enough up there?

Nephew Yes.

Beat.

Granny What do you see?

Nephew Same as before. Nothing. No wait – the smoke from the other side of the wood has gone out.

Pause.

Nephew This is the longest game I've ever played.

Beat.

Granny You know it's not a game don't you.

Nephew Yes.

Pause.

He begins to whistle.

Granny Stop that – it's bad luck.

Nephew Sorry.

Pause.

The **Grandmother** *takes some cheese from a bag and eats a piece – she hands a bit to the* **Mother** *who shakes her head.*

Granny Eat it.

*The **Mother** puts it in her mouth and chews distractedly.*

Granny (*to herself*)   There is no law but the law of the –

*The **Grandmother** eats another piece, then goes to the box where the mouse is kept – she looks in it, around it and then goes to the **Mother**.*

She speaks quietly.

Granny (*to **Mother***)   The mouse is gone.

Mother   What?

Granny   The field mouse – it's chewed a hole in the box and gone.

Mother   Oh.

Granny   They'll both be really upset. He won't last five minutes in these woods – if it's not a fox or a bird it'll be a boar that gets hold of him. Maybe we can try and catch another one.

Beat.

Granny   Are you listening?

Nephew   I can see them.

Mother   Who?

Granny   Who do you think?

Mother   Where are they?

Nephew   Behind our house . . . now they are walking past the school . . . they're ducking down below the wall . . . I can see her looking through the gate, she looks so tiny – I could almost hold her in my hand . . . The school gate seems to be locked.

Granny   There's no one there – the teachers have all gone.

Mother   And the students – everyone's gone but us.

Granny   Is there anyone else about?

Nephew   No one. It's a ghost town.

Granny   What are they doing now?

Nephew   Just looking at the school playground.

Mother   You keep watching them – you make sure you watch over them – their every move. Tell us everything you see.

Nephew   The clouds are rolling across the sky fast – it must be very windy.

Pause.

Mother   We should have harvested by now.

Pause.

Granny What now?

Nephew They are still there – no wait – they seem to be moving . . . Around the side . . . they've gone out of view I can't see them . . . And now the sun's gone behind a cloud – I can't see anything.

Mother Look harder – look harder – can you see them?

Nephew I'm trying – I can't.

Mother Oh no.

Pause.

Nephew Yes, it's very windy – the tree in the school yard is getting blown about like mad – it's like its possessed – or dancing – crazy dancing.

Pause.

Mother If I was at home we'd have done the windows by now – as it is it'll be too cold when we return – and we won't have aired anything properly for the winter months. Everything will get mouldy.

Pause.

Mother And how can I make my preserves? – All the fruit will be bad. It's such a waste.

Granny Can you see them yet?

Nephew No.

Beat.

Nephew Wait, I think I see her – yes, just behind our shed – there they are peeping round – looking at the house. They're looking at our house, uncle's going inside now.

Mother Through the front door?

Nephew No, the back door.

Beat.

Nephew He's stopped –

Granny Why?

Nephew He's petting the goat.

Mother Silly fool – get inside.

There's a huge gust of wind which blows the tree.

Nephew He's gone in.

Mother Be careful.

Pause.

Nephew Now she's moving in the field – she's picking flowers.

Mother What if someone sees her?

Nephew It's OK, the grass is long. She must be picking them for you, Auntie. Cousin is watching her – don't worry.

There's another huge gust of wind, the boy cries – he nearly falls out of the tree. The **Grandmother** *and* **Mother** *rush to the foot of the tree.*

Granny Are you OK?

Mother What happened?

Nephew The wind – I lost my footing.

Granny Hook your foot over the branch below – there that's better.

The women draw back.

Mother What do you see?

Pause.

We now simultaneously see the camp area where we have been and the **Cousin** *and* **Daughter** *hiding behind the shed near the family house waiting for the* **Father** *to come out. The* **Daughter** *has a handful of wild flowers.*

There is a long pause with everyone's attention focused on the back door (whether they are actually seeing it, or seeing it in their mind's eye willing the **Father** *to come out of it). This pause continues and continues, longer than seems possible . . .*

And then the **Father** *comes out of the back door very, very slowly and quietly, closing it silently behind him and walking past the* **Daughter** *and* **Cousin** *towards the woods. They look bewildered and they follow him. Only now the boy begins to relate what he sees.*

Nephew He's come out and he is walking back – they are following him.

Granny What does he have with him?

Nephew Nothing. He is walking very straight.

Mother Come down from there now.

The boy climbs down and goes to the women who are standing looking into the forest to catch a glimpse of them coming back.

Long pause . . .

Eventually the **Father** *strides in at a pace. He looks different. He goes to his bed and sits.*

Mother Are you OK? What happened?

The **Daughter** *and* **Cousin** *come bounding after trying to keep up with him. The girl goes to her* **Mother** *with the flowers.*

Daughter I saw it – it's still there – it looks much smaller than I remember it. But the gate was locked and there was no one there, but it's still standing – real as you or I. And the goat says hello.

Mother What happened?

Cousin I don't know.

Nephew Come over here – what did you see?

*The **Daughter** and **Nephew** sit in their area talking quietly – the **Father** has begun to slowly gather together his bedding. The women watch in surprise, as does the **Cousin**.*

Granny What are you doing?

He continues to pack things away at some pace.

Mother Husband – what are you doing?

Father Everyone – pack your things.

They all look at him in amazement.

Father NOW, come on.

Cousin It's not safe to go back to the house.

Father We're leaving the village.

Beat.

Father Come on!

Mother But what about the crops?

Granny And the livestock.

Cousin Do as you're told, collect your things.

Granny Must we go now though?

Mother Surely we can wait another day.

Father I told you – you aren't to challenge me – if you want to stay behind you can with your boy and your mother – but I'm taking my daughter – come on girl get your things.

*All the women, the **Daughter** and **Nephew** begin to pack their things together.*

*The **Cousin** takes the **Father** to one side.*

Cousin What was it, Cousin – what did you see?

Beat.

Father (*to himself*) We saw no one enter or leave the house.

Cousin This is how they work – by stealth – they are clever. Had they killed an animal? They did that in one house in our village and smeared everything with its blood.

Father No, not that.

He looks close to tears.

Cousin Was it a body – had they left a corpse in your house?

Father No.

Beat.

Daughter He's gone.

She is frantically looking around everywhere.

Daughter Where's Mousey gone? I can't find him.

Nephew He's chewed a hole in the box. He escaped.

Daughter Oh no! What will become of him! We can't leave him behind.

Cousin Come on, children, gather up your things – we need to go.

Daughter I need to find him.

Cousin He's clever – he can look after himself – he's gone – come on we need to go too.

Daughter But my mouse.

Granny Don't cry – come on – we all have to leave things behind.

The **Grandmother** *looks at the white stone and then at the* **Mother**.

Nephew It's just a mouse.

Daughter It's my mouse . . . Where are we going?

Mother Away from here – come on, pack your bedding.

Daughter But how will he find us?

No reply.

Daughter What if the cat gets him again?

Granny He has to learn to take care of himself. Now come on –

Father Quickly.

Granny Gather up your things, we mustn't forget anything important.

Gradual fade down of lights as they collect together their things. We can hear the girl softly sobbing all the while.

Lights down.

Part Five

*Scene: We are in the kitchen area of another house, which is similar to our family's house. The **Mother** is sat at the table with her head in her hands. The **Father** stands smoking at the window looking out. An **Old Man** comes into the room.*

Old Man They seem to be settled. They got into the one bed and wrapped their arms around one another and fell asleep straight away. Like a couple of babes in the wood.

Beat.

Old Man So alike – like peas in a pod.

Father I can't thank you enough for your kindness, we won't bother you for too long.

Old Man Please – we always welcome travellers. And this is a frequent occurrence in these sad times.

Beat.

Old Man Is she alright?

Father We lost her mother on the way.

Old Man Oh dear.

Father My cousin has gone back to find her.

Old Man Does he know where you are?

Father Yes – he walked us to the gate.

Beat.

Old Man Would you like some water dear?

*The **Mother** doesn't respond.*

Father A cigarette?

Old Man Oh – well – don't mind if I do – I haven't had such a thing in years. My wife didn't like it.

Father Is she dead?

Old Man Yes – thirty years, God rest her.

*The **Old Man** lights his cigarette from the **Father**'s one. He takes a drag.*

Old Man Very nice.

Beat.

Father You never married again?

Old Man   I thought about it – but I couldn't do it. She still filled my head. She used to stand out there and pick lemons from the tree in the yard. I'd stand right here and watch her. And at night she smelt of them. Her hair, her skin, her blood, her bones . . . When she died I cut a branch that was covered in leaves and took it to my bed. I put the leaves in my nose and tried to breath her back . . .

Pause.

Old Man   What have you seen? Is it all true?

Father   It's strange – there are buildings that have been destroyed, and craters in the ground – trees uprooted. And people – lines of people walking East. Or North. They were told to go, and they went. That's all.

Old Man   Amazing.

Beat.

Old Man   A disaster.

Father   Yes.

Beat.

Father   But it can't last – we'll be able to go home soon.

Old Man   It will blow over.

Pause.

Father   We saw one man sitting beside a pile of rubble crying. We told him to come with us but he said he wouldn't leave his family – they were all inside. We helped him to take out their bodies and bury them and then he lay on the soil and cried. He wouldn't come.

Old Man   What happened to him?

Father   I don't know. He just kept saying the same thing over and over – 'You can't cut a man's roots, you can't cut a man's roots'.

Beat.

Father   In a way he is better off.

Old Man   What do you mean?

Father   He has nothing to lose now – no house, no family.

Old Man   Only his country.

Father   They can't take that away.

Beat.

Father   They can't . . .

Beat.

Father This won't last for long.

Beat.

Old Man And you? What happened to you?

Pause.

Father We'd be staying in the woods and I went back to collect some things . . . I went in and the house felt warm, the sun coming in the window and as I closed the door I had decided that this was all nonsense. I was going to go outside again and fetch my family, bring them back to the house because this is madness, we can't be hiding from nothing. But then I noticed something – a new smell – something I didn't recognise. Not a smell of my house or of my family or of my people. And I walked into the kitchen and that's where I saw it. There. Him. A man. Sat at my table. The one I made. Smoking a cigarette with one foot on the chair. He had just eaten something and the plate was pushed away from him. He heard me come in and he turned and looked at me, looked right at me. He almost smiled. And then I thought he was going to get up – I could feel a scream rising in my throat. But he didn't get up, he turned away from me, leaned back in the chair, pulled on the cigarette, closed his eyes and put his hands behind his head. He turned away from me. As if I wasn't there.

Beat.

Father And I quietly walked out of the room.

Beat.

Father In my chair. My plate. My table. My knife. My house. It was as if I didn't exist – as if I had never been born. A catastrophe.

Pause.

Father You know they seem to be moving in this direction – you should come with us – travel with us – there is safety in numbers. We have family over the border we can stay with until the wind changes.

Old Man I can't leave my home.

Father That's what I said.

Pause.

They both look at the woman who seems to have fallen asleep on the table.

Old Man How did you lose the mother?

Father I don't know – she just vanished. One minute she was there mumbling away about something or other and the next she was gone.

Old Man You don't think?

Father No. I think she was up to something – crafty old thing. She had a gun with her – she'll be OK.

Old Man How long ago was this?

Father Yesterday – she (*looking at the* **Mother**) wanted to search immediately, wanted to go back, but it wasn't safe for the children. My cousin persuaded her to keep going, said he'd search for her himself.

Old Man Perhaps she forgot something?

Father The only things that mattered to her were her husband's picture and her gun – and she had both of those.

Beat.

Old Man Oh dear. Sorry business.

Beat.

Old Man You see I couldn't leave without that tree – but you can't take a tree with you can you? (*He smiles.*)

Beat.

Old Man I'm afraid I don't have any other beds – I've put the children in mine – I'll sleep up there too, on the floor – so you will have to stay down here.

Father That's fine – a roof over our heads is luxury these days.

Old Man Wait.

He goes to a drawer and takes out an old service revolver.

Old Man You might need this old lady.

Father Where did you –?

Old Man Look at the date on it.

Father (*looking at the inscription on the gun*) Where did you get it?

Old Man We used to need her . . . It seems she'll have to come out of retirement. Take her.

Father I couldn't – you might –

Old Man No, no, I'm a man on my own – you have a whole nest to protect.

Father Does it even work?

Old Man Now, now, old she may be, but she's up to a fight – never let me down before.

Father If you're sure . . .

Old Man The wife never liked it in the house, thought it was dangerous (*he yawns*).

Father You go up – it's late. Thank you for everything.

The **Old Man** *shakes his hand and goes to leave the room. At the door he turns back to look at the woman and then goes up to bed.*

*The **Father** sits at the other end of the table and stares at his wife, asleep with her head on the table. He lights another cigarette and smokes it.*

When he has finished, he sits on the chair with his arms crossed and gradually falls asleep on his front.

Pause.

*The **Daughter** appears at the door. She walks over to the table and looks at her sleeping parents. She places a hand on her mother's head. Then she pulls up a chair and sits down.*

Pause.

*She ties her hair up in a knot in the same way her **Grandmother** used to.*

Pause.

*The **Nephew** enters, he sees the **Daughter** and approaches her, speaking quietly so as not to disturb the sleeping adults.*

Nephew   Was his snoring keeping you up? Do you want me to try and turn him over?

Daughter   No, I'm waiting.

Nephew   What for?

Daughter   Granny.

Pause.

Daughter   I knew I should have held her hand.

Nephew   It's not your fault.

Daughter   She did have the gun didn't she?

Nephew   Yes – no chicken in the land is safe – she's probably walking up the path now with armfuls of dead poultry.

Beat.

He goes to the window and looks out hopefully.

Daughter   Poor Mousey's out there somewhere too.

Nephew   Maybe he met a friend who helped him escape.

Daughter   Escape – what from? He was at home . . .

Beat.

*The **Daughter** moves to stand behind her **Father**.*

Daughter   I'm sorry he's been so mean to you – he's just worried about us all, you know.

Nephew   About his family?

Daughter   Yes, us.

Beat.

Nephew   There's more walking tomorrow, you should sleep.

Daughter   So should you.

Pause.

Nephew   Come up – let's go back up – we don't want to disturb them – we can wait up there.

Beat.

Nephew   You'll get cold here.

Beat.

Nephew   Come on.

Reluctantly she gets up. They both look at the adults for a moment and then head upstairs together.

Stillness.

Many hours of the night pass . . .

*Suddenly the **Mother** wakes with a start, she gets up and goes to the door. The **Father** wakes now too.*

Father   What is it?

Mother   He's back.

*She opens the door and watches the **Cousin** walk in.*

Cousin   How did you know I was coming?

Mother   Did you find her? Where is she?

Cousin   No, I asked everywhere – someone said they had seen her heading North along the stream a few miles from where we lost her.

Mother   Why would she go there?

Cousin   Doesn't she have family in the valley beyond there?

Mother   I don't remember.

Father   Now you mention it – she does – your old uncle? Her brother?

Mother   I thought he died.

Father   No – not that one. She must have wanted to check on him.

Mother   Without telling us?

Cousin   She knew we'd never let her go alone.

Father   Silly old thing.

Mother   I don't know – we should go there then – find her.

Father   But we are so close to the border – we'll cross it by nightfall tomorrow – let's take the children to safety and then we can come back for her.

Mother   Are you sure?

Father   Yes, of course.

Cousin   I think that's a good plan.

Mother   But what if she –

Cousin   We must think of the children first – it was her decision to go.

Father   She'd never want you to leave them.

Mother   No, of course. Where are they?

Father   Asleep upstairs – why don't you go and get in with them – you've an hour or so before we need to leave.

Mother   OK, I will.

She hugs the **Cousin***.*

Mother   Thank you, Cousin.

She goes upstairs. We hear her footsteps. The two men look at one another. The **Cousin** *sits down.*

Pause.

The **Father** *is looking at the* **Cousin** *but doesn't want to ask.*

Pause.

The **Cousin** *places the gun and the empty jewellery pouch on the table.*

Pause.

The **Father** *hands him a cigarette. The* **Cousin***'s hand is shaking so much he can't light it. The* **Father** *takes the matches and does it for him.*

Beat.

Cousin   She was in the forest. Near our camp.

Beat.

Cousin   She must have gone back for whatever was in this (*indicating the pouch*).

Father   We'll go over the border tomorrow and stay there until this has all passed.

Cousin   I'm coming back – to fight.

Father   Fight who?

Cousin They'll come – once we have all disappeared, they'll come.

Father They are just trying to teach us a lesson. Show us who's boss. We'll all be back home by spring.

Beat.

Cousin They shot her.

Beat.

Cousin The animals – in the forest – ate her. I buried what I could find with his picture.

Father Where?

Cousin Near the clearing. I marked it with a big white stone.

Father Thank you.

Beat.

Father We'll know where to look when we go back.

Beat.

Cousin Next spring.

Father Yes, next spring.

Beat.

Father You'd better get some rest, we've a long journey ahead of us.

*The **Cousin** nods and puts his head on the table. The **Father** takes the gun and goes to stand by the window, looking out.*

Pause.

Lights gradually fade to black, but not until we see the silhouette of the lemon tree and the man.

Playwright's Outro

Plan D was my first professional full-length theatre show and was an exhilarating, exhausting and terrifying experience. I had no idea how people would respond to the play. Or even if they would come. But they did, including the critic Michael Billington; in fact, it was his first ever visit to the Tristan Bates Theatre in Covent Garden, our brilliant PR Liz Hyder later told me. More importantly though, we had people from many different backgrounds in the audience, many of whom sought me out in the bar after the show to talk to me about the play and relate their own family's experiences of displacement. These people were not just Palestinians but from many different backgrounds – memorably a young woman from Afghanistan told me how strongly the play resonated with her own experience of her family home being occupied and reoccupied during the war. I gathered up all these tales and felt a responsibility to bear witness, pass them on, keep them alive.

Scenes from 73* Years

Scenes from 73* Years is a snapshot of Palestinian life under occupation. A picnic interrupted by soldiers. A never-ending queue at a checkpoint. Sunbathing in the shadow of a tank. How do people get by when every day feels constrained?

Thirty+ characters, can be performed with a minimum of six, 3 males and 3 females.

The play was first performed as *Scenes from 68* Years* at the Arcola Theatre, London, on 6 April 2016, a production by Sandpit Arts. Directed by Chris White, designed by Paul Burgess and produced by Alia Alzougbi, it had the following cast:

Maisa Abd Elhadi
Yasen Atour
Taghrid Choucair-Vizoso
Janine Harouni
Pinar Öğün
Mateo Oxley
Peter Polycarpou

A note on the title: the asterisk (*) in the title denotes the fact that the number should be amended as appropriate – it is a measurement of the time since the Nakba, or 'Catastrophe', as Palestinians call 1948 when partition happened with the creation of the State of Israel.

Playwright's Intro

After the performances of *Plan D*, many audience members approached me with their own stories, including those of life under occupation. I held all these amazing tales close, along with other snippets and family anecdotes that I had heard over the years that had stayed with me. For example, the story of my surname. Around the time I was getting married and making it publicly known that I was absolutely keeping my own name and not taking my husband's family name, I got a surprising email from my Dad. In it he told me he had updated his email address – nothing particularly unusual there – but the address included his first name and another name I did not recognise: Musleh. When I asked him why he had included Musleh he responded, 'Because that's our name'. I nearly fell off my chair. My passport, my birth certificate, all my documents are in the name Khalil. My Dad's passport too – so what was the story? Well it seems when Dad went to get his first passport in Jerusalem in the 1960s, the official behind the desk deemed his name 'too long' so cut the last few words. My Dad became a Khalil rather than a Musleh just like that. Of course that story had to go into the play, and duly did, along with many others. I checked first with all the people who had given me their stories that I could include them in a play, and they kindly agreed.

Production Note

The dates in the stage directions are for the performers' information and it's possible but not necessary to include them in the performance, at the discretion of the director. Note also that although the scenes are not numbered, they must only be performed in the order as set out here.

Scene: (2010) The stage is in complete darkness, everything is still. Perhaps we hear a gentle sigh or the sound of a body turning in a bed. [Pause] Suddenly everything changes. The sound of a door being broken down with one hard smash. The sound of feet moving and voices – but the stage should still be in complete darkness throughout this scene.

Voice 1 (*shouting*)   Get up, get up now, where is he, where is he?

Voice 2 (*shouting*)   Move!

We hear a child scream and begin to cry, it's not clear if this is from this house or next door.

Voice 3   My wife is not dressed.

Voice 6   I have no clothes on –

Voice 2   HE SAID GET UP, GET UP NOW, GET UP, GET UP, GET UP!

Voice 4   We are civilians –

The sound of a door opening and a gun being cocked, then a child screaming and crying in fear; the child continues to cry throughout the rest of the scene.

Voice 4   Don't point that at him he is a child.

Voice 5   Get him out then.

Voice 1   Where is he? Tell us!

Voice 2   Move, we want to talk to your husband.

Voice 6   I'm not leaving him alone with you.

Voice 2   Get the fuck out and take your –

Voice 3   We don't know anything.

The sound of someone falling over; the soldier has kicked the man to the floor.

Voice 6   Leave him!

Voice 4   I'm filming this.

Voice 5   What?

Voice 4   I have a camera and I'm going to show the world.

Voice 5   PUT THAT DOWN IMMEDIATELY!

Voice 3   Please calm down.

Voice 5   STOP FILMING!

Voice 3   I'll come with you – let my wife and child –

Voice 2   GET THEM OUT!

Voice 5   IS HE STILL FILMING?

Voice 1 Where is he?

Voice 2 WHO? WHO's filming.

Voice 5 Him.

Voice 2 WHO THE FUCK IS FILMING!

Voice 5 Him.

*Suddenly a film projection appears of what the **Cameraman** sees as his night vision comes into focus, a **Soldier** in full army fatigues right in front of him, pointing a gun at him.*

Voice 2/Soldier PUT THAT FUCKING CAMERA DOWN OR I'LL SHOOT YOU!

*Scene: (1948) In the middle of the space there is a body – it is a **Boy**. His face and hands are both bandaged, as is one of his legs. One arm is in a sling.*

Pause.

Boy Mama!

Beat.

Boy Mama! Come here! I need you!

Beat.

*The **Boy**'s **Father** rushes in.*

Father What is it?

Boy Where's Mama?

Father She's hanging the washing – why are you shouting – be quiet!

Boy I need her, I can't breath – you did it too tight.

Father Let me see.

*He examines the bandages on the **Boy**'s face and moves them around his nose area.*

Father Is that better?

Boy Not really.

Father Breath through your mouth.

Boy I'm hot. When are they coming?

Father Any minute.

Boy You said that half an hour ago.

Father They will be here. They said they would and they will. You know it's not easy for them to move around.

Beat.

Father Now please stop shouting, be a good boy. They will be here. Be good.

Boy What can I do? I want to play but I can't like this.

Father Then think. Think about how lucky you are. To have both your parents here with you, about what you want to do with your life, what you will study at university. I think you should be a doctor, don't you?

Boy Because you are a doctor, right?

Father Not only because of that, but because you have an instinct for it. Remember the bird you found, made the bed for him, kept him warm.

Boy It died.

Father Comfortably. And dignified. Thanks to you.

Boy But a doctor should make people better, not help them die.

Father If things are beyond help, then it is better to make it easy to go.

Boy Like Sayed?

Father Yes.

Beat.

Father Now be good and quiet, I'll bring them here when they come, OK?

Boy OK.

Father And don't call your mother, she has a lot to do.

Boy She doesn't know they are coming does she?

Scene: (2003) A pavement. A **Shopkeeper** *sits outside his shop on a folding chair. He is smoking a cigarette. Either side of him is a tank. He shifts his chair a little to the left to move out of the shadow cast by one of them. He sees the* **Soldier** *looking at him and smiles.*

Shopkeeper Hello, my friend. I'm just getting the sun. Very good for you, you know. Healthy. Vitamin D.

He sits finishing his cigarette and enjoys the sun a little more. Then he takes out his mobile. He dials a number.

Shopkeeper Where are you? I've got nothing to do here. I'm sitting in the sun. I know but a shop with no food is like a blunt pencil – pointless. (*Beat.*) Come on have a sense of humour! I know. I know. How long have you been there? No. You can't have been. That's bad even for Huwara. Are there lots of people? Really. I hope you locked the car. People could steal the things. They're desperate. And you know what the soldiers are like.

As he says this he looks up at the tank, wary they may have heard him, they haven't.

Shopkeeper I know it's not your fault, I'm not blaming you – but I don't want it all to go bad in the heat, why don't you try another way – how about you turn around and try Awarta checkpoint? I know it's meant to be for trucks but your car is full isn't it? So tell them it's a mini truck . . . try it – you may as well. What have you got to lose? I need those things – maybe I should ask Fouad next time, eh? He'd manage to sweet talk his way through, Yulla Awarta, try it –. OK, OK, bye.

He hangs up the phone and leans back in the chair again.

Friendly Soldier *(from top of tank)* Well?

Shopkeeper He's stuck at Huwara checkpoint. So no Coca Cola for a few hours . . . you should call one of your friends down there – he's the one with the blue hatchback.

Friendly Soldier Sorry, mate, I'd help if I could – but I'm just a lowly Turai – a Private.

Beat.

Friendly Soldier Shame, I could kill a coke . . .

Shopkeeper I know – these checkpoints hurt everyone, eh? I tell you what, how about a nice *shay bin nana*? That will refresh us?

Friendly Soldier Well – I wouldn't say no.

Shopkeeper I make it really good – I have a pot of mint on the back step and it tastes so fresh. You wait – you have to try it to believe it. We'll all have a cup. It will make us feel refreshed and revived. The best. Trust me.

Friendly Soldier OK, thanks.

He gets up and goes into the shop to make the tea.

Scene: (2005) We are outside a house, it is old but well kept. There is a small gate and front garden, outside which stand two people.

Translator Are you sure about this?

Beat.

The other **Man** *nods.*

Beat.

Translator And it's definitely this one?

The **Man** *nods.*

Translator OK. But I'll warn you again – you must be prepared for – well you know.

The **Man** *nods.*

Translator Right then – you stay here. I'll go.

The **Man** *stands by the gate, the* **Translator** *walks up to the door and knocks. He looks back at the* **Man** *and smiles weakly.*

Eventually the door is opened by the **Resident**.

Resident Hello.

Translator Hi, I'm sorry to bother you, I'm a translator, I'm working with the Orchestra, you know the . . .

Resident Oh yes, they are wonderful – I have tickets for tomorrow night.

Translator Oh, that's good. Well this man here . . .

He points to the **Man**.

Translator   is one of the musicians and, believe it or not, his mother used to live here.

Resident In Jerusalem?

Translator In this very house.

Resident Oh, I see.

Translator And well, he wondered if he could have a quick look inside,

Pause.

The **Resident** *looks at the man with the* **Translator**, *who stares back – he neither smiles, nor frowns. He wears a blank expression on his face. The* **Resident** *considers this face.*

Resident And he's a musician?

Translator Yes. A very good one. The best.

Resident Of course he can come and have a look, come on.

Gesturing to the **Man**.

Resident Come in.

The **Translator** *gestures to the man, who tentatively approaches the front door. They all go in and the door closes behind them.*

Scene: (2016) A girl in Palestine has left a message on Skype.

Rula Ya Nadia – not there? Shoo? It's 10.20 with me, we agreed . . . oh right – the time difference . . . yes you're two hours behind me. Imagine Palestine being ahead of the West in something. I'll try you later. I'm waiting for you, Cousin . . .

She blows a kiss to the screen.

Scene: (2003) Huwara checkpoint. A huge group of people stand waiting in the heat. People with cars have got out and are milling about. They are all looking at one female **Soldier**, *stood there.*

Blue Hatchback Man *approaches her.*

Blue Hatchback Man What's the situation?

Soldier Step back, please.

Blue Hatchback Man How long will we have to wait here?

Soldier Step back, please. I'm waiting for orders.

Blue Hatchback Man I have a car full of food, it's going to go bad in this heat. That's my one there – see? The blue hatchback? I've got Coca Cola – want one?

The **Soldier** *doesn't reply.*

Blue Hatchback Man I just want to know if you think it's worth me waiting. I don't want to leave if it's going to be fifteen minutes, but I don't want to wait if it's going to be closed all day. I need to get to Ramallah. With my supplies. I'm delivering them. It would be a shame if they went bad.

Beat.

Blue Hatchback Man So what do you think? I know all this isn't your fault – should I stick it out a bit longer or go?

No answer.

The **Man** *looks despondent, he's not sure what to do. He takes out his mobile and moves away from the* **Soldier** *– he makes a call.*

A young **Woman** *in a hijab walks forward and hands her papers to the* **Soldier**.

Soldier What's this?

Woman My papers.

Soldier The checkpoint is closed.

Woman But it's three o'clock.

Soldier And?

Woman You told me yesterday . . .

Beat.

Woman to come back – remember? I'm the student. I study here and my parents live over there – ten minutes' walk. I haven't seen them for a month because this checkpoint is always closed on the days I'm not studying.

Beat.

Woman You told me to come back here with my papers today at three and you would let me go and see my parents.

Beat.

Woman   They're old.

Beat.

Woman   I miss them.

Soldier   I think you have me mixed up with someone else. You probably think we all look the same.

Woman   No, I know it was you. I remember.

Soldier   You must be mistaken.

Beat.

Woman   Please.

Soldier   Step back. This checkpoint is closed.

Woman   But –

Soldier   Step back.

*The **Man** has finished his phone conversation and approaches again.*

Blue Hatchback Man   Is it worth trying Awarta? I know it's usually for trucks but – ?

No answer.

Blue Hatchback Man   We don't want to bother you – really just let us know if it's worth us waiting or not.

*The **Soldier** turns her back on them. The two re-join the throng of people, watching and waiting to see if the checkpoint will open.*

Scene: (1948) A group of male soldiers are inside a house. The house is empty but there are signs that it has only recently been vacated; the table is laid for dinner. The soldiers look at the things in the house.

Soldier 1   Look at this picture.

Soldier 2   It's very nice isn't it?

Soldier 1   It is. Colourful. Do you want it?

Soldier 2   No – no you saw it first – you can have it.

Soldier 1   Are you sure? Do you think it will get ruined in the jeep – that would be a shame.

Soldier 2   I tell you what – let's take it out of the frame and roll it up – then you can get it reframed when you get home.

Soldier 1   Good idea.

The two men very carefully take the picture down and proceed to remove it from the frame and roll it up.

Soldier 3 (*from off-stage*) They've got a gramophone! I haven't seen one of these for ages! Listen!

Umm Kulthum's 'Fakarouni' plays.

The soldiers stop and listen.

There is the sound of the needle sliding off the record.

Soldier 3 (*still off-stage*) Sorry about that.

Soldier 2 What a racket!

Soldier 3 Try this.

On comes Eric Satie's 'Gymnopodie no. 3'

Soldier 1 That's more like it.

Soldier 3 *comes on-stage.*

Soldier 3 It's in really good condition. We should bring it with us, give it to the captain for the mess.

Soldier 2 Good idea.

Soldier 3 And the kitchen is fully stocked – try this jam – it's delicious.

Soldier 1 What kind?

Soldier 3 Quince – it's lovely.

Soldier 1 It's heaven – is there much there?

Soldier 3 I'll collect up the jars, I've never tasted anything like it.

He goes back next door.

Soldier 2 There's some lovely embroidered bedding next door as well, I'll pile it up to bring.

Soldier 1 See if you can get something to wrap it in, we've got to be careful with this stuff on the jeep. It could get ruined.

Soldier 3 (*from off-stage*) Chaps, there's a whole cake in the larder – get in here!

Scene: (2002) We are in a small studio flat, a **Woman** *is there, with a dressing gown on. She sits on the bed applying makeup. There is the sound of a buzzer. The* **Woman** *gets up, hurriedly puts away her makeup and turns off the radio and answers the entry phone.*

Woman Hello? Come up.

She checks her hair and face in the mirror.

She takes off her dressing gown to reveal a modest but sexy negligee.

There's a knock at the door.

She opens it, and there is a man there. He is the **Friendly Soldier** *from the tanks outside the shop scene.*

Friendly Soldier   Hi.

Woman   Hi, come in. How are you?

Friendly Soldier   Oh, fine, a bit better.

Woman   And your mother?

Friendly Soldier   Getting worse.

Woman   I'm sorry to hear that . . . Would you like something to drink?

Friendly Soldier   No, thank you.

Woman   What's the matter?

Friendly Soldier   Nothing, I'm sorry I'm late. The traffic was a nightmare. Almost a standstill on Ayalon. There was a bomb scare. Then I had a run in with this taxi driver.

Woman   Arab?

Friendly Soldier   No, Israeli.

Woman   What happened?

Friendly Soldier   I clipped his tail light – it was an accident – you could hardly see it – but he went crazy asking me where I was going. He wanted my number.

Woman   What did you do?

Friendly Soldier   Drove off. I couldn't give it to him. You know I'm signed off for stress – I have to avoid anything like that . . .

Beat.

Friendly Soldier   Did you get my message?

Woman   No, I didn't – but it's OK. When you are coming I normally clear my afternoon.

Friendly Soldier   I didn't know that. You didn't get my message?

Woman   No. But I don't mind. You're here now.

Beat.

Woman   You seem really shaken. You're not yourself.

Beat.

Woman   Did the taxi driver bother you that much?

Friendly Soldier Check the message I left you.

Woman Why?

Friendly Soldier I asked you something in it. Check it.

Woman Why don't you just –

Friendly Soldier Check it.

Woman OK, OK.

She gets up and finds her mobile.

Woman Are you sure you won't have a drink?

He shakes his head.

She listens to her voicemail. She hangs up.

Woman I see.

Friendly Soldier Is it OK?

Woman What do you mean?

Friendly Soldier Do you mind?

Woman Why would I mind? If it's what you want.

Friendly Soldier It is. Very much.

Woman I'm a little surprised.

Friendly Soldier So am I – but I thought I should be honest with you. If I can't be with you, then –

Woman Yes. But I'll need you to be more specific.

Friendly Soldier What?

Woman You need to tell me what you want.

Friendly Soldier Oh. Well. Perhaps I – hold on.

He takes a jotter and pen from his pocket and writes for a moment or two.

He then hands the paper to the woman.

She reads, then nods.

Woman What does that say?

Friendly Soldier Wall.

Woman Oh.

She continues to read.

Woman OK. Well, it's not exactly – I mean it's unusual.

Friendly Soldier If you are uncomfortable –

Woman No, no, it's OK. But it's going to be double.

Friendly Soldier I'll pay you triple.

Woman Do you want me to change?

Friendly Soldier Would you mind?

Woman What shall I wear?

He goes to her drawers and looks at the clothes. He takes out a pair of dark tracksuit bottoms and denim shirt with a faint military air.

Woman Really?

He nods.

She takes off the negligee and puts on the tracksuit bottoms and shirt and faces him.

Friendly Soldier Good. Do you have any boots?

She takes out a pair of heeled boots.

Friendly Soldier They're a bit trendy.

Woman It's all I have.

She puts them on.

Friendly Soldier Can you tie your hair back, and take off your makeup?

She shrugs and does so. He looks around the space for the props he wants. He brings a chair centre-stage and takes some of her tights out of the drawer. He's warming to the task, getting into it.

He takes a pillow off the bed.

Woman Ready.

Friendly Soldier Great. Now here's what I'm thinking.

He whispers into her ear; she raises an eyebrow but nods.

Friendly Soldier Understand?

Woman Understand.

He takes off all his clothes except for his underpants.

Friendly Soldier No talking.

Woman Understand.

Beat.

Friendly Soldier Go!

She pushes him into the chair and ties his hands to it with a pair of tights. He is acting scared. She then takes another pair of tights and stuffs them into his mouth so he can't talk. Finally she takes a pair of black tights and blindfolds him.

Beat.

She stands on his foot. He moans loudly.

She then pushes the chair so it falls backwards – he cries out.

She gets a small table and throws it upside down on his chest, he yelps in surprise. She sits on it crushing his torso, again he makes a noise.

She bounces up and down a little, knocking the wind out of him.

Finally, she hesitantly picks up the pillow from the bed and holds it above his face for a moment. Then she presses it down hard.

He moans and struggles a little.

She silently counts to four, then lifts it up.

Beat.

He is breathing hard and moaning.

She presses the pillow down on to his face again, more moaning and gentle struggling ensues. Again she silently counts, this time to five, then lifts the pillow up.

Beat.

More hard breathing and moaning from the man.

She gets the pillow and presses it harder still on his face – she's getting a taste for this.

He moans and struggles.

She silently counts to 4, 5, 6, 7 – the moaning and struggling has stopped. She is frightened. She casts the pillow aside.

Woman   Are you alright?

She pulls the gag out of his mouth.

Friendly Soldier   I told you, NO TALKING.

Scene: (1992) A group of women sit on a rug outside, they have a bag with food in it and are sharing a picnic.

Woman 1   Right, has everyone got a glass of tea? I want to say congratulations to Fatima, we wish you a very happy healthy married life.

Woman 2   Here, here.

Woman 1   With lots of children.

Laughing.

Woman 1 Boys!

Woman 2 Why boys?

Woman 3 Thank you. This is such a nice idea.

Woman 1 Did you see the house yet?

Woman 3 No, not yet. Why?

Woman 1 Everyone's saying that Fouad has gone to sooo much trouble to make it perfect for you.

Woman 3 Really?

Woman 1 I heard he got a new mattress, imported from Italy.

The women laugh, **Woman 3** *looks embarrassed.*

Woman 2 You mean from Abu Riyad's warehouse!

Woman 3 I feel very special.

Woman 1 You even got to choose your own husband – lucky girl.

Woman 2 And such a handsome one, eh?

Two soldiers who are passing stop.

Soldier 1 Good afternoon, ladies.

Woman 1 Good afternoon.

Soldier 1 What are you doing here?

Woman 3 We're having a picnic.

Soldier 2 Nice day for it.

Soldier 1 On your own?

Woman 1 Yes. As you see.

Soldier 2 What's in the bag?

Woman 3 Just some pastries and mezza.

Soldier 1 And the flask?

Woman 2 Tea. With mint.

Solider 1 Would you mind opening the bag?

Woman 1 *opens it,* **Soldier 1** *peers in.*

Soldier 1 Looks nice, eh?

Soldier 2 Wish my wife could cook like that.

Beat.

Soldier 1 Enjoy your afternoon.

They move off.

Woman 2 Pass me the tea.

Scene: (2003) Inside the shop, it looks pretty empty. The **Friendly Soldier** *and the* **Shopkeeper** *sit drinking tea, the* **Soldier** *on a folding chair, the* **Shopkeeper** *on an empty olive oil can.*

Friendly Soldier Then my father died.

Shopkeeper *Yaboyay*, what bad luck. How did he die?

Friendly Soldier He had a heart attack, in his sleep, so it would have been completely painless they said.

Shopkeeper And your mother? How did she take it?

Friendly Soldier That's the worst part, she was devastated, crying and crying. But when I went back the next day she was fine, then I realised she'd forgotten – that's the disease you see, so I had to tell her again, and her reaction was exactly the same, awful. This happened every day for a week until the nurse said, 'Don't tell her anymore, it's not worth it'.

Shopkeeper Poor woman.

Friendly Soldier And now I have to lie to her. She says, 'Why hasn't that bastard come to see me, tell him I'm getting a divorce'. And I say, he's busy with work, or he's at the dentist or anything that comes into my head. It makes me feel really bad. I got signed off work for stress last year you know.

Shopkeeper That's bad, how old is your mother?

Friendly Soldier Seventy.

Shopkeeper And to think my old mum is eighty-seven and still climbing olive trees, I am blessed . . .

Friendly Soldier You are, mate, you are.

Beat.

Friendly Soldier Does she really climb –

An **Arab Man** *comes into the shop, then sees the* **Soldier** *and turns to go.*

Shopkeeper Yusef, hello! How are you my friend, *yulla* come and try don't be shy!

Nervous Man I'm in a hurry.

Shopkeeper What are you after?

Nervous Man   Nothing. (*Looking pointedly at the* **Soldier**.) Nothing.

Friendly Soldier   I better be going, thank you for the shay.

Shopkeeper   It's OK, you don't have to go.

Friendly Soldier   I better – don't want anyone to steal my tank.

The **Soldier** *leaves.*

Nervous Man   What was he doing here?

Shopkeeper   Drinking tea, probably going to buy something until you came in like a ticking bomb.

Nervous Man   What do you mean?

Shopkeeper   Look at yourself, Yusef, you are a twitching mess. A bundle of nerves.

Nervous Man   What the hell do you expect, there's bloody tanks parked in the streets!

Shopkeeper   We've all got our problems, my friend, my supplies are stuck at Huwara! What's the matter?

Nervous Man   I've only got a few hours before they re-impose curfew but how will I know when they do it?

Shopkeeper   You'll know,

Nervous Man   How?

Shopkeeper   When everyone else disappears,

Nervous Man   Every other Palestinian in Ramallah seems to have an inbuilt clock – they instinctively know when the curfew is starting – except me,

Shopkeeper   Just look around to see who's about,

Nervous Man   I do that but then by the time I've realised, I'm the only one left, it's too late and those sons of bitches start taking pot shots at me,

The **Shopkeeper** *is laughing,*

Nervous Man   It's not funny – look,

He pulls up his shirt to show a bandage in his stomach.

Shopkeeper   Shit – you were shot?

Nervous Man   Yes, I was shot. Why are you surprised! There are men with guns, tanks!

Shopkeeper   You should be careful – get inside when there's a curfew.

Nervous Man   I KNOW! That's what I try to do but I never know when it is.

Shopkeeper   Relax, what can I get you? Tea?

Nervous Man   I'm in a hurry – but I need . . .

Shopkeeper   Yes?

Nervous Man   You know –

Shopkeeper   Oh. I don't have any.

Nervous Man   Don't lie! Before all this they were as common as olives, now you can't find them anywhere. Please.

Shopkeeper   What do you want it for?

Nervous Man   Why does it matter? Do you have any or not?

Shopkeeper   I have but it depends what you want it for.

Nervous Man   Do you have any or not? Stop wasting my time.

Shopkeeper   How many do you want?

Nervous Man   One, two.

Shopkeeper   Well it can't be for cooking then.

Nervous Man   What difference? Is there one kind for cooking and another kind for . . .?

Shopkeeper   No, they are all the same but the price is different. I'll get them.

He goes to the back of the shop and comes back with two onions.

Nervous Man   Thank you.

He hands over a note, the **Shopkeeper** *gives him his change.*

Nervous Man   What's this?

Shopkeeper   Your change.

Nervous Man   Where's the rest?

Shopkeeper   Prices fluctuate my friend – it's the economy.

Nervous Man   Two onions!

Shopkeeper   They're in demand at the moment.

Nervous Man   You've charged me three times the regular price.

Shopkeeper   Because I know you – anyone else would have to pay five times. Do you want them or not?

Nervous Man   It's a lot of money.

Shopkeeper   I'm the shopkeeper, I can charge what I like.

The **Man** *gives him a cross look.*

Shopkeeper   If you don't want, give them back.

Nervous Man   Let me think.

Shopkeeper   You better hurry up, the curfew is not far away.

Nervous Man   What? How do you know?

Shopkeeper   Can't you tell? The street sounds different.

Nervous Man   Oh my god. I'll take them, this time.

Shopkeeper   Send my regards to your wife – tell her she'll get a better price if she comes in.

Nervous Man   Why?

Shopkeeper   Because she uses them for cooking . . . Get home safely.

The **Nervous Man** *exits.*

Scene: (1948) The **Boy** *covered in bandages sits centre-stage. There is a group of young men around him, and his* **Father** *stands behind him.*

Father   Mohammed, what is that?

Man 1   My gun.

Father   I told you I didn't want guns in my house.

Man 1   But I might need –

Man 2   No – go and put it by the door with the others.

Man 1 *goes off to dispose of his gun.*

Father   If my wife saw that, with the boy.

Man 2   I'm so sorry. It won't happen again.

Beat.

Man 1 *returns.*

Man 2   You were saying?

As the **Father** *speaks, he undoes the bandages from the* **Boy**'s *head and then his hands and leg.*

Father   I was finished actually. I just hope you were all listening. I know some of you will think that this is women's work, but it's 1948, not 1928. This is the modern world. A new era for us and it is vitally important for all of you to understand the principles of first aid, it may make the difference between life and death. You need to practise, so why don't you pair up. As there's an odd number, one of you can use my son here, the rest of you work on each other, just pick one part of the body to bandage and have a go. I'll come back in ten minutes and let you know how you've done. There's more supplies in this box here.

*The **Father** leaves the room. The men get in pairs,* **Man 1** *goes to the boy.*

Man 1 Do you mind if I bandage you up again?

Boy No, just so long as it's not my head.

Man 1 How about I do your arm and put it in a sling?

Boy OK.

*The **Man** starts.*

*The **Boy** watches him critically.*

*The **Man** notices.*

Man 1 What is it? Too tight?

Boy No, not nearly tight enough. Remember what he said, it has to stop the swelling and the flow of blood, so it needs to be really tight. Start again.

Man 1 Right.

He does.

Boy That's better.

*The **Man** continues to work.*

Man 1 So I suppose you are going to be a doctor like your father?

Boy Why do you say that?

Man 1 You seem to know what you are doing.

Boy Only because he always uses me as the test dummy.

Beat.

Boy I don't want to be a doctor.

Man 1 No?

Boy No. Ask me what I want to be.

Man 1 No.

Boy Why?

Man 1 Because I already know. And it's a bad idea.

Boy Why?

Man 1 It's too dangerous. And you are too smart.

Boy I'm not. I want to help. Let me hold your gun.

Man 1 No.

Boy Please! Why?

Man 1 Because you are a boy. But according to them you are a man.

Boy   What do you mean?

Man 1   Their law says any one of us over the age of 10 with a weapon will be treated as an adult.

Boy   So?

Man 1   So maybe you aren't as smart as I thought. You'd go to prison, maybe even be executed. Just for being caught holding a gun. Understand?

*The **Man** has finished and looks at his handiwork. It's a bit messy but does the job.*

Boy   I'm not afraid.

Man 1   You should be.

Boy   I want to help.

Man 1   How's your counting?

Boy   I can do it.

Man 1   How many can you count to?

Boy   As many as you like.

Man 1   Well if you want to help, maybe you could count some bullets for me.

*The **Boy** smiles.*

Boy   What happens if they catch me with bullets?

Man 1   What use are bullets without a gun?

*The **Father** re-enters the room.*

Father   Right let's see how you are doing.

He goes to two men, one of whom has a bandage on his head.

Father   What's this?

Man 2   He has a head wound.

Father   He'd be dead by now if that's the best you can do. Come on, all of you, I keep telling you, this is life and death. You need to pay attention. Right, Wallad, come here, I need your head.

Boy   Oh!

Father   You're saving these men's lives. Now everyone watch.

He begins to bandage up his son's head again.

*Scene: (2005) We are now inside the house where the **Man** and **Translator** are being shown round by the **Resident**.*

Resident And finally this is the kitchen, which is pretty much as it would have been in 1948, in your mother's time.

Translator This is the kitchen, similar to how it would have been in 1948.

Resident The windows have been re-done, obviously. And I think there used to be a wall here which was demolished to give the place more space, open it up and make it lighter.

Translator There are new windows and a wall may have been removed here.

Resident Oh, he's looking at those tiles? They have been here as long as the house, I think that wall was covered in them once. Most of them fell off, but those four clung on somehow, refused to fall off, my wife hates them, wanted me to remove them but I insisted we keep them. They are authentic.

Translator He saw you looking at the tiles and says that they are originals, most have fallen off.

Resident Would you like a glass of wine?

Translator We wouldn't want to impose on you any more – you've been extremely kind.

Resident Nonsense, come on, have a glass with me.

*The **Resident** takes out three wine glasses and a bottle from the fridge, pours wine and ushers them to sit at the table. The three drink for a moment in silence.*

Translator I'm very surprised you let us in. Do you mind me asking how long you have lived here?

Resident Seven years, we came from the Loire Valley, in France.

Translator Oh, it's beautiful there – all the vineyards.

Resident That's right. But my family were only there for a generation, they were originally from Krakow in Poland.

Translator I see.

Resident So you know what happened to them. Except my grandmother, she got out. Hid in a suitcase. Only got as far as Paris and then the war ended.

Beat.

Resident I still have that suitcase, it's an heirloom. You wouldn't believe someone could fit in it. She must have been so small. Desperate.

Translator Yes.

Resident My grandmother always wanted to come here, but she didn't make it. So my wife and I brought the suitcase here, a kind of pilgrimage and fell in love with it. You know when you feel you belong somewhere? We decided we should move here. To Jerusalem, my mother was furious, she said 'Don't you want a quiet life?'

Beat.

Resident I'd like him to know that we love this house. We loved the place as soon as we saw it. We stood outside and put our arms around one another and thought, this is it, OK maybe my father, or grandfather or great grandfather didn't live here, but my ancestors did and that's in the bones, you know. This is the end of the journey started by my grandmother. And now we, she, can have peace. It's like it was built for us. Home.

Beat.

Resident Maybe don't translate that – it might seem insensitive.

Pause.

Translator You feel at peace? Even with everything that's going on?

Resident Peace comes from inside you. If I didn't feel peace I wouldn't have let him in, would I? But I'm not surprised, that he came. I knew he would.

Translator How?

Resident It's like the final bit of the puzzle: this house has always had a feeling, a presence.

Translator A ghost?

Resident No, not that – it's like it has a memory. Sometimes you feel it in some of the rooms – a breeze like the echo of someone who was once there. It sounds stupid I know. My wife says I'm crazy, but I'm not. I knew it. I knew someone would come, sometime.

Translator And he did.

Resident I've looked forward to it actually, knowing that would be the full stop. The end, he'd see we belong here, and he could move on with his life and us ours, be at peace.

Pause.

Resident Do you want to translate that?

The **Translator** *drains his glass awkwardly.*

Translator Perhaps later, thank you so much for your hospitality, we really should go, there's a rehearsal in a while and he can't be late.

Resident OK, well I hope that he's – you know he could have taken photos if he'd wanted.

They get up and move towards the door. The **Man** *and the* **Translator** *step outside.*

Resident Goodbye then, I hope the concerts go well, I'm really looking forward to them.

Translator (*to* **Man**) He hopes the concerts go well. (*To* **Resident**.) Thank you.

Resident   Oh, hold on, wait a minute. Just wait there.

The **Resident** *closes the door on the men and goes inside.*

Translator   He told us to wait for a moment.

Pause.

The **Resident** *opens the door beaming.*

Resident   I found it – look, it's one of the tiles from the wall. I threw most of them away but I remembered I kept one. Maybe he'd like to have it. (*Directly to the* **Man**.) Here – take this – it would have been on the wall when your mother was here.

The **Resident** *looks directly at the* **Man** *and hands him the tile which the* **Man** *takes and stares at.*

Translator   Thank you.

Resident   I thought he'd like it. Goodbye then.

Translator   Goodbye, thanks.

The **Resident** *shuts the door.*

The **Man** *stares at the tile, then looks at the house. He continues to stare at the house until the* **Translator** *gently takes him by the arm and leads him away.*

Scene: (1960) There is a long queue of people from one side of the stage to the other, waiting, smoking, looking bored.

Scene: (2010) Inside an office. A male Western **Charity Worker** *is talking to a an Israeli female* **Official**. *Both hold lists in their hands, which they consult periodically.*

Official   What else?

Charity Worker   Toilet cleaner,

Official   OK,

Charity Worker   baby wipes,

Official   OK,

Charity Worker   female hygiene products,

The **Official** *looks at the* **Charity Worker** *– he's a little embarrassed, she smiles a little.*

Official   Tampons?

Charity Worker   And sanitary towels.

Official   OK.

Charity Worker Toothpaste,

Official OK,

Charity Worker toothbrushes,

Official OK,

Charity Worker bath sponges,

Official OK,

Charity Worker candles,

Official OK,

Charity Worker blankets,

Official OK,

Charity Worker mineral water,

Official OK,

Charity Worker plastic combs,

Official OK,

Charity Worker sticks for brooms,

Official OK,

Charity Worker tea,

Official OK,

Charity Worker coffee,

Official ummmm – oh yes, here – OK,

Charity Worker canned tuna,

Official OK,

Charity Worker canned beans,

Official OK,

Charity Worker canned pineapple.

Official No, sorry.

Charity Worker What?

Official You can't bring that in.

Charity Worker Why?

Official It says so here.

Charity Worker I can't bring in canned pineapple?

Official Nope.

Charity Worker What about canned peaches?

Official No, sorry – no canned fruit.

Charity Worker Oh. Right. OK. So the canned tuna and beans is OK, but not the canned fruit.

Official You got it. No canned fruit.

Charity Worker Right. OK, so I'll –

Official You'll have to offload it. Anything else.

Charity Worker A few other things, yes.

Official Go on then.

Charity Worker Tahini,

Official Yes,

Charity Worker Zaatar,

Official yes,

Charity Worker olives,

Official yes,

Charity Worker pasta,

Official yes,

Charity Worker sesame seeds,

Official yes,

Charity Worker black pepper,

Official yes.

Charity Worker Salt.

Official Oh – wait – I can't – no I can't see that here.

Charity Worker No salt?

Official I don't think so – hmm, odd one – I can check on that if you like.

Charity Worker Please. What about chicken stock powder?

Official Yes, that's OK.

Charity Worker And I've got some clothes.

Official Of course.

Charity Worker Shoes,

Official fine,

Charity Worker and some chocolate and toys and that's it.

Official No.

Charity Worker No?

Official No. You can't bring those last two things in. I'll check on the salt.

Charity Worker I can't bring in chocolate or toys, why?

Official Not on the list I'm afraid.

Charity Worker. Why?

Official I didn't write it, friend, I'm sorry.

Charity Worker But why – in your opinion – why would the state want the children of Gaza to be denied toys?

Official Good place to smuggle guns I guess.

Charity Worker What about chocolate?

Official I understand your frustration but please, I'm just doing my job.

Charity Worker You realise that there are 1.5 million people who are effectively imprisoned in Gaza and half of them are children – it's going to be your problem when they all come of age don't you think?

Official Don't take that fucking tone with me – you Westerners, you're so fucking self-righteous. Wake up! We're just doing your dirty work – the shit you don't have the courage to do yourselves.

Pause.

Charity Worker I'm sorry. I – it's hot and it was a long drive. I'll, I'll offload the toys, chocolate and canned fruit. Would you check the salt situation for me?

Official I've just remembered – salt's off the list too. So you better offload that as well. Then you can be on your way.

Scene: (2016) A girl in Palestine waits in front of a computer.

Rula (*quietly*) *Bastana el daw el akhdar* . . . Waiting – for the green light, for the little noise it makes. To show she's there. Everyone here is watching me, so I'm pretending I'm already talking to her. But there's no one there yet. She's not online. No one is listening. Well I'm going to talk anyway. And my English is better than any of the hameer in this library, so they don't understand what I'm saying. *Yalla Nadia! Weinik inti?* I hate waiting. I will never get used to waiting. Waiting. To talk to my cousin, on the other side of the world. England. While I'm here in Palestine. I shouldn't be nervous of her. Not when I live here and there are actual dangerous things to be scared of. Like the dark. Outside. At night. It's dangerous. But I go out anyway. Wait until everyone else is in bed. And then I sneak out. In my black hoodie.

Armed. Sneak down the backstreets. My hair is hidden, so is my face. I want them to think I'm a ghost. A phantom. I go looking for my target. I always know where it will be. I plan in advance. I'm organised. Decide the best way to get there without being spotted. And once I arrive and make sure no one is around, I take out my weapon and start. Spraying. Red. Green. Black. White. Those are my colours. I have one picture – logo – tag. Not like Handala the barefoot Palestinian boy – mine is a tree. I use a stencil. It was sent to me by a woman in Syria. She used it there. This tree's branches spell out words – whatever I want them to say – so this way it's an original and a copy at the same time. I like that. Sometimes I write 'tahrir'. Freedom. Sometimes I write the names of people in prison – people who everyone thinks are forgotten, sometimes the names of the dead. It depends. On what's happening. But the most exciting part is the next day when someone discovers this new drawing on the wall. They all start talking and wondering who is this new Palestinian Banksy! *Khally wally Banksy* . . . His pictures are considered art. No one would dare touch them . . . but mine are gone by the end of the day. Painted over. Gone but not forgotten. I need to make sure they're not forgotten. So, I'm waiting for my cousin Nadia to call me . . . to ask her . . .

She turns to someone nearby who has said something to her.

No I'm still using it – sorry this is an important call – from London.

Scene: (2002) An attractive **Woman** *stands outside Tel Aviv airport, she is waiting for a taxi. She sees the* **Taxi Driver** *in his car and approaches him.*

Woman   Are you free?

Taxi Driver   Depends – where you going?

Woman   Home.

Taxi Driver   Where's that?

Woman   Ramat Aviv.

Taxi Driver   Oh – OK, I should warn you the traffic's a nightmare today – there was a bomb scare in town and everyone's acting crazy.

Woman   I don't care how long it takes – I just want to get back to my house.

Taxi Driver   Let me help you with your bag.

He lifts it into the boot.

Woman   What happened to your taillight?

Taxi Driver   Like I said, there are crazy people out today.

They get in the car – she in the front seat. He starts the engine and they drive a little while in silence.

Taxi Driver   So you been on holiday? Lucky you.

Woman Sort of.

Taxi Driver Where were you?

Woman Poland.

Taxi Driver No wonder you don't have a tan.

Woman It was cold.

Taxi Driver Should have gone to the Red Sea – that's where I always go.

Woman It wasn't just a holiday.

Taxi Driver No?

Woman I had to go – for my service.

Taxi Driver Oh, oh right. I did that – years ago – I remember they took my fingerprints on the first day and pictures of my teeth – I thought – hey I'm not the prisoner here!

Woman Where did you serve?

Taxi Driver Ended up a driver! All over. Chauffeuring Generals – all sorts. What I'm good at . . . Poland – so did they make you go to –?

Woman Auschwitz.

Taxi Driver Ah. Have you been before?

Woman No.

Taxi Driver That's a tough one, eh? Seeing the actual place . . . what happened there . . . really gets you. Never affected my family – they came here in the 1920s, but it's a terrible place. Eerie . . . you can feel the presence of all those poor people, don't you think?

Beat.

Taxi Driver I kind of also always wondered why? You know, why send us there? It's a terrible thing and it's important to remember, but it's too late to change that now. I mean did you feel it was relevant to you?

Woman What do you mean? Of course it's relevant.

Taxi Driver Excuse me, I mean to your day-to-day work – on the front. I mean it's important to remember like you say, that people want to destroy us and all that, but when you are in the service you are reminded of that every day aren't you? When you live here you are reminded of that every day. Why send the young people to Auschwitz, or Belsen, it's depressing.

Woman That's offensive.

Taxi Driver Oh, I don't mean to offend you – I'm just trying to say it's a shame a nice young girl like you has to go and experience all that. See it. I dreamt about it for months afterwards.

Beat.

Woman So what happened with your taillight?

Taxi Driver Oh nothing much – some guy was in a real hurry – you'd think his pants were on fire, and he clipped it. But when I got out and asked for his number he just drove off . . . what's the world coming to eh?

Woman Arab?

Taxi Driver No, Israeli. People are so disappointing aren't they? Israeli and Arab, there are good ones and bad ones and this one was a bad one.

*The **Woman** begins to sob.*

Woman Stop the car.

Taxi Driver We're in the middle of traffic – do you feel sick?

Woman I need to get out, I can't breathe.

Taxi Driver What is it? You're white.

Woman Just STOP!

Taxi Driver I think you're having a panic attack.

Woman STOP THE CAR!

He stops the car and she gets out. We hear other drivers beeping at him.

Taxi Driver HEY, HEY, easy pal! She's not well! Same to you!

*While the **Taxi Driver** waits for the **Woman** to sort herself out, this scene bleeds into the next and we simultaneously see:*

Scene: (2002/2007) A man is shown into a room where he sits down on a chair to wait. He is the man who had the blue hatchback in the checkpoint scene. He is alone. He goes to light a cigarette but sees a no smoking sign. He puts away the packet and waits. He hums a few bars of Umm Kulthum's 'Fakarouni'.

*As both **Taxi Driver** and **Blue Hatchback Man** wait, they say in sync:*

Taxi Driver/Blue Hatchback Man What a day. All I want is to drive around but there's always something in the way. Imagine to be in America. The open road, Route 66, miles and miles of clear road as far as the eye can see. No traffic jams, checkpoints, road blocks, diversions, nothing. Just a straight clear road all the way to the horizon. Not even another car. You could fall asleep at the wheel and nothing bad would happen. Imagine. Driving off into the sunset . . . A dream.

*Scene: (2010) A **Woman** with a camera and a bag stands outside a house, and knocks on the door.*

Woman Haitham, come on – it's time. Are you ready?

Voice from Inside No – I can't, I can't come today.

Woman What do you mean? Open the door, are you OK?

Voice from Inside I'm busy – not well.

Woman But it's Friday – and it was your idea – it's great, come on open the door.

Voice from Inside I think it's a bad idea.

Woman It's not, it's brilliant – open it – everyone else is waiting for you. They all look fantastic honestly.

Voice from Inside Really?

Woman Really. Open up.

The door opens a little, then more and a **Man** *stands there looking sheepish. He is dressed up as one of the characters from* Avatar *and his skin is painted blue. He has false pointy ears and a long black wig in plaits.*

The **Woman** *looks at him and nods encouragingly, then starts to laugh.*

Man I knew you would laugh.

Woman It's just – you look – great. Come on. It's a great idea – it'll definitely get the world's attention.

Man You think so?

Woman Of course, come on they're waiting.

Man I'm not the only one dressed like this, am I?

Woman No – Mohammed, Kamila and Hameed – loads of people.

Man OK – hold on a minute.

He gets his Palestinian flag from inside the door.

Let's go then.

They begin to walk to the bottom of the street, and as they do more people join them, some dressed as Avatar *characters, some with their faces covered with scarves, others in more traditional Western clothes. The* **Woman** *begins to take photos with her camera.* **Nervous Man** *appears.*

Man Yusef! What are you doing here?

Woman You said you weren't coming again.

Man What did the doctor say?

Nervous Man That my stomach ulcer is worse than the bullet wound.

Woman That's the third time you've been shot in as many years – you are so unlucky.

Nervous Man   What do you mean unlucky – I'm alive aren't I?

Man   You shouldn't be here, you aren't even from Bil'in.

Woman   You're like a dog with a bone, always back for more.

Nervous Man   I have to stand in solidarity with you.

Man   What did Hanan say?

Nervous Man   She thinks I'm visiting my mother, if she knew I was here she'd really kill me, seriously – Hanan is scarier that the whole of the IDF, so no photos please? Eh?

They approach a barrier where there is a partition marked by barbed wire and metal girders. Several people put on gas masks including the **Woman** *with camera. We do not see the soldiers but they are on the other side of the partition. The villagers of Bil'in begin their peaceful protest chanting:*

'No wall in Bil'in.'

They wave their Palestinian flags and a couple of men begin to shake the barrier with their hands.

Suddenly a tear gas grenade is fired at them – it lands at the feet of the **Woman** *with the camera.*

Man   Shit! I knew I forgot something –

Nervous Man *takes an onion from his pocket and a small penknife and cuts it in half.*

Nervous Man   Here.

The two men hold the onions to their noses.

Avatar Man *picks up the canister and throws it back in the direction it came from.*

The **Woman** *begins to take photographs.*

More tear gas canisters are thrown as someone shouts from the crowd:

'Shame on you! This is a peaceful protest!'

The protestors scatter to avoid the tear gas.

The stage is now empty but covered in smoke.

Scene: (2011) A little **Boy** *is in bed sleeping, it is dark, the early hours of the morning. He is young. His* **Mother** *enters the room and gently tries to wake him up.*

Mother   Majeed, Majeed – wake up. It's time.

Boy   Huh? He's mine . . .

Mother   Darling.

Boy   I'm taking him home.

Mother   Majeed, wake up, darling . . .

The **Boy** *stirs.*

Boy   Oh, Maama. I was dreaming.

Mother   Not bad ones again?

Boy   Is it time for me to get up?

Mother   It is, my boy it is.

Boy   But it's too early.

Mother   The bus is coming soon, now come on, up you get.

She encourages him to get up and fetches his clothes. He talks as she does this, and begins to dress himself, she helps him a little now and then.

Boy   It was such a nice dream. There was a cat. A kitten. He was tiny, I could pick him up in my hand. He was a tabby and he liked to be grabbed by the back of the neck because that's what mummy cats do isn't it? But his wasn't there. His mummy. She was gone somewhere else and I found him in the car park, just wondering about. And I put him inside my jacket and he was all warm, and I could feel him moving as he breathed next to my heart. And I showed Sami and Lamia and they were jealous, they tried to take him away but I said you can't because he's mine. He's my cat now.

Mother   Did you give him a name?

Boy   No, you woke me up, I didn't get that far.

The **Mother** *is now beginning to brush his hair.*

Mother   Now you remember what you have to say today?

Boy   Yes. Are you coming, Maama?

Mother   Darling we've been over this. You know I'm not allowed. You have to go. Be a brave boy. You've done it before.

Boy   I know.

Beat.

Mother   There – you look all smart, now go and brush your teeth.

The **Boy** *goes to brush his teeth, the* **Mother** *brings out several bags for him to take with him.*

Mother   So in this one is your breakfast, try and have a little sleep on the bus first, then when you wake up at the first checkpoint eat something, OK?

Beat.

Mother Aren't you excited?

Boy I want you to come.

Beat.

Boy Sami says Daddy is in Israel.

Mother What – when?

Boy He said the bus takes so long because I have to travel to a whole 'nother country.

Mother Did he?

Beat.

Mother I can't come. You know they don't let me. That's why you have to go. You are the man of the family now, what are you going to say?

Boy 'Mother sends her love and devotion, we both think of you every day and before we eat a meal we say a silent prayer.'

Mother Good, what else?

Boy 'Sitti is healthy, the olive oil is nearly ready, Farouk is engaged and I got ten in my English test'.

Mother Bravo – clever boy.

Boy But why can't you come? I don't like the checkpoints alone.

Mother You are with the other children and Mr Red Cross. Come on now – you have to be brave. What would your father do if you didn't visit?

Boy What will happen when I'm sixteen?

Mother That's a long way off – why?

Boy Sami says when I'm sixteen I can't go and see him anymore – who will see him then?

Mother Oh, don't worry about that, you silly billy – Daddy will be home long before that. Now come on, I think the bus is here.

Scene: (1960) The long queue of people reappears from one side of the stage to the other – it has moved slightly. People continue to wait, smoke, looking bored. A man whistles Umm Kulthum's 'Fakarouni'.

*Scene: (2002) A **Man** stands outside Tel Aviv airport, he has a couple of suitcases and is waiting for a taxi. The **Taxi Driver** approaches him.*

Taxi Driver Looking for a taxi?

Man Yes, please.

Taxi Driver Over here, that's my car, let me take your bag.

Man That's kind, thank you.

Taxi Driver No problem, where you going to?

Man It's a bit of a journey.

Taxi Driver Where you headed?

Man Nazareth.

The **Taxi Driver** *stops and puts down the bag.*

Taxi Driver Are you kidding me? I can't believe this day.

Man No. Nazareth, it's where I'm from.

Taxi Driver It's another country.

Man Its only 100 kilometres.

Taxi Driver 102.

Man I'll pay you whatever you like.

Taxi Driver I don't go there.

Man Please – there are no other drivers around – I'm in a hurry.

Taxi Driver I'll need protection money.

Beat.

Man I need to get home to see my father. He's not well.

Beat.

Taxi Driver I think you need an Arab driver. I just don't know that area at all. I never get fares out of Tel Aviv. Besides the traffic's bad today and there are loads of crazies about.

Man Please. I need to get there.

Taxi Driver But I told you I don't know the way.

Man I do, I'll show you.

Taxi Driver I don't have a map that goes that far.

Man I have it all up here (*gesturing to his head*).

Taxi Driver How can I trust that? When was the last time you were in Israel?

Man 1988.

Taxi Driver Well it has changed a lot since then. You won't remember.

Man I can't forget – honestly, it's etched on my memory, this is my home.

Beat.

Taxi Driver   I really think you should wait for an Arab driver. You know what's been going on – there was almost a bomb today. Nazareth isn't safe for me.

Man   You'll be with me.

Taxi Driver   How can you protect me? What if we are pulled over by gunmen?

Man   You keep quiet and I'll talk. In Arabic, to them. I'll tell them who I am, that my father is unwell. We will be fine.

Beat.

Man   It'll probably never happen anyway.

Taxi Driver   That's the trouble with you Arabs, you always look on the bright side – don't see the bad things that could happen.

Beat.

Man   I'll pay you double what it says on the meter.

Taxi Driver   Danger money.

Man   Danger money.

Beat.

Taxi Driver   And you are sure you know the way?

Man   Like the back of my hand. Don't be afraid.

Beat.

Man   Trust me.

Taxi Driver   Oh alright then, come on, before I change my mind.

Man   What happened to your taillight?

Taxi Driver   Don't ask.

The two men move to the car, and we hear the engine starting, then a radio comes on with a news report, which we hear as the car drives away.

BBC Newsreader   Tomorrow is Israeli Independence Day and the one day a year when the Israel government allows Palestinians to visit the sites of their former homes. Israel says it will put the IDF on alert for any terrorist activity that may occur . . .

Static as the **Taxi Driver** *retunes the channel.*

Taxi Driver   Is that the real reason you're back then? To visit the site of your former home? Cause trouble?

Man   No, I told you I'm from Nazareth, my father's sick.

More static as the **Taxi Driver** *tries to tune it.*

Taxi Driver   And now I can't find any music . . . come on you piece of crap.

More static.

Scene: (1978) Inside a very, very basic house, almost a shack. An **Old Man** *holds a radio, it is battered and the batteries are taped to the back. He is trying to get a reception to hear the news.*

He keeps trying.

Nothing but static.

It begins to get something – it is a recording of Umm Kulthum's 'Fakarouni' – he smiles, and begins to slowly sway and mouth the words. He gets into it, and puts down the radio to dance more, but as he does so it loses the signal and becomes static noise again.

He tuts, annoyed, and turns it off. He then moves to a stool and sits down. He takes out a cigarette and begins to smoke it. Suddenly he moves his hand to his head, something has dripped on it. He looks to the ceiling, there's another drip. He moves his chair to one side and looks at the floor to see if he's right – if there's a drip from the roof. He watches, he waits, he's right – there is. He watches one, two, three drips. He gets up and takes a cooking pot and puts it under the drip. He sits smoking and watching it.

Pause.

Suddenly a young **Boy***, his grandson, runs into the room.*

Boy   Seedi Seedi, did you hear the news? They've liberated our lands!

Grandfather   What?

Boy   We are free, we can go home! Anytime we like! They've liberated/

Grandfather   Thanks be to God! (*He jumps up and grabs the radio.*) When did you hear that?

Boy   Just now – come on – we can go back.

Grandfather   I knew it was coming – patience – that's what I said.

He gets a bag and begins to fill it with his clothes and things.

Grandfather   Didn't I tell you all, I knew it. It couldn't last forever, liberated . . . free at last.

The **Boy** *begins to laugh.*

Grandfather   What?

The **Boy** *is laughing hysterically now.*

Boy   You believed it!

Grandfather   What! You little bastard . . . come here.

The man picks up the stick and chases the **Boy** *– he hasn't a hope in hell of catching him.*

Grandfather You little bastard.

The **Boy** *runs away from his* **Grandfather** *still laughing and then runs out of the room.*

The old man stands, out of puff.

Grandfather You little bastard.

He lowers himself back into his chair and lights another cigarette. He watches the drip again as his breathing gradually returns to normal.

Pause.

A **Man** *walks in.*

Man You didn't fall for that again?

Grandfather He's a little bastard.

Man He knows you will always go for it.

Grandfather The next time it'll be true and I won't believe him.

Man You will.

Beat.

Man There's a drip?

Grandfather I know – that's why I put the pot there.

Man You can't continue to live like this, it's been thirty years – I'm going to get some iron from Mohammed, lay it on the roof and . . .

Grandfather No. Leave it.

Man You need a proper roof. Dad.

Grandfather No.

Man Please – let me – I worry about your health . . .

Grandfather No.

Man Having a proper roof doesn't mean anything –

Grandfather This is not where I live. It's temporary.

Man But it's been temporary for –

Grandfather What would your mother think, eh? Defeat? Not yet.

Man It's just a roof, Dad.

Beat.

Grandfather   Tell that boy of yours next time he pulls that stunt I'll be ready – and if I catch him he won't be able to sit down for a week.

Beat.

Grandfather   Nothing better to do . . .

Scene: (1960) The long queue of people from one side of the stage to the other reappears. The order has changed slightly – it has moved a little. More waiting, smoking, looking bored. Suddenly a man jumps forward and breaks into a loud and fevered rendition of 'Fakarouni'. His wife clips him round the ear to shut him up. More bored waiting in line.

Scene: (1992) The women sit on their rug outside, continuing their picnic.

Woman 2   Can you believe Hanan has been married ten years?

Woman 3   Really?

Woman 1   It's true, I have.

Woman 2   What a wedding!

Woman 1   It wasn't a wedding.

Woman 3   Why?

Woman 2   Curfew.

Woman 3   Oh, yes.

Woman 1   You were just a girl so you wouldn't remember, but we had to be indoors.

Woman 2   And the bastards cut the electricity too.

Woman 1   That's right.

Woman 2   Well at least your first time was in the dark – just like you!

They laugh, **Woman 3** *looks embarrassed.*

Woman 1   And my mean mother-in-law was pleased because she didn't have to feed the guests all night!

The soldiers are passing again and stop.

Soldier 1   Good afternoon, ladies.

Woman 1   Good afternoon.

Soldier 1   Still here?

Woman 3   We're having a picnic.

Soldier 2   Nice day for it.

Soldier 1   What's in the bag?

Woman 1 Just some pastries and mezza.

Woman 2 Just like before.

Soldier 1 And the flask?

Woman 2 Still tea.

Soldier 1 Would you mind opening the bag?

Woman 1 *opens it,* **Soldier 1** *peers in.*

Soldier 1 Nearly finished it all.

Soldier 2 Didn't leave any for us.

Beat.

Soldier 1 Enjoy your afternoon.

They move on.

Woman 3 Shall we go?

Woman 2 No.

Woman 1 Fadia.

Woman 2 What? I haven't finished my tea.

Scene: (2010) A kitchen where a **Mother** *is putting the finishing touches to dinner and puts it on the table. Her* **Son** *is watching TV in the next room; there is a news story about the protests in Bil'in and images of men dressed as the characters from Avatar.*

Mother Come on everyone – dinner is ready!

The family come into the kitchen, there's a young **Son**, *a* **Father** *and* **Mother** *and a teenage* **Daughter**.

They all sit and the table and begin to pour glasses of water.

Father Shall I serve Tabbouleh?

Daughter Not much for me.

Mother If you aren't eating meat anymore, you need to eat vegetables.

Daughter I've changed my mind.

Mother What do you mean you've changed your mind? I bought some really expensive vegetarian cheese for you.

Daughter It doesn't seem right.

Mother That's what you said – and we respected that but, Raquel, if you want us to take you seriously as an adult you have to – (*to her husband*) speak to her.

Father Your mother's right. We respect your choices, you are nearly an adult, but –

Daughter I'm sorry, it just seems wrong to choose not to eat meat when there are people not a million miles away who don't get any choice about what they eat.

Pause.

Father That's fine. You must do what you think is right – but try and take your time to make a decision – particularly when it affects the rest of the family.

Daughter How does me being a vegetarian affect –

Mother If you cooked occasionally, you'd understand.

Beat.

Daughter OK. Sorry, Mum.

Son So you're not a veggie anymore?

Daughter No.

Son Oh. Did you see the news, Dad?

Father What news?

Son There were some crazy people dressed up as that movie.

Father Which one?

Son The 3-D one?

Daughter *Avatar.*

Mother What's that?

Son They painted themselves blue – isn't that funny!

Mother Mm. Do you want more chicken?

Son And they were all sniffing onions but that's not in the film.

Mother Eat your food.

Daughter The onions help with the tear gas.

Son How?

Father Anyone want water?

Daughter Tear gas makes you feel like you can't breathe but the onion helps.

Son Awesome, I'm going to do that for Yoav's party! It'll be really funny.

Mother Do what?

Son Dress up as one of those blue guys.

Father I think it's best to stick with your cowboy outfit.

Son But –

Father It's already up there in the cupboard, otherwise your mother will have to find blue paint.

Pause.

Father I noticed the envelope's still there on the counter.

Mother I can post it for you if you like?

Daughter No – I'll do it.

Father Just remember there is a deadline.

Daughter I know.

Father Don't imagine you are the only girl in the world who wants to go to Oxford.

Daughter I don't.

Beat.

Daughter I don't want to go to Oxford.

Son Uh oh.

Beat.

Son I've finished – can I go to my room.

Mother Don't you want more Tabbouleh?

Son No.

Mother Dessert?

Son What is it?

Mother Ice cream.

Father What do you mean you don't want to go? We spent a month on your personal statement.

Mother Let's talk about this later.

Father Did you know about this?

Mother I had a feeling . . .

Father But if you stay you'll have to do military service.

Mother You are not doing that.

Daughter I don't want to leave.

Father What are you saying? You want to stay here, go to university here, over my dead body.

Mother   It's not safe.

Daughter   Yes, it is.

Mother   What about the rockets?

Daughter   How many people have died from the Hamas rockets, Mum?

Son   Can I go upstairs?

Daughter   How many? You don't know do you? I tried to find out – I looked on the IDF website. I know how many rockets have fallen here – but there's no record of how many people have died.

Son   Why?

Father   Go upstairs.

Son   Why?

Daughter   Because they didn't kill anyone.

Mother   What about Mrs Silverman's niece?

Daughter   She's alive.

Mother   Thank God – but she was in hospital for two days.

Daughter   That's because she threw herself down in the middle of the road when she heard a car backfiring.

Father   We live in a climate of fear – they've made that. That's why we want something better for you.

Mother   Where is she getting all of this from? Who have you been talking to?

Daughter   No one. There's a thing called the internet.

Son   Can I take some ice cream upstairs?

Father   So what exactly is your plan for your life?

Daughter   I don't know. I just don't want to go to Oxford.

Father   I dreamed of going to Oxford, but we couldn't afford it, I've saved all my life so –

Daughter   Let him go.

Son   Me – no! I don't want to go to England.

Mother   No one's going to send you there.

Daughter   Yet – you better watch out.

Father   Go upstairs.

*The **Boy** leaves the room.*

Daughter I haven't even got in yet. It'll probably never happen.

Father Is that what this is about? Of course you will get in.

Beat.

Daughter I'm not going to Oxford, I'm going to the West Bank to see for myself.

Father The West Bank?

Daughter Maybe Gaza, too – you can't stop me. I'm nearly 18. I need to know what is going on.

Mother Don't go there, look on the internet . . . watch TV. It's too far.

Daughter Further than Oxford?

Mother Yes.

Father Go upstairs,

Daughter I'm not a child you can order around.

Father You are still my daughter. And you are still underage.

She goes.

Beat.

*The **Father** stands up and picks up the envelope.*

Father I'm going to post this.

*Scene: (2016) We hear a Skype ring tone, then see two faces on the screen. They are cousins **Rula** and **Nadia**. **Rula** is a twenty-year-old Palestinian woman living in the West Bank and **Nadia** is a thirty-year-old mixed-race Palestinian British woman living in the UK. When the picture comes up both women scream and wave madly at each other.*

Rula *Marhaba,* Nadia.

Nadia Hi, hi! Oh my god I can't believe we managed to Skype, yay we did it!

More maniacal waving.

Nadia Where are you?

Rula At university! What about you?

Nadia In my house – do you want to see it?

Rula Sure.

Nadia OK, I'll just pick up the laptop and show you around. Don't get excited, it's a tiny flat! So here's the kitchen area, you see, all my herbs and things, the fridge . . .

Rula You have a washing machine in the kitchen?

Nadia That's a dishwasher actually. Then this is the sitting room, TV, sofa and the sofa opens into a bed, it's where I sleep. And then through here the bathroom, that's it! Tiny isn't it?

Rula It looks so clean and lovely. Everything is so new and shiny. Modern.

Nadia Enough about me, how are you doing? How's your studying going?

Rula Good, although I hate Shakespeare.

Nadia What? Say that again, I can't hear you properly.

Rula I can't speak too loudly, I'm in the library – I said I hate Shakespeare.

Nadia WHY? He's amazing.

Rula Very hard to understand.

Nadia It's easier when you see it on stage.

Rula Did you lose weight? Your face looks so thin.

Nadia Not at all. What about you – how are you? (*Low voice.*) Why are you covering your head? I didn't know you did that? Your mother doesn't does she?

Rula *types a message at the bottom of the screen which* **Nadia** *can see. It says: 'My father thinks it's safer for me to cover when I'm out.'*

Nadia I understand.

Beat.

Nadia It's so nice to see you! To speak to you!

Rula You too!

Nadia It was such a good idea of yours! I didn't even know you had access to Skype!

Beat.

Rula Actually, there's something I wanted to ask you, that's why I wanted to do this, it's nicer face to face than the phone isn't it?

Nadia Much nicer, what did you want to ask?

Rula I'm shy – but my mother told me I should ask . . .

Nadia You can ask me, come on what is it?

Pause.

Rula I don't want you to feel like you have to – oh I'm embarrassed to ask.

Beat.

Rula Oh I wish you could speak Arabic.

106 Scenes from 73* Years

Nadia I think I know what you are going to say . . . Is it about coming here Rula? Because I don't have the space really or any money, it's just really really hard for me. I want to help but you know it's –

Rula No, no, it's not that. Uncle Hameed said you had a new iPhone and I wondered if I could have your old one –

Nadia Oh. Oh god.

Rula But maybe you still need it.

Nadia No, no, I'm sorry. I'm embarrassed, of course you can have it –

Rula Only if you don't need it.

Nadia I'd love you to have it – shall I post it?

Rula No, a friend of my father is in London in two weeks – can I give him your number? Then he will meet you and bring it for me, it's much faster. You remember when we used to write to each other and it would take months.

Nadia And we had to write in our special code.

Rula Exactly. Is it OK?

Nadia Of course. It's a bit scratched.

Rula But the camera works?

Nadia Perfectly.

Rula Oh my god, I'm so excited! Mahmoud is going to go crazy with jealousy.

Beat.

Nadia I'm sorry I thought you –

Rula Don't worry – when will you come to visit? We would love to have you here.

Nadia I want to – but my mum says it's too danger – (*She stops herself.*)

Rula What did you say? You cut out.

Nadia It's too expensive.

Rula Too what, I can't hear you? Hello.

The image of **Nadia** *has frozen,* **Rula***'s internet connection has gone.*

Rula Hello? Hello? Nadia? (*To someone who is waiting.*) No, I'm not finished, I got cut off . . . you have to wait.

Scene: (1960) The long queue of people from one side of the stage to the other reappears. But now we can see the front of the line. There is an **Official** *at a desk. Pause. Eventually the man at the front has been dealt with and the second* **Man** *moves to the desk.*

Official Just a minute.

Pause.

Official OK, give me your form.

The **Man** *hands it over.*

Official You want a passport?

Man Yes. This is the right line?

Official Yes.

He looks over the form.

Official Your name?

Man Saeed.

Official Full name.

Man It's on the form.

Official Full name.

Man Saeed bin Hameed Al Hassan bin Ibrahim al Faisal Walleedi.

Official Too long.

Man Sorry?

Official Too long.

He draws a line across the paper.

Man Why did you do that?

Official I just told you – it's too long. So I've cut the last few words – your passport will be in the name Saeed bin Hameed al Hassan.

Beat.

Man But that's not my name.

Official Listen son, five names are enough for anybody.

Man But it's not my name.

The **Official** *eyeballs him.*

Official You've been waiting five hours. One name per hour. I thought you wanted a passport.

Man I do.

Beat.

Official So what's your name?

Man Saeed bin Hameed . . . al Hassan . . .

Beat.

Official Good. NEXT.

Scene: (1992) The women sit on their rug outside, packing up from their picnic.

Woman 3 You went to so much trouble – thank you I've had a lovely time.

Woman 1 Good. Well it's too important an occasion to miss – engagement, a wedding . . . babies.

Woman 3 Stop talking about babies! You make me embarrassed. You know Saleh's mother put her hand here and said she thought I would be very fertile.

Woman 2 She didn't! Old witch.

Woman 1 Mothers-in-law!

The women laugh, **Woman 3** *looks embarrassed.*

Woman 2 How dare she, god they just think we are baby machines don't they? It makes me sick.

Woman 1 I quite like it.

Woman 3 What?

Woman 1 Making babies!

Woman 2 Stop it, you're embarrassing Fatima again.

Woman 3 Stop raising your voices.

The soldiers are passing again and stop. The women stop packing up.

Soldier 1 Good afternoon, ladies.

Woman 1 Good afternoon.

Soldier 1 Still here?

Woman 2 Still here.

Soldier 2 Nice day for it.

Soldier 1 Bag empty yet?

Woman 1 More or less.

Soldier 1 And the flask?

Woman 2 Empty.

Soldier 1 Would you mind opening the bag?

Woman 1 *opens it,* **Soldier 1** *peers in.*

Soldier 1 Nearly all gone.

Soldier 2 Didn't leave any for us.

Beat.

Soldier 1 Are you going soon?

Woman 2 Why, shouldn't we be here?

Soldier 2 It's a free country. We're just asking.

Woman 1 We are just talking.

Soldier 1 Well you've finished your picnic, so you must be going home soon . . . enjoy your afternoon.

They move on.

Woman 3 Shall we go then?

Woman 2 Sit back down. We'll go when we are ready.

Scene: (2007) The interior of a house, IDF soldiers destroy everything (there should be male and female soldiers here), overturning tables, scattering things from drawers, breaking crockery may be even putting a bullet or two into the cushions so feathers fly everywhere. It should feel like wanton, deliberate destruction, not an act of rage.

*Scene: (2013) A kitchen where a **Mother** is putting the finishing touches to dinner and puts it on the table. Her nineteen-year-old and thirteen-year-old **Sons** sit at the table.*

Mother OK. It's ready. Go ahead.

Son 2 (13) Tabbouleh again? I'm sick of tabbouleh.

Son 1 (19) (*hits him across the back of the head*) Eat it.

They sit in silence eating tabbouleh with bread.

Son 1 Is there Zaatar?

*The **Mother** gets up and fetches some, putting it on the table.*

Mother I was thinking of making Mousakkan on Friday, Umm Mazin said we can have a chicken in return for some of my soap.

Son 2 Brilliant!

Son 1 I won't be here.

Mother Why?

Son 1 I've got uni.

Son 2 On a Friday?

Son 1 Yes.

Mother We'll wait till the following week then.

Son 2 Oh! Can't we do it without him? Leave him leftovers?

Mother No. A family meal needs to be the whole family.

Son 2 It's never the whole family though is it?

At this point **Son 1** *clips* **Son 2** *across the back of the head again.*

Son 2 You better stop that you know!

Son 1 Or what?

Son 2 I'll pay you back.

Son 1 What you going to do, shortie?

Son 2 You wait.

Beat.

Son 2 I've put you in hospital before.

Mother STOP, you know you're not to bring that up.

Son 1 Be careful.

Beat.

Son 2 Are you scared?

Mother Stop it!

Son 1 Of a few grape seeds?

Son 2 The doctor said if I'd pushed them in any further you'd have been permanently deaf.

Son 1 At least I wouldn't have to listen to your singing.

Son 2 I'm good. Everyone says I'm good. I'm good aren't I, Mum?

Son 1 *starts a rendition of Mohammed Assaf's 'Al Keffiyeh'; it's a mocking imitation of his brother singing it and when he has finished he puts his hand out like he is begging for money.*

Son 2 *storms out of the room.*

Son 1 He'll cool off. Always had a hot head.

Mother I do worry about him though. What will he do?

Son 1 Think up another scam to make money.

Mother In future I mean. I can't see him getting a scholarship and going to Birzeit University like you.

Beat.

Son 1 Birzeit isn't everything.

Mother It's a huge achievement. The first person in our family to go to university, and with no father to support you.

Son 1 I know you are proud.

Mother Proud! You have no idea. You always make me proud and happy I don't know what we would do without you.

Son 1 You'd be fine.

Beat.

Mother Are you really going to university on Friday?

Son 1 Of course.

Beat.

Mother What is it then . . . what's the lecture?

Son 1 Oh, it's something about international law.

Mother You're lying, oh my God, what are you really doing? *Yaboyay!* What have I done to deserve this!

Son 1 Stop, Mother.

Mother My son lying to me.

Son 1 I'm not lying.

Mother You are, you are, oh what will I do if something happens to you, I can't bear to think of it.

Son 1 Nothing's going to –

Mother My own son, lying to his mother – who has made you do this? Yes, you have been sneaking around – I pretended it wasn't happening. *Ya Allah!* I can't bear any more tragedy in my –

Son 1 Stop, stop, I'll tell you – I'm not lying, I am going to uni but it's not a lecture . . . It's an interview. On Skype. The internet. With UCL.

Mother UC?

Son 1 University College London. I've applied for a transfer to do my final year there.

Mother London?

Son 1 Yes. If I can go and study there then /

Mother But it's so far away . . . for a whole year.

Son 1 Well I was thinking once I'd finished my course I could get a job there – the pay is really good – then I could –

Mother Move there?

Son 1 Yes. My English is pretty good.

Mother But you are Palestinian –

Son 1 There are plenty of /

Mother Don't you know what that means?

Son 1 Of course. I've lived here all my life . . .

Mother So you understand you have to be here. What if everyone left? They'd win.

Beat.

Son 1 Mum, there are more Palestinians living outside of Palestine than in it – it's not our fault – this happened to us, there's nothing we can do.

Mother What are we doing then? Come on, let's go – all of us, let's tell everyone in the street, it's too late we've lost, all the years of hardship, being murdered, imprisoned, having our homes taken, our jobs, our fields, our olives, our ability to move from one place to another – everything we have endured has been for nothing. They've won. So let's just leave it to them, disappear. It's what they want. You are doing what they want. You are an educated young Palestinian man. We need you here. Stay.

Son 1 I can't. I can't bear it any more. I need to go.

Beat.

Son 1 I'll come back – to visit.

Mother They won't let you. It's a one-way door.

Son 1 They will. They'll have to. I'm Palestinian.

Mother If you leave you won't be.

Son 1 Yes I will. I'll achieve more out there for us than I can in here – this is suffocating me.

Beat.

Son 1 Do you understand?

Mother No.

Son 1 I have to go.

Mother No you don't, you want to.

Son 1 It's impossible.

Beat.

Son 1 I shouldn't have told you . . . anyway I've got to pass the interview first. It'll probably never happen.

Scene: (2002 and now) People approach a clearing. They position themselves in a formal grouping facing on point in the space, like a congregation in a church. A formal pre-theatre hush goes over the crowd and a middle-aged man stands up to address the crowd. He is the **Man** *who was trying to get home in the taxi scene.*

Man Welcome everyone on this, the sad occasion of Nakba day. Take a good look around at what once was our village and retain every sight, smell and detail of our home, because, as Israeli law states, we will not be permitted to re-enter this place until Nakba day next year. This is our one day to reflect and remember our past, what happened in this place. The things we must none of us ever forget. I'd like to welcome Abu Zaman, who is the oldest living member of our community. Abu Zaman.

An **Old Man** *gets up and stands in front of the crowd.*

Old Man Our village. Stood here. We had a simple but prosperous life, four main farming families for whom everyone worked or was associated. There was no records office – we didn't need one, everyone knew who owned what, where the borders of land lay, these things were ingrained, in the blood and the hearts of every man, woman and child from this place. Over here in the centre of the village was the communal taboon oven. Each house would take turns to make the bread for the village. We all shared.

Beat.

Old Man I was born in 1925, in June. My mother was working in the fields, she came back to the house which stood over there, gave birth, handed me to my grandmother and returned to the fields.

Beat.

Old Man When I was twenty-three everything changed. Of course there had been rumblings beforehand, suggestions, the wind was changing . . . But here, so close to the border we felt safe and protected. Then, on 25 April 1948, soldiers entered this village. They went from house to house and ordered everyone out, into this central square. Where you are standing now, that is where we all stood. Waiting. We were not afraid. We had nothing to hide. They could turn our houses upside down, they would only find oil, blankets, bread and chickens, we had no guns or bullets. We waited. Here.

Beat.

Old Man Once everyone was gathered they took men of age to one side, over there, the women and children were on the other side, there. They were told to go. Walk. Everyone looked confused. When this woman's grandmother – Umm Hameed – tried to go back to the house to get another blanket for her baby daughter, the solder hit her in the face with the butt of his gun. She had a scar for the rest of her life, god rest her.

Beat.

Old Man So the women and children began to walk, the men were taken to a field to the west – over there – and left to sit in the sun, with no water or food. We sat and sat. Then we began to get angry. We were hungry and thirsty and worried about our women. One of the village elders tried to speak to the soldiers. They were all going into the houses, we couldn't see what they were doing. The soldiers wouldn't listen to him. Then Fareed Khalili stood up – he was eighteen. He went to the soldier who was guarding us by the gate. He said this is enough. Fine you are in our village, do what you want but let us go – we have families, mothers and children who need us. The soldier took out a gun and shot him in the head. They wouldn't let us bury him, they threw his body into the well by the fourth field.

Beat.

Old Man   Two days later we were all put into a van and taken south – the opposite direction from our families. We were driven for seven hours and then let out. We did not know where we were. We did not know how to contact our families. We began the walk home.

Beat.

He is overcome.

*The **Man** who introduced him gets up to help him.*

Old Man   Sorry – no, I'm OK.

Beat.

Old Man   We began the walk home.

Beat.

Old Man   We are still walking.

He sits down. There is a silence and a pause.

Man   Thank you, Abu Zaman. Thank you very much. Now I need Kamil al Samuh.

Beat.

Man   Where are you, Kamil?

Mother (*whispering*)   Go on, do you want me to come with you?

Little Boy   No.

He gets up and moves to the front.

Man   OK, Kamil?

Little Boy   Yes.

Man   This, as you all know, is Kamil Al Samuh – the youngest speaking member of our community. Now, Kamil, you understood everything Abu Zaman said, didn't you?

Little Boy   Yes.

Man   Well we need you to tell us what he said so we know that you remember – so you don't forget – so you can tell everyone.

Little Boy   OK.

Beat.

The **Man** *steps back to give the* **Little Boy** *the floor.*

Little Boy   This is where our villages was before the Nakba. There were lots of farmers. And here in the middle was the oven, which everyone shared to make the bread. In 1948, the catastrophe happened. On 25 April 1948, soldiers came and made everyone go out of their houses and stand in the middle – like you all. All the boys went over there. All the ladies had to leave or the soldiers would shoot them – her granny was hurt by a soldier. She's dead now. But not 'cos of that.

Pause.

Little Boy   The soldiers shot a man for asking to go to his family. He was put in the deep well. Then all the boys were put on a truck and driven far away from here and their families.

Pause.

He looks like he is about to cry.

Man   Are you OK? – don't get upset.

Little Boy   They were driven far away from their . . .

Beat.

Little Boy   They were driven away from their . . .

Beat.

Little Boy   They . . .

He begins to sob.

Little Boy   I can't remember any more! Mum – sorry, I can't.

Man   It's OK.

The **Mother** *begins to get up but the* **Old Man** *gets up first and goes to the* **Boy** *and whispers in his ear.*

Little Boy   Shall I say that?

The **Old Man** *continues to whisper.*

Little Boy   They began the walk home. (*He listens.*) We are still walking. (*He listens.*) And so will our children, and our children's children, until we are back in this place, our home, for good.

Beat.

The **Old Man** *has stopped whispering to him. The* **Boy** *looks at the* **Old Man**.

Little Boy   Is it finished?

The **Old Man** *smiles at him sadly.*

Playwright's Outro

Scenes was an even more terrifying experience than *Plan D* when it first opened at the Arcola Theatre in London. Yes, *Plan D* had been about Palestine but in it I had obscured time and place to create what I hoped was a universal story about what happens to ordinary people during world-changing events. But *Scenes* was absolutely, categorically a play about the experience of life under occupation. One that I hoped would undermine an audience's preconceived ideas. I was very pleased that people did laugh at the moments of humour in the play. And I was surprised by how emotional audiences were at the end. I have also been delighted that this play has found further life. It's the first of my plays to be remounted: in San Francisco by Golden Thread, directed by Michael Malek Najjar as *Scenes from 71* Years* in 2019. It was also translated into French in 2018 as *70* ans de Fragments* by Ronan Mancec, which subsequently led to a new Tunisian version of the play in 2019/2020. This new incarnation of the play was called *Trouf* and a very different piece, as I wrote several new scenes specifically set in and about Tunisia. It was performed in Tunisian Arabic, Palestinian Arabic, French and English between 2019 and 2021 and was directed by Ghazi Zaghbani and Chris White. The production was supported by British Council Tunisia, L'Artisto, AFAC and Nabeul Cultural Centre. I'm very grateful also to Imed Belkhodja for his commitment and passion to the piece.

A Negotiation

In *A Negotiation*, an Iraqi woman puts herself in danger in order to protect something she loves.

One female character only.

A Negotiation was first performed at Rich Mix, London, on 11 March 2017, as part of Arab Women Artists Now (AWAN) Festival, produced by Arts Canteen and directed by Chris White. The cast member was:

Taghrid Choucair-Vizoso

Playwright's Intro

I discovered a few things about myself while home-schooling during the first UK COVID-19 lockdown. One of these things was that I am horribly impatient. This was not news to my loved ones apparently, but it was a bit of a shock to me. And it strikes me that this monologue, *A Negotiation*, is very much a result of my impatience. I wrote it while working on *A Museum in Baghdad*. That play was many years in the writing, and I became very frustrated that it hadn't been produced, while also fearing it might never reach production because of its size and ambition (my producer's head told me it would be too expensive). So I channelled some of the themes of *A Museum in Baghdad* into this – and I hope it makes an interesting companion read to *Museum*.

Scene: There is one **Woman** *in the space.*

Woman Don't!

Leave her alone!

Don't touch her.

She's old.

Please – leave her!

NO wait . . . listen.

Let me tell you.

I've seen it –

Heaven.

Beat.

A line . . . it's just a line. One above, one below, but together they make . . . magic.

And then two holes – oval – dark inside.

Holes where her eyes should be.

Empty – should make me feel empty – somehow though they look inside me.

The shape.

The lines.

The first face.

Beautiful, beautiful.

And in my pocket I touch –

But that's too far . . . why am I here? . . .

I thought about joining the army.

Don't laugh.

They have plenty of women. And they'd want me. I speak Arabic. Know the customs.

But coming here as part of the British Army? The occupying force in my country? Too much.

Parents would disown me.

And truth is, I have no stomach for destruction – of any kind. Even to protect what I love.

So I bided my time . . . went to university instead.

No, but that's not far back enough . . . wait . . .

Father . . . yes – my father, a pharmacist – went to university in the capital – respected. Always working. A worker.

Only saw him at Ramadan. Big man. Loved his food.

Religious too – like (you) . . .

Respected Ramadan. But it killed him. Fasting. A torture. Someone of that size should be OK for a few hours on water – but not him. It was agony. He would wait for Iftar, staring at a clock with the date in front of him. When the second hand hit the hour . . . (*mimes gobbling up a date*).

Eid was the only holiday. Father, mother and brother – all get into the car and drive to his special place, with a picnic . . . (*she is in the car, she sings an Arabic song*) baba beeps the horn in time.

We're there, our valley – bags of food on a mat and eat.

And eat.

And eat.

'I'm full.'

'I can't move.'

'Urrrgh' (*Ali groans in pain from overeating*).

But Father takes time.

'Mama, we're bored.'

'I'm reading.'

'We're bored!'

'In this heavenly valley? Go and hunt – this place is generous – filled with gifts. The peasants call it "*melagit*" – seek and you will find.'

She's right.

I find a coin.

Mama said we must bring it to the museum in the capital. Where it belongs.

The woman at the desk said I'd done something important.

That the coin belonged to all of us.

Tarath: heritage.

Every Eid it was a tradition to try and find something.

The final time we went – just before we left – you guessed that I think – that my family and I left and went to the West? I find something.

Small and shaped like a – like a very, very tiny rolling pin.

It has engravings on it.

I don't know what it is.

I want it.

I keep it.

In my pocket. Always.

This isn't fiction you know . . . it's the truth. I know my skin is pale but we're the same – I'm from here too . . .

'You're so white.'

'Are you mixed?'

'Your accent is strange.'

I am from here. This country – a town in the south that's famous for its perfumes – ah! You know it . . . don't you? It's not there anymore.

So now a little girl. England. Cold. Wet. No cheeks pinched. No hair gently tugged. No one *sees* me.

So I look elsewhere. Books. Try to find out what my mini rolling pin is. The history teacher at school sees me holding it.

'Where did you get that?'

'A Kinder egg.'

'It doesn't look like plastic. Show me.'

I'm afraid.

He'll take it.

He holds out his hand.

I shake my head. It's mine.

'Please.'

I squeeze open my fist and his eyes light up.

In his office, a big book, pictures.

'Here!' he cries triumphant.

'It's some kind of seal.'

A cylinder seal.

'It might be Assyrian – you'd have to go to the British Museum to check . . .'

So my mission to get to London was born.

I had to go.

I had to know.

Find out more. Learn about my treasure.

But they say, 'No'.

Baba has lost weight –

'the food tastes different in England.'

He's a supermarket assistant now.

Mum just disappears into her books.

When history teacher offers to take me to London, Baba says he will do it. He has some pride left.

So a military operation. Ali stays with a friend. We get two trains. Plan the route. Buy the tickets.

They're nervous. Never liked travelling since the big trip here.

Lazem nenzel. Yulla (*We get off here*).

Mo hnana, bi Holborn (*Not here, at Holborn*).

Shino ra-ek ya binti? (*Daughter, what do you think?*)

I look away. Pretend not to hear.

Mum hates the escalator.

'Bismilahe rahmanee Rahim, Bismilahe rahmanee Rahim' (*she says the Arabic prayer*) –

I don't want people to think I'm with them.

I'm relieved to get above ground and weave through the streets until there –

it opens up in front of us –

the British Museum, a fortress, strong, permanent, like it's always been there.

Will always be there.

Comforting to think that.

I look at my parents – they look . . . Scared.

Like this is a place of interrogations – torture – not beauty and history.

I drag them in.

A security guard checks us.

They look guilty.

The bag is full of food.

He looks at the food.

Then lets us in.

And heaven.

I see it. Her.

That face.

A line. Then one above, one below, lips. Softer lines trace the distance from lips to nose.

Two holes – oval – dark inside. Her eyes.

The mask of Warka. Earliest representation of a human face it says.

The first face.

My hand goes to my cylinder seal.

Habit.

Then a flash.

This is where it belongs.

With all the other seals.

With all the other history.

It will be safe here.

I turn to find my father – tell him what I want to do.

Leave it where it belongs.

But he's in the corner. Face to the wall. Like a child.

My mother whispers to him.

He – he's crying.

They go.

I don't want to leave her. That face. But I have to.

126   A Negotiation

He's calmer outside.

'Did you see what you needed to see?'

'Why are you sad?'

'All those things belong to our people. But they're never going home. They're like me. They do not belong here.'

And he cries again.

'But, Baba, it's not safe there now but when it is, both you and the antiquities will return *inshallah*.'

Then the crying stops.

His face changes.

He looks at me – differently. As if I'm not me anymore. Not his daughter.

'You sound like them.'

I don't know what he means.

'You are becoming one of them.'

And with that he walks away.

We lose him for a while. And even when he comes back a part of him is missing.

But the seal. The seal is still in my pocket.

We travel home in silence. I'm relieved. No more evidence of our Arabness to embarrass me.

But there are looks. Lots of looks. From the people.

They never fitted in there. My parents. They couldn't change.

They didn't belong there.

They die within a week of each other. And as the English soil pours over them I feel so sorry that they will be stuck in a place they don't belong – forever.

My hand goes to the seal – in my pocket – habit – it doesn't belong there either.

It belongs in my country.

And I have to bring it back home one day.

But how?

Army? No.

I think about her. The first face. And I know.

That's how I will go back.

Serve my people.

Protect my heritage. Archaeology.

That's why I'm here.

Back home.

I'm working for them.

The British Museum.

I'm returning. The seal. Myself.

You're right – I don't pray. I don't believe in God.

But these things. These things I believe in. These statues and bricks, seals and coins that were made thousands and thousands of years ago. They are heaven – heavenly – divine. They're why I'm here. To make sure that these things, these wonderful things that prove we are more than animals, that we are dignified, developed people, are preserved.

That's why they're important. Do you see?

Legacy.

Tarath.

Heritage.

As vital as blood.

So kill as many people as you want – we all die anyway.

But leave her.

Leave that beautiful woman there.

That old woman made of stone.

Don't hurt her.

She is part of us – you and me, part of both of us – all of us – our history.

Leave her.

I mean it.

Leave her.

And if you want to do something –

come.

Come here.

I'm not scared.

Playwright's Outro

A Negotiation was performed as part of AWAN, Arab Women Artists Now festival. The festival is the brainchild of Aser El Saqqa, the man behind Arts Canteen, a wonderful organisation that promotes and produces the work of Arab artists. Aser inadvertently inspired my radio writing. He invited Chris and I for dinner on 25 January 2011 and we were all surprised when we started getting messages from Egypt – the revolution had started. Aser was worried about a family member who was trying to leave Cairo, but as a Palestinian this was not going to be easy. He told me about the notorious deportation room Palestinians from Gaza are subjected to at Cairo airport and this led to my first radio play, *The Deportation Room*. As for *A Negotiation*, I hope one day it might be presented as a sort of curtain raiser to a production of *A Museum in Baghdad* as I'd love to see the two pieces side by side, and understand how they speak to one another in performance.

A Museum in Baghdad

In 1926, the nation of Iraq is in its infancy, and British archaeologist Gertrude Bell is founding a museum in Baghdad. In 2006, Ghalia Hussein is attempting to reopen the museum after looting during the war. Decades apart, these two women share the same goals. But in such unstable times, questions remain about who and what this museum is for? Whose culture are we preserving? And why does it matter when people are dying?

Ten characters, 5 males and 5 females.

A Museum in Baghdad was co-commissioned by the Royal Lyceum Theatre and the Royal Shakespeare Company. It premiered at the Swan Theatre, Stratford Upon Avon, on 11 October 2019. Directed by Erica Whyman, designed by Tom Piper and with Arabic translations by Hassan Abdulrazzak, Nourredine Bessadi, Yasmeen Ghrawi and Rasoul Saghir, it had the following cast:

Leonard Woolley	David Birrell
Layla	Houda Echouafni
Gertrude Bell	Emma Fielding
Kidnapper/Prime Minister	Ali Gadema
Ghalia	Rendah Heywood
Salim	Zed Josef
Nasiya	Nadi Kemp-Sayfi
Sam York	Debbie Korley
Mohammed	Riad Richie
Abu Zaman	Rasoul Saghir

Playwright's Intro

Sometimes you think a play is one thing – but later discover it's actually something else entirely. *A Museum in Baghdad* started life as a play about a woman called Gertrude Bell. It all began when *Plan D* was on in London and I went for a stroll around the National Portrait Gallery. There was an exhibition of Victorian Women Explorers, in which a picture of Gertrude caught my eye. The description card said something like 'aristocrat, explorer, diplomat, spy: travelled widely in the Middle East, spoke every dialect of Arabic and set up the Museum of Iraq in Baghdad'. I had never heard of Gertrude and set out to find out more – I read all her letters and diaries thanks to the University of Newcastle's online archive. Her life was so fascinating I decided I wanted to write about her. Then, not long after, the brilliant Arab British Centre in London hosted a talk by an inspiring Iraqi archaeologist, Dr Lamia Al-Gailani Werr. She was part of the team spearheading the 'clean up' job at the Iraq Museum in Baghdad after the American invasion and subsequent looting. Her talk presented images of artefacts stolen, destroyed, damaged and some returned. I was engrossed. Then at the end of the presentation her final slide was of a man in a blue boiler suit – the caretaker of the museum. She said, 'I always end my talks with a picture of him, because it feels as though he has always been there and as though he will always be there'. At that moment an idea crystallised in my head. My Gertrude Bell play wasn't about Gertrude: it was about the Museum in Baghdad and it needed to cover two times, the original opening by Gertrude in 1926 and the re-opening post-looting in 2006. These two times would be linked by a timeless caretaker who I would name Abu Zaman, in Arabic 'the father of time'. So began a huge rewriting and editing process that eventually became *A Museum in Baghdad*.

Cast

1926:
Gertrude Bell, *57, from Durham, presently an archaeologist*
Salim, *20, Iraqi, Gertrude's assistant*
Professor Leonard Woolley, *46, British archaeologist*

2006:
Ghalia Hussein, *55, Iraqi archaeologist and Director of the Museum*
Mohammed Abdullah, *25, Iraqi curator*
Layla Hassan, *31, Iraqi archaeologist*
Private Sam York, *27, American (from the Deep South)*

Other characters:
Abu Zaman*
Nasiya, *an Arab woman who is timeless*

Production Note

The set should be sparse apart from a large glass exhibition case. It is empty. In addition, the space should begin sandless but gradually more and more sand is introduced throughout the play – emanating from pockets, things being moved, being brought in on people's feet. Camera flashes can be just that or could be moments to reveal images from antiquity or the war that has raged outside.

*A note on Abu Zaman. He is a character who straddles time and space trying to affect the future. At certain points denoted with an asterisk (*), we have a chorus of members of the company speaking Arabic and English.

A Museum in Baghdad

We are in the Museum of Iraq in Baghdad. **Abu Zaman** *is on stage flipping a coin (ideally as the audience enter). When the moment comes, he stops and says:*

Abu Zaman   It's time.

People are conjured to the stage. We are Then (1926), Now (2006), Later (this could be 50, 100 or 1,000 years in the future).

The space is filled with dignitaries and perhaps the odd soldier from then, now and later.

There are three ribbons, three pairs of scissors, three important people. Each important person cuts their ribbon.

Important People   I officially open this museum.

Abu Zaman* (*with chorus made up of* **Nasiya**, **Ghalia**, **Layla**)   Again.   مرة أخرى

Abu Zaman   What if

Gertrude   You could play a moment

Ghalia   Again,

Abu Zaman   *Maratan Okra,*

Ghalia   And again.

Gertrude   What if you could change the future?

Then

The space clears of people and **Professor Woolley** *and* **Gertrude** *are left. Meanwhile,* **Ghalia** *and* **Layla** *are in a corner of the space with a working laptop.* **Abu Zaman** *is fiddling with a coin – he knows he will need it soon.*

Woolley   You can't be happy here . . . Surely you'd prefer to be on site? Up to your elbows in dirt – I know you, Bell.

Gertrude   I'm perfectly happy, there's just a lot to do, but I've my system. Do you think I'll make it for the opening?

Woolley   You, woman, will achieve anything you set your mind to. But letting the King tell you when to open? I never thought I'd see the day . . .

Gertrude   It's not just him. The Government too. You know that.

Woolley   You're not losing your touch are you, Gerty?

Gertrude   Careful, Professor Woolley, or I may decide to come back to your dig at Kish . . . a bird told me there are some lovely artefacts being found, perfect for my 'little' museum.

Woolley   Has he been? The king – seen what you're doing . . . how much is left to do.

Gertrude I expect him any day. But I'm not worried – if you agree to help me plan this place, I'll surely make the opening in time.

Woolley The question is – what's in it for me?

Gertrude The Englishman's mantra. What do you want?

Woolley Well once you are open perhaps you'd consider loaning us a few items? Your goddess, for example (*indicating empty glass cabinet*).

Gertrude I won't lend her unless I have it in writing that she'll return: I know your 'borrowing' and don't forget the Iraq laws of antiquities.

Woolley How could I? You and your laws, like a little girl who changes the rules of the game to suit her.

Gertrude What are you complaining about? Before my laws you could barely dig here.

Woolley Yes, but now *you* get the pick of the finds.

Gertrude This isn't about me – it's about creating unity, nationhood.

Woolley Isn't that why we've crowned a king?

Gertrude It's about galvanising an identity for the people of Iraq.

Woolley Ha! There was no such country till five years ago –

Gertrude That's exactly my point.

Woolley From what I hear they don't think your laws are stringent enough.

Gertrude Of course they are. What is found in their country belongs to them. But you lot do need an incentive to dig in the first place.

Woolley I predict it'll all be back to the British Museum in time for tea when civil war erupts again and they go back to their tribes.

Beat.

Gertrude Let's ask our caretaker – what do you think, Abu Zaman – as an Iraqi?

Woolley He's no fool – he knows she'd be safer in Blighty.

Abu Zaman Safer? أكثر أماناً؟

Gertrude Don't you be swayed by him. Come on, let's do this the Arab way – *maktouba* – let's toss a coin for it.

Abu Zaman Allow me.

Abu Zaman *tosses a coin, and in doing so he affects the timeline. You can indicate or mark this 'magical' moment in production or not as you see fit.*

Gertrude *calls 'heads'. He shows them both the coin – tails –* **Woolley** *is ecstatic.*

Woolley Tails! I win! She comes to England!

Gertrude But my statue!

Woolley Ah, ah! It's not yours – it belongs to the 'people of Iraq', remember?

Gertrude Abu Zaman – how could you?

Woolley Don't blame the poor chap, he can't control the toss of a coin –

Abu Zaman She'll be safer in England – Professor Woolley said so.

Gertrude If she survives the journey in one piece. She doesn't belong there.

Abu Zaman It's dangerous? خطر؟

Woolley Don't panic him! Come on, old boy – I'll give you the shipping details.

Gertrude But the opening.

Woolley You can keep her for that, Gertie, send her after. Why are you so upset?

Gertrude I have high hopes for this place. I don't want you interfering – it could be a great museum.

Woolley Don't be a bad loser.

Gertrude First her – what next? It's a slippery slope . . .

Woolley You could always chaperone her.

Abu Zaman She WILL be safer in England, won't she, Professor Woolley?

Woolley Relax, old boy, we treat our treasures with nothing but respect.

Woolley *has gone.* **Gertrude** *continues to work.*

Abu Zaman Safer. What if you could play a moment. Again. Maratan Okra. What if you could look into the future. See what was to come. What will happen. To people you care about. People who could make a difference. To a museum. A country. Would you try? To make the future the best it can be? To change it?

Of course you would . . . so yalla, let's try . . .

Abu Zaman *places his coin on the floor and goes behind the glass cabinet to see what will happen.*

Gertrude *stands staring at the glass cabinet from one side.*

Ghalia*'s attention is also captured by it.*

We are simultaneously Then/Now/Later.

Abu Zaman *looks through the glass as though it is a crystal ball – a vision of what's to come.*

Abu Zaman *goes behind the glass cabinet and looks through it as though it is a crystal ball – a vision of what's to come.*

Through it he sees **Mohammed** (*Later*). *He is older. He is smoking a cigarette – on a break from his work at the Museum he wears a lanyard around his neck – it says he is the Director of the Museum, he holds it and looks at it then spots the coin and bends to get it. As he does so, three masked men enter and approach him.*

They grab him, put a pillow over his head and hustle him out of the space.

Abu Zaman *bangs his hand on the glass frustrated.*

He comes out from behind glass.

Abu Zaman Not this time . . .

Ghalia *leaves.*

A camera flashes.

Now

Layla *and* **Mohammed** *are working – logging items –*

Gertrude Bell *writes in a corner.*

A female soldier, **York,** *fiddles with a pack of playing cards.*

York Sure is hot.

Beat.

York Like an oven.

Layla Shame your colleagues didn't realise.

York What?

Layla That while they sat back and watched, the looters were taking pipes and wires as well as artefacts, making the building unpleasant for you now.

Pause.

York The Director sent me back here. She had to see the Minister. Is there anything you want me to do?

Layla A tank would have been nice. But it's a bit late now.

Beat.

York I don't know much about the ins and outs of what happened here yet, I wasn't part of the initial force, but I do know one tank on its own wouldn't have been able to do much.

Layla What are you talking about – a huge US tank on the grass outside would have the same effect as an ugly guard dog.

York What most civilians don't realise is a stationary tank is like a death trap, they have blind spots like a car . . . you need at least two.

Mohammed (*to* **Layla**) You've been schooled. By an American. Ouch!

Layla Well then, two would have been nice.

York   And infantry as well – and once you get infantry you get a big shoot up and I can tell you for nothing this here museum'd be a big old pile of rubble if that had happened.

Mohammed   At least this historic building is still standing.

Layla *looks annoyed.*

Layla   Historic building!

York *lays the cards out on the floor for a game of patience.*

They continue their individual tasks in tense silence.

Pause.

York   Hey, awesome.

Beat.

Mohammed   I'll bite. What is so awesome?

York   I just saw this mask in the amnesty room, someone brought it back.

She shows him a picture on the back of one of her playing cards.

Mohammed   The mask of Warka.

York   She made it home.

Layla   One of the first representations of a human face . . . amazing she came back – there are some who would call her sacrilegious.

York   She looks perfect to me.

Layla   Depictions of beings with souls are *haram*.

Mohammed   Forbidden – but only crazy zealots think that . . .

Layla   How do you know I'm not one of those.

Mohammed   I know.

Beat.

Mohammed   I heard they were giving you cards with sites and artefacts on – I never saw them – can I look?

York   Sure – let's play, you know rummy?

Mohammed   Rummy?

York   It's easy, I'll teach you, you need seven cards –

Mohammed   I know how to play.

York   Fine, I'll deal.

Mohammed   I'm at work.

York   Me too – come on – lighten up. Don't you wanna see the cards?

Mohammed   Alright.

York   Shall we make it more interesting?

Layla   Now she's trying to hustle you.

York   I am not – forget it.

Layla   He's got no money – we've none of us been paid for months.

York   Well why'd ya come into work then?

Mohammed   Because it's my job.

They begin to play.

York   Can't imagine that happening back home, if people didn't get paid they wouldn't go to work.

Beat.

York   You folks should get paid extra – danger money in this place it's not even safe to get up in the morning, I don't feel safe in a Humvee so what you civvies must feel like –

Layla   Your concern is touching.

Mohammed *begins to laugh.*

York   What's so funny?

Mohammed   It says here 'Drive around – not over – archaeological sites'.

Layla   Isn't that common sense? Or don't soldiers get that in their basic training?

York   Hey, we don't have things that old in the States.

Mohammed   Look, Layla! A picture of the Statue of Liberty saying, 'How would you feel if someone stole her torch' – it doesn't even come close.

Layla   Let me see.

He shows it to her.

York (*to* **Mohammed**)   We're supposed to be playing a game here. You don't know the rules at all – do you?

Beat.

She takes the cards back and returns to her game of patience.

Gertrude *is showing* **Salim** *the method of logging with enthusiasm.*

Gertrude   So this is my plan: every object must have a running museum number besides its number in its particular room – the latter for making a catalogue easily usable by the public. As yet we have only the excavators' numbers, Ur 1 to 4,000, say, and Kish ditto; while objects that don't come from an excavation – like these wonderful things – have no number at all. The new arrangement will be chronological not geographical, except in the downstairs rooms where all the big, heavy stone objects, too heavy to carry upstairs, will stand – a Babylonian room, an Assyrian room and an Arab room are what we begin on downstairs when the necessary fittings are made. Do you see? Tell me if it's unclear.

Salim   I understand. And this is YOUR system?

Gertrude   It is. I borrowed from another I set up in France during the war to help trace the missing and wounded. Strange there should be an overlap here – one about burying, the other digging up the past. But it's satisfying isn't it – bringing order where there is none . . .

Salim   Many would find this work boring – but it seems to fire you.

Gertrude   Of course! Look at these things . . . what a legacy. While palaces, laws and complicated administrative systems were being built here, bronze age Britain was grappling with basic pottery. It's my duty to make sure the world knows.

Salim   The Assyrian kings had foundation stones for their palaces on which their achievements were inscribed. I'd suggest we had one made for 1926 listing your achievements to go under the museum, but I don't think we'd be able to find a stone big enough.

Gertrude   You flatter me. I foresee that I shall make innumerable mistakes and that I shall be very boring about museums for some time to come! You mustn't let me bore the King when he comes. I can get carried away.

Salim   The King is coming? Here?

Gertrude   Yes so we'd better get on.

They fervently return to their work.

Mohammed *watches* **York**.

Mohammed   Do you think those cards worked?

York   I dunno, but I sure like them better than the last ones.

Mohammed   Naked ladies?

York   Nope, the top fifty most wanted Iraqis, it's hard to keep a poker face with Chemical Ali leering at you.

Mohammed   So you'd know Chemical Ali would you – if you saw him?

York   I reckon so.

Mohammed   Describe him.

York   Why?

Mohammed   I'm just interested to know what the image on the card looked like.

York   He was King of Spades.

Mohammed   Is that all you remember?

York No, he just looked like an old man, with grey hair and a moustache, he was wearing a suit and tie and his mouth was open so you could see his bottom teeth.

Layla Sounds like a million other Arabs.

York It's hard to describe, but I can see the picture in my head.

Mohammed Clear enough to be sure? So if you saw him you'd know it was him, not just another innocent Iraqi with a moustache.

York Sure. I'm not just going on the moustache thing. You guys have all got those.

Mohammed That's what worries me.

York I have had a whole bunch of training you know.

Beat.

York What are you two so pissed at me about?

Layla Look around.

York The Iraqi army used this as cover – not us.

Mohammed You just shot at it.

York I wasn't even here then.

Ghalia *returns – she is in a foul mood.*

Ghalia And you may as well not be here now if you just came to play cards and distract my staff from their work, they've a lot to do. You're supposed to be helping. I've seen no evidence of that so far.

York Yes, mam, No, mam.

Ghalia Go down the basement and help Abu Zaman clear up.

York *goes to leave but stops.*

Ghalia Well? What are you waiting for?

York The basement door.

Ghalia What about it?

York Where is it, mam?

Ghalia Don't you know yet?

York I don't have a great sense of direction . . .

Layla Oh for goodness sake, come on – I'll show you.

The two women exit.

Ghalia *slams around a bit.*

Mohammed What's the matter? The soldier said you went to see the Minister.

No answer.

Mohammed Did something happen?

Ghalia You knew, didn't you? You could have warned me. It put me on the back foot entirely. I didn't have an argument ready. I suppose you wanted that though, didn't you?

Mohammed What do you mean?

Ghalia We've only a few weeks – it's impossible.

Pause.

Ghalia The opening.

Mohammed Oh that.

Ghalia Yes, that.

Mohammed It's not a big deal, it's just a soft opening for journalists, show them we are doing something. Give them a taste that this museum is going be great again, able to rival anything in the West.

Beat.

Mohammed Better than the British Museum.

Ghalia I'm the Director – I should decide when we open.

Mohammed It's just a couple of rooms.

Ghalia This place will be great. I believe that. It's why I'm here. But we shouldn't rush. The Minister doesn't seem to get it.

Mohammed My uncle just wants things back to normal.

Ghalia Yes, but we need to do things properly. We need TIME.

Beat.

Ghalia Can't you speak to your uncle, put him off, just for a few months?

Mohammed It would be pointless, his mind's made up. Besides, I think it's a good idea. Don't worry – you need to be more Iraqi about things.

Ghalia I am Iraqi.

Mohammed I didn't say you weren't.

Ghalia What did you mean then?

Mohammed You have to pick your battles here . . .

They continue to work.

Then/Now/Later

Abu Zaman* (*with chorus*)

> What if –
> You could play a moment
> Again.

He tosses a coin.

> And again.

He tosses a coin.

> And again.

He tosses a coin.

> Torture
>
> Unless
>
> You could unpick the stitches.
>
> Be ready to start again.
>
> Try again . . .
>
> Make it better. . . .
>
> The past you can't change
>
> But the future . . .
>
> we must all try to make the future the best it can be. For who knows what's to come?
>
> *Fatahit Al Fahl* – A fortune teller
>
> What if it was this person's job to predict the future – not with a looking glass or magic but with
>
> A clear sight of what had happened in the distant past, as well as recent history, with an understanding of human nature – patterns of behaviour.

ماذا لو
بِأمكانِكَ ان تُعيدَ اللحَظَة
مرةً أُخرى

ومرةً أُخرى

ومرةً أُخرى

تَعذيب

الا إذا

يُمكِنُكَ ا تنزيلَ الغُرَز

وكُنتَ مُستعداً أن تَبدءَ من جَديد

وان تُحاوِلَ مرةً أُخرى

وان تَجعلَ كُلَ شيءٍ أفضل

لا أحَدَ يُمكِنُه تغييرُ الماضي

لكِنَّ المُستقبل...يَجِبُ علينا جميعا
ان نَجعلَهُ أفضَلَ ما يُمكِن فمن يَعرِفُ ماذَ
ا سَيحدُث؟

سوى الشَخصِّ الذي يَتَنَبأُ بالمُستقبل

وماذا لو كانت تِلكَ مِهنَتُها، مُعتَمِدَةً لا على مرآه ولا على تَعاويذَ
سِحرية.
وإنما على الحِسابات...

ورؤيَةٍ واضِحَةٍ لِما حَدَثَ في الماضي البَعيد والتاريخ الحديث،
وفَهم لطَبيعةِ الإنسان - لأنماطِ سُلوك البَشرْ...

And what if this person was
asked routinely –
What do you think will
happen next?

وماذا لو سُئِلَ هذا الشخص بصورَةٍ روتنة
مالذي سَيحدثُ فيما بعا؟

All eyes on **Nasiya** *and* **Abu Zaman**.

A leader gone.	القائدُ سَقَط..
Showers of bombs.	أمطارٌ من القذائف..
Enemies uniting.	أعداءٌ يَتحدّون..
People in hiding.	أناسٌ مُختَبِئون..
The wrong kind of aid.	مُساعداتٌ فاشِلة
Military heroes made.	أبطالٌ عَسكَريون يُخلَقون..
Families fled.	عائلاتٌ هاربة
Children dead.	أطفالٌ مَيتون.
Seas	بحار..
Bodies	أجساد..
Perhaps.	رُبمّا...
All possible. Of course.	كُلُ شيءٍ مُمكن. بالتأكيد
But in the end. They won't dig down far enough	لكن ،وفي النهاية لن يَتَعمَقوا بما فيه الكفاية
Can't imagine.	لم يكونوا قادرين على تَخيُلِ
What's to come.	ما سيأتي
What will happen next . . .	ما الذي سَيحدثُ فيما بعد..

Then

Gertrude *works on an article.*

Gertrude   Has someone come?

Abu Zaman   No. Are you expecting?

Gertrude   Nothing concrete. My mind keeps wandering from the task at hand. I'm trying to devise a clever premise for an *Illustrated London News* article. They're publishing piece after piece about Woolley's exploits in Ur – do you see (*she proffers article*). But nothing about this. Us. Here. The Museum. I want to change that (*she looks at the goddess*). If only the statue could talk. Share her secrets. Give them a real story.

Abu Zaman   Maybe not that goddess – but . . .

He encourages her onto a stool.

Abu Zaman   What's your story?

Gertrude   Oh you know. The usual: girl grows up, goes to Oxford, climbs a few mountains, travels the desert.

Abu Zaman   No. Not that one. The one inside you. The one you'd like to be remembered for in future. By future goddesses.

Gertrude   Ah. Well, that's a bit harder to get at. You'd have to take one of these brushes and dust away all the layers of desert sand to really see me.

Abu Zaman   I see you ... in your heart. Underneath it all ... You are truly an Arab.

An intense moment between them.

Ghalia   Stupid idiot!

Abu Zaman   Another one?

Ghalia   Yes – Cretins! If you are going to buy antiquities on eBay at least get an expert to verify it first!

Abu Zaman   How much?

Ghalia   This *h'mar* (*looks for his name on screen*) calls himself 'the appreciator', just paid a thousand dollars for a fake cylinder seal.

Abu Zaman   Do you follow the real ones or only the fakes?

Ghalia   I report the real ones – breaking the laws of antiquities, I laugh at the donkeys who buy the fakes!

Layla   I'm amazed you make the time, Professor. The basements are still in chaos – trying to get a list of everything stolen or damaged will take a lifetime – and now we have to open in a few weeks.

Ghalia   These people need to be brought to justice. They can't just take what they want. This is our country and we have to protect it.

Ghalia *exits.*

Salim *enters holding a brown box as* **Gertrude** *steps down from the chair.*

Gertrude   Abu Zaman, will you order those seals for me – chronologically ... (*Seeing* **Salim**.) Aha. How is the labelling coming along?

Salim   Like counting grains of sand. This was delivered for you.

Gertrude   From the palace? At last!

He hands her the box. It has an object wrapped in paper that has a word written on it in Arabic script.

Gertrude (*reading*)   *Melagit*? 'Not found'? What does it mean Salim?

Salim   I don't know, Miss Bell.

Gertrude   Not from the King then . . .

He watches as **Gertrude** *carefully unwraps the item. It is a magnificent crown, bejewelled and breath-taking. They both stare in wonder.*

Gertrude   Look at this crown, Salim . . . it's beautiful! Magical!

Salim   It is, Miss Bell.

Gertrude   And someone just brought it here, handed it in, just like that.

Salim   This is where it belongs,

Gertrude   What wonderful people. What a place. Anywhere else they'd have kept it – but not here.

Salim   If they'd kept it, it would have come back later, another time. Everything eventually ends up in its rightful place, don't you think?

Abu Zaman *sees the crown and smiles.*

Abu Zaman   *Melagit.*

Salim   What is it, Abu?

Abu Zaman   It's a tradition. After any heavy rain when the earth washes away from the surface of ancient mounds, exposing archaeological objects, the locals in the area surrounding these mounds pick whatever the earth has given up; *Melagit*. Beads and cylinder seals made from semi-precious stones, carnelian, onyx or lapis-lazuli. But I have never seen something so beautiful as this come to light . . . These objects are considered to have magical powers, a good omen. They are meant to be a promise of marriage, children.

Salim   It's good luck then, a marriage – how wonderful!

Beat.

Gertrude   I have been in Baghdad all this time, and Basra before that, I've travelled across the desert, been to Syria and Palestine, *ana ahchi kl allahjat al arabiat wal farisia* [*I speak every dialect of Arabic and Persian*]. What's more I've seen more archaeological sites than Salim's had hot dinners and yet I have never heard this tradition. How is that possible?

Abu Zaman   There are many rituals and sayings – hundreds for each tribe, every time someone new invades new traditions appear, we adapt, things change a little. You could never learn them all, you'd have to live through it all . . . it would take several lifetimes, being born again and again –

Abu Zaman* (*with* **Nasiya** *who speaks in Arabic*)   You'd have to live forever.
يجب أن تعيش إلى الأبد

Gertrude   Impossible – when there are so many ways to die. Pneumonia, typhoid, bullet to the heart, drowning, suffocating, being buried alive.

Beat.

She realises they are looking at her she is gripping the crown very tightly like she might damage it.

Abu Zaman Let me put that back in the box for safekeeping, Miss Bell.

Gertrude Thank you, Abu Zaman. You're like an old tree, or, like one of our pieces of antiquity here – isn't he, Salim? Perhaps you should be the next director of the museum, Abu Zaman.

Abu Zaman Oh no.

Gertrude Why not? You know more about these things than anyone.

Abu Zaman Such positions are for the likes of you, Miss Bell. I'm just an 'Iraqi'. For now.

Beat.

Abu Zaman It takes one a little while to get used to one's new hat. The most important thing is to remember what colour your hair is underneath.

Gertrude Is that an old Arab saying?

Abu Zaman No, but it should be, don't you think?

Salim *smiles.*

Beat.

Gertrude I'll never get to the bottom of all this will I / – won't dig down far enough.

Abu Zaman / If you dig down far enough.

Salim I'm sure there are many English traditions we will never understand – I can never remember when to put the milk in tea – our tea is much simpler just with cardamom.

Gertrude I prefer it like that.

Abu Zaman We all drink it the same way.

Salim *mimes drinking tea from a china cup with his pinkie up,* **Gertrude** *smiles.*

Salim Shall I make some for you?

Gertrude That would be very nice. Thank you.

Salim *goes to make the tea.*

Gertrude (*indicating crown*) That thing may well have magical powers, it has me under its spell . . . thinking strange thoughts . . . You'd better take it and lock it away somewhere, Abu Zaman, till we can get a display cabinet that's secure enough to hold it. The broom cupboard has a lock, doesn't it? It seems sacrilegious but it will have to do.

Abu Zaman   Don't worry – I know where it will be safe.

He takes the box and removes some letters from his pocket.

These came for you.

Gertrude   Wonderful! – Just what I've been waiting for! Thank you.

She opens a letter and begins to read. It annoys her and she puts it down. She stares into space considering the letter's contents.

Abu Zaman   Not what you were hoping for?

Gertrude   I'm waiting for news from the Palace, instead all I get is requests to go back there.

Abu Zaman   To England? I didn't think you took orders, Miss Bell.

Gertrude   It's always useful to know what people want you to do when trying to make a decision.

Abu Zaman   So you can do the opposite?

Gertrude   Sometimes.

Beat.

Now

Layla *has returned,* **Ghalia** *is working on her computer.*

Abu Zaman   Your office would be cooler.

Gertrude/Ghalia   I prefer to be amongst the artefacts – that's why I'm here.

Abu Zaman (*proffering box to* **Ghalia**)   This was left for you.

Ghalia   Thank you. Who by?

Abu Zaman   I don't know.

Beat.

Abu Zaman   Aren't you going to open it?

Ghalia   Later – I'm busy.

Abu Zaman   It could be important.

Ghalia   This is important.

Abu Zaman   More fakes?

Ghalia   No, an authentic seal, I'm emailing to report it.

Beat.

Ghalia Imagine the hands that seal has passed through. What it's seen – an invaluable tool which was in the ground for 5,000 years, then carefully excavated, put in a museum and admired before being grasped by greedy hands and exchanged for cash. Dealers stood outside those doors with price lists of how much they'd pay on their car. They let the thugs do the smashing. And they smuggled the pieces to the States. Or Europe. It's sickening.

Abu Zaman There are thousands of those seals out there, you can't find every one.

Ghalia I know, but cylinder seals are my speciality, without them what am I?

Abu Zaman A camel without a desert.

Ghalia Exactly.

Ghalia/Gertrude Will you set up a meeting with the Chief of Police?

He nods.

Gertrude We need to ensure everything on display for this ludicrous opening is secure.

Abu Zaman *Bil khidme.*

Gertrude *is looking at the glass cabinet.*

Gertrude/Ghalia Thank god she's not damaged. (*Indicating the invisible statue.*) So beautiful.

Mohammed Beautiful but heavy – I nearly got a hernia lifting her into that case. (*To statue.*) No more baklava for you young lady – diet time.

Layla *smiles.*

Ghalia She's very important, don't mock her!

Mohammed I'm only joking.

Ghalia It starts with teasing and disrespect and ends with battery and destruction.

Layla That's quite a leap . . . What's the matter?

Ghalia I knew what to expect here but it's still a shock. It's like a rollercoaster, you must have ice water running through your veins to take it all in your stride. Every time I see something that has been destroyed it's like a knife in my flesh, doesn't it break your heart? Layla?

Beat.

Layla There are bodies in the streets. It puts broken statues into perspective.

Beat.

Ghalia Your brother. I'm sorry.

Beat.

Layla Besides – one piece on its own means nothing. It needs to be in context.

Ghalia Such an archaeologist.

Mohammed You're both archaeologists.

Woolley *enters and looks at the statue in the cabinet.*

Woolley There she is.

Ghalia But Layla is a purist – she believes artefacts should be left where they are found, experienced in that context. Taking them out of the ground is probably a step too far.

Mohammed WHAT?

Layla Well it's too late now – they *have* been dug up. But they won't survive. Gradually eroding –

Woolley I'm not sure she's happy here.

Gertrude (*indicating glass cabinet*) It's where she belongs.

Layla Now they're above ground they should be where they belong, where they were found as part of a community museum – not this globalized, commodified, Western version of a museum, shaping historical narrative in the way that suits those in power. Artefacts as trophies.

Mohammed I love it when she gets all academic.

Woolley She'd look better in a nice secure display cabinet at the British Museum. I'm glad you got her back in one piece. I heard Smith carried her in a rucksack

Gertrude That's a lot of tosh, you should not listen to rumours Len, she was carefully wrapped in a trunk. I wouldn't be so careless.

Woolley Who'll see her here though, eh? Goddesses are for worshipping.

Ghalia You'd prefer to leave them in harm's way? No. She should be locked in the basements where she will be safe and secure.

Mohammed Next you'll say she should be back at the British Museum. But people must see her – HERE. We want this to be a tourist destination! Change the way people think about Iraq! Layla – help me.

Layla Help you?

Woolley Let me take her to safety.

Mohammed To convince her not to lock the goddess up, we need her! For the opening!

Layla She has no business being in Baghdad. This isn't her home.

Gertrude It's out of my hands. It's the law.

Woolley You made the law you can break the law . . .

Ghalia She's been here since the original opening, bar a loan to the British Museum . . .

Mohammed It's amazing they ever let her come back.

Layla That woman. She was obsessed. Too many artefacts were taken from their rightful places. Half of everything went to the people who organized the dig as payment, i.e. The West.

Ghalia Half of it stayed here. She was ground-breaking.

Layla Nonsense. What about Egypt?

Ghalia What about Egypt?

Gertrude Would you rather we adopted the Egyptian laws?

Woolley Native inspectors? Nothing allowed out of the country? NO THANK YOU.

Ghalia Many items were ruined there because the locals didn't have the expertise to dig and preserve properly.

Layla Say what you like – that woman was out for her own ends.

Ghalia Without 'that woman' there'd be no museum. Gertrude Bell did everything she could to keep artefacts in Iraq.

Layla We were better off with the Ottoman laws. Duplicates were all that was allowed to be taken then. She basically put herself in charge and shared the spoils with her mates

Gertrude Stop staring at her and make yourself useful – check my cylinder seal groupings are right before we put them in the cabinet.

Ghalia If it weren't for her all these things would be in London or New York or Berlin.

Layla They are.

Ghalia No, we have a Museum in Baghdad despite everything.

Mohammed Exactly and people should know about it, that this is the greatest Museum in the world, or will be . . . if the artefacts are all locked up it's no better than under Saddam.

Ghalia What happened to this museum must never happen again.

Layla I'm telling you there is much, much worse than the looting to come . . . Besides, broken statues have their place too. A reminder. Attempting to mend them, make them look new is a form of cover up.

Mohammed Layla you aren't helping my argument. Come on – I can get a better glass cabinet – reinforced – from my cousin in Najaf. Then she'll be safer.

Beat.

Mohammed The world should see her.

A Museum in Baghdad   151

Ghalia   Bring the case then. I'll get Abu Zaman to look at it. But I'm not promising anything.

Nasiya (*to* **Ghalia**, *who doesn't see her*)   Because we need her story – it mustn't be forgotten . . .

Abu Zaman *gestures to* **Nasiya** *offering her the floor.*

Nasiya   Let me tell you how it was.

Then/Now/Later

Abu Zaman* (with chorus)

There was a group of women.	كانتْ هُناك مجموعةٌ مِنْ النسوةِ
You might call them a tribe.	ممكن أنْ تُسَمُّنَهُنَّ قبيلةً
Who lived in isolation.	عِشنَ في عُزلة
Solved problems.	وَحَلَلنَ المشاكلَ
Documented their findings in writings.	وَوَثَّقنَ نتائجهُنَّ بالقلم
Discovered medicines and cures as yet unknown.	أكتَشفنَ أدويةً وعلاجاتٍ لم تُعرفْ بعد
Could hear the Earth's language understand her.	يَسمَعنَ لغةَ الأرضِ وَيَفهَمنَها
Of course they needed men for one particular task.	وكُنَّ في حاجةٍ إلى رجالٍ لغرضٍ واحدٍ لا غير
But in that eventuality all they had to do was ask.	كُلُّ ما كانَ عليهِنَّ فِعْلهُ هوَ الطلب
Their role fulfilled, the men were dismissed.	وبعدَ ما قامَ الرجالُ بدورِهم تَمَّ صَرفهُم
The women could return to their lives.	كُنَّ قادِراتٍ على العودةِ إلى حَياتِهِنَّ
But soon the men grew suspicious and raged.	ولكنْ سُرعانَ ما ارتابَ الرجالُ واعتَرَضوا
They didn't like being on the outside.	سَئِموا البقاءَ في الخارج
They agreed that the time had come to unseat these women.	وَاتفَقُّوا على الإطاحةِ بهؤلاءِ النسوة
Clearly the only way to do that was to kill them.	وما مِنْ طَريقةٍ لفعلِ ذلكَ الا بِقتلِهِنَّ

So they stole into the tribe in the dead of night	إِذا تَسَلَّلُوا إلى القبيلةِ في جَوفِ الليل
And set everyone and everything alight.	و أَحْرَقوا كُلَّ شيء
The smell of burning hung in the air for days.	وبَقِيَتْ رائحةُ الاحتراقِ تَحومُ في الهواءِ لِعدَّةِ أيام
No woman survived, the bodies dumped in a grave.	لَم تَنْجُ أيُ امرأة وأُلقِيتْ الجُثَثُ في قبرٍ
The children they spared, and took back to their land.	لَم يُؤذوا الأطفال، وأخَذوهم مَعَهُم الى بلادِهِم
They never told them of their history.	لم يخبروهم أبداً عن تاريخهم
And so those children – the girls	وهؤلاءِ الأطفال- الفتيات
Grew up into women in this masculine world.	أصبَحْنَ نساءَ في هذا العالمِ الذكوري
They followed the rules.	اتَّبعْنَ القواعد
Because the truth about their past they never knew.	لأنَّهنَّ لَمْ يَعرفْنَ الحقيقةَ عَنْ ماضيهنَّ
Not of the tribe who had changed the world for a time.	ولا عَنْ القبيلةِ التي غيَّرتْ العالمَ لبعضِ الوقتِ
Although many of these young women would often pine	على الرغم مِنْ إنَّ هَؤلاءِ النسوةِ الشاباتُ غالباً ما يَتَحرَّقنَ شَوقاً
For what, they weren't entirely sure.	إلى شيءٍ لَمْ تَفْهَمْنَه
But their feet would carry them	لكنَّ أقدامَهُنَّ سَتَحملُهُنَّ
into the woods to a particular place.	إلى الغابةِ، إلى مكانٍ مُحدد..
They never knew why they were drawn to this space	لم يعرفْنَ أبداً سببَ تَواجدِهنَّ في هذا المكان
But the terrible truth they did not know	ولكنَّهُنَّ لَمْ يَعرفنَ الحقيقةَ المأساوية
Was that their history was deep below	إنَّ تاريخَهُنَّ أسفلَ
Their feet.	أقدامِهن
Burned and buried with their mothers.	محروقٌ ومَدفونٌ مَعَ أمهاتِهن.
Forgotten.	وَفي طيِّ النسيانِ..

Then

Woolley *looks up from his work.*

Ghalia *exits at some point in the next section.*

Woolley   Before I forget – I have news – from the Caliph.

Gertrude   You mean His Highness King Faisal. He's sent word with you? Why didn't you tell me sooner?

Woolley   Slipped my mind.

Gertrude   I've been expecting him to come and see my progress.

Woolley   Kinging is a weighty business.

Gertrude   Perhaps he wants it to be a surprise. At the opening.

Woolley   Perhaps he's busy with the ruminations of monarchy –

Gertrude   You don't need to tell me – I've sat by him and helped him draw up laws on oil concessions, medical practices, dredging the river, and more. I was intimate with every stitch of this young country's vestments. But now . . .

Beat.

Gertrude   I wish the King would invite me to *majlis* as he used to, I never know what's going on in the cabinet these days and I have an uneasy feeling that no one is controlling things.

Woolley   There's the King.

Gertrude   What's a King without his advisor?

Woolley   He has advisors.

Gertrude   His ENGLISH one.

Beat.

Gertrude   What did he say?

Woolley   Talk of the weather – the floods.

Gertrude   Tell me what he wants you awful man!

Woolley   Well, there's something important he wants you to do.

Gertrude   I knew it! They want me to negotiate with the Turks about the oil fields don't they – I was surprised they didn't ask me in the first place I'll message the maid to pack.

Woolley   No, no, Gerty, not that – that's in hand. No, it's about this place.

Gertrude   Oh.

Woolley   I wonder if I should tell you – now I've been here.

Gertrude What's wrong with it?

Woolley Nothing – but you've still such a lot to do.

Gertrude I have time.

Woolley He asks if you can do it by 14 June?

Gertrude Do what?

Woolley Have it finished –

Gertrude That's just a few weeks away.

Woolley He thinks it's important – let the people know we are doing something . . . that sort of thing. He will come. Cut a ribbon, make a speech –

Beat.

Woolley You'll have to tell him no.

Gertrude Out of the question.

Woolley Quite – too much to do.

Gertrude No it's out of the question to say no – he's right of course, it's important – let the people know we are doing something . . .

Beat.

Gertrude Faisal sent no letter to me?

Woolley No. Just the message. Open the museum. Then your work here will be done.

Gertrude Is that your opinion – or his? Besides – it will never be done.

Woolley Well then you can pass on the mantle as planned. I must go, I've a report to write on Ur for the BM – wretched white ants ate my first effort. We've all got responsibilities back in Blighty, eh?

Beat.

Woolley You really think you can do it – the fourteenth?

Gertrude Len, the museum is a life-long task, but I know I can make the Babylonian stone room ready for an opening, make the King proud, remind him what I'm capable of. The rest of the museum will take much longer to be finished. Just logging these items is taking forever, though my system is good. It's all rather Sisyphean – and the rooms upstairs look like a bomb site –

Woolley Archaeological site surely. Let's not conjure more wars Gerty . . .

Now

York I've done a bad thing. I need to tell someone about it.

Layla *appears as if summoned*

York That mask got me thinking. The Warka one . . . that came back.

Layla Look, I'm not really qualified – you should speak to the Director or don't you have counsellors at your base or something?

York Oh not that kind of bad thing, it's to do with an artefact.

Layla Something stolen? Go on.

York Well, in my first week here I was patrolling on the Friday, on Mutanabi Street, and I came across the book market there, what an incredible sight, as if the street was paved with books, and cars covered in books too and people all gathered around reading – not buying just reading like they were eating up the pages . . .

Layla They can't afford to buy.

York I guess not, but it was amazing and as I walked I saw one guy with these beautiful maps. Maps of the Mid East with Arabic writing marking different places, archaeological sites, cities, the rivers, so decorative . . . He saw me looking and called me inside – said it was one of the first maps of Iraq, just after it became a country over eighty years ago, it belonged to the first King, King Faisal. He said he could see I'd take care of it, he didn't want it to get destroyed here –

Layla How much did you pay?

York Five hundred dollars . . . I couldn't help myself, it was so beautiful, it seemed like the right thing to do – to save it.

Beat.

York But pretty quick I knew it was wrong, what I done. And when I heard I was getting posted here to the museum it seemed like fate, you know, I could return it. Thing is, if my Commanding Officer found out – well I'd get in some hot water you know, we're not supposed to buy stuff like that.

Layla Where is it?

York Here . . .

She takes it out and gives it to **Layla**.

York I thought maybe you could take it – say it was handed in anonymously. So many things are being handed in every day – no one needs to know.

Layla I could do that –

She is studying the map.

York I'd appreciate it – it's been on my conscience since I bought it.

Layla Really? After all the things that you must have seen and done *this* has been on your conscience?

Layla *smells the map –* **York** *looks bemused.*

York Sure. Civilians don't get it, but it's different when you are told to do something, it's sort of not you, you know – even the really bad stuff. But that, that's something I chose to do, myself, I have to take responsibility for it.

Beat.

Layla *hands the map back to* **York**.

She takes out a camera.

York What are you doing?

Layla Photo for posterity. Then you can have it back.

York Huh?

Layla It's a fake.

Layla *takes a photo and there's a flash.*

Abu Zaman *holds the coin up to the light examining it for dirt, then wipes it on his clothes to shine it.*

Abu Zaman If only every problem was so easy to solve.

Then

Woolley The question is – what's in it for me?

Gertrude The Englishman's mantra. What do you want?

Woolley Well once you are open perhaps you'd consider loaning us a few items? Your goddess, for example.

Gertrude I won't lend her unless I have it in writing that she'll return: I know your 'borrowing' and don't forget the Iraq laws of antiquities.

Woolley How could I? You and your laws, like a little girl who changes the rules of the game to suit her . . . anyway I predict it'll all be back to the British Museum in time for tea when civil war erupts again and they go back to their tribes.

Beat.

Gertrude Let's ask our caretaker – what do you think, Abu Zaman, as an Iraqi?

Abu Zaman Maybe things would be different – better if she stayed here . . .

Gertrude Tell you what. Let's do it the Arab way – *maktouba* – let's toss a coin for it.

Abu Zaman Allow me.

Abu Zaman *tosses a coin, again he affects the outcome and this can be marked or not in production at the discretion of the creative team.*

Gertrude *calls 'heads'. He shows them both the coin – heads –* **Gertrude** *is ecstatic.*

Gertrude   It's heads! I win! She stays!

Woolley   Show me that coin!

He inspects it – it isn't a trick one.

Gertrude   She stays with me.

Woolley   With the 'people of Iraq'; you mean. I was sure I'd win – like I'd dreamt it before . . . Why do I feel I've been had Abu Zaman?

Gertrude   Don't blame the poor chap, he can't control the toss of a coin –

Abu Zaman   She'll be safer *here* – won't she? Where she belongs.

Woolley   As long as the Iraqis aren't revolting . . . and I'm afraid they are.

Gertrude   Professor Woolley!!

Woolley   What? It is less than a decade since the uprisings and the only way we quashed them was with air power.

Abu Zaman   You predict another civil war, Professor Woolley?

Woolley   Look around, man. The tribes are twitchy – Sunnis, Shias, Kurds, Jews – all vying for supremacy. Imagine taking an Englishman, Scotsman, Welshman and a Paddy – telling them they are one family – making them share one house and locking the door on them. Go back in a week and they'll each have barricaded themselves in a room – the English in the drawing room, Scottish in the bedroom, Welsh in the kitchen and the Irish in the latrine. And when the Welshman kindly asks if he can use the facilities the others will barge into the kitchen devour the luncheon meat, pour flour all over the floor and destroy every plate in the house. The Welshman will be cleaning for a week.

Abu Zaman *looks worried.*

Gertrude   Ignore him he's just a sore loser.

Abu Zaman   But we want our plates intact – our flour in the jar! What would no kitchen mean for the future of everyone? With no kitchen . . .

Woolley   No one gets to eat.

Gertrude   For goodness sake.

Abu Zaman   But if things were changed. If she (*the statue*) stays here. Educates people – things might be different . . .

Abu Zaman* (*with chorus of* **Nasiya/Salim**)   The future might be better.

لامستقبل فأضل دكيون

Woolley   *Ma-tigdar.* You can't change the future old boy.

Abu Zaman   You are wrong, Mr Woolley. It's the past you can't change. But the future . . . we must all try to make the future the best it can be . . .

Abu Zaman *nods to the audience to indicate he is going to try to change the future once more.*

Gertrude and **Woolley** *regard the statue from one side.*

We are Then/Now/Later.

Abu Zaman *places the coin on the floor as before and moves to look through the glass to the future once more: a future he is hoping might now be different.*

Through it we see **Mohammed** *again (Later). Again he is older and toys with his lanyard while smoking a cigarette – on a break from his work at the museum.*

Beat.

Mohammed *spots a coin on the floor – he bends over as he did before to pick up the coin and now a group of people who are masked enter. They get to* **Mohammed** *and grab him as before,* **Abu Zaman** *hits the glass with his hand in frustration.*

Abu Zaman   WHY NOT THIS TIME?

York *enters sweeping up sand – she sweeps them away.*

She continues to sweep.

Now

Ghalia *enters, she is carrying the box that* **Abu Zaman** *gave to her previously.* **Mohammed** *and* **Abu Zaman** *follow.* **Gertrude** *is writing an article in a corner.*

Ghalia   Everyone. Come here. Come on. Who knows about this?

They all look at her in curiosity.

Ghalia   It just appeared – look!

Ghalia *opens the envelope to reveal the crown from before. It's from the 4,500-year-old royal cemetery at Ur.*

York   Sweet lord, I've never seen anything like it.

Layla   Who from?

Ghalia   Abu Zaman?

Abu Zaman *looks blankly at them all.*

Abu Zaman   Melagit.

Ghalia   If 'not found' – then what?

Mohammed   All that gold!

York   Funny, you'd think someone would steal that – not return it, right?

Layla   Maybe they just wanted it off their conscience.

Mohammed   It's not exactly common is it? – It'd be a nightmare to sell. Maybe whoever took it was just looking after it – keeping it safe.

Layla   You can be so naïve.

Mohammed   That's my youth and optimism for you – attractive isn't it?

Layla *smiles in spite of herself.*

Ghalia   When I opened it – it gave me a surge of hope . . . despite all the destruction things can get back to where they belong . . . Isn't it WONDERFUL?

Abu Zaman   Shall I take it to the basement – lock it up safely there?

York   How old is it?

Layla   Is it from Ur?

Ghalia   Yes – 4,500 years old give or take –

They all stare at it looking beautiful.

Mohammed   It's going to look amazing at the opening.

Ghalia   What?

Abu Zaman   No!

Mohammed   We have to find the best way to display it.

York   Someone could model it.

Ghalia   No, no, it goes under lock and key, it isn't being displayed.

Mohammed   This is ridiculous, you are being far too over cautious. A museum needs its public or it's just an archive – dead.

Ghalia   But you saw the looting.

Abu Zaman   They were possessed, the pounding – thuds – bangs – they broke down the door – a wave –   موجةٌ عارمةٌ من الدمار

They smashed everything in their way! We need these things intact for the future.

Gertrude   / a tidal wave of destruction /

Mohammed   No ordinary Iraqis will be at the opening, it's only for dignitaries and journalists.

Ghalia   Forget the opening, what about when we lock those flimsy doors at night, who's to say they won't break them down again?

Mohammed   You are being paranoid. It has to go on display.

Ghalia   No it doesn't.

Mohammed   Did you just come back here to lock everything up?

Ghalia   Your uncle may be the minister but I'm still the director of the museum and I say NO.

Mohammed I'm going to call the Minister now.

Ghalia I'm right behind you – let's get him on speaker phone. My office. Abu Zaman, come with me, back me up.

Abu Zaman The crown?

Ghalia It has an American soldier guarding it. Come on.

The three exit leaving the crown behind them.

Gertrude *steps forward and picks it up.*

Gertrude, **Layla** and **York** *all look at it.*

Pause.

York It's incredible.

Layla Must have belonged to a queen,

Gertrude Beautiful.

York I want to hold it.

Layla You shouldn't touch it without gloves.

York Almost doesn't look real, like a costume.

Beat.

York It's a darn shame . . . it was meant to be worn.

Layla By a queen. A goddess.

Beat.

Layla Can you smell –?

Gertrude Burning?

York Why don't you try it on?

Layla Don't be ridiculous.

York Let's get a glimpse of what it would have been like . . . what about it? Don't be a stick in the mud.

Layla My skin could damage it.

York What are you? Bionic woman?

Beat.

York It was made to be worn.

Beat.

York Come on! It survived the looting – why not? I won't tell.

Beat.

Layla *looks it at.*

York   I'll shut the door . . .

Layla *slowly proceeds to take off her head covering, revealing long black hair,* **York** *respectfully turns away.*

Layla   It's OK, you can look, you're a woman aren't you?

She unties her hair and it is loose around her shoulders.

York *takes the crown out of* **Gertrude**'s *hands.*

For **Gertrude** *it vanishes.*

Gertrude *is looking around for the crown – she can't see it.*

Gertrude   It's gone!

Layla   Come on then, quick.

Gertrude   Where?

York *lifts the crown ceremonially.*

Gertrude   It belongs here!

York *places the crown on* **Layla**'s *head.*

York *steps back to look at her – an in-breath – she looks incredible, regal and beautiful, like a ghost from the past. Her whole demeanour changes – she is transformed.*

At this moment **Gertrude** *sees her too, she places her hand over her mouth in shock, at this vision.*

Gertrude   The goddess!

Layla   I can smell burning . . .

Gertrude   SALIM! SALIM! ABU ZAMAN!

Pause.

York *has picked up the camera which is used to log items and held it up to take a photo of* **Layla**. *The camera flashes. As soon as this happens* **Gertrude**'s *vision vanishes, and she collapses shaking into a chair, her breathing ragged.*

Layla   What are you doing?

York   I was just taking a picture so you could see.

Layla   Put that camera down.

Suddenly **Abu Zaman**, **Mohammed** *and* **Ghalia** *enter the room.* **Layla** *is affected by the crown – it's as though she's wading through sand.*

Abu Zaman   I told you – look – it wasn't safe!

Ghalia   What are you doing? Hey!

Layla   Be calm.

Ghalia   Take it off!

Layla   I am.

Mohammed   So beautiful.

Ghalia   Layla! How can you – be so disrespectful. I'm shocked. What were you thinking?

Layla *takes her hijab and leaves to go to the bathroom and put it back on.*

York   It was made to be worn . . .

Abu Zaman   It needs to be preserved – to inform future goddesses.

He takes it carefully from her, checks it for damage, wipes it and returns it to its box.

Mohammed   Future goddesses? Are you feeling OK, Abu Zaman?

Beat.

York   Did you see her – she looked incredible. You should totally display it like that . . . like a statue, a goddess . . . I'm going to help her.

She exits.

Ghalia   Unbelievable. If the staff can't be trusted to safeguard the artefacts then what hope is there? –

Abu Zaman (*the truth dawning*)   What hope is there?

Mohammed   Without her hijab she looked . . . amazing (*he catches himself*) – the crown – looked amazing . . . it was alive.

Ghalia   Where are you going?

Mohammed   To try and get a mannequin and a wig.

Ghalia   What for?

Mohammed   To display it.

Ghalia   It can't be displayed. I won't allow it I told you it's not safe. What is wrong with you people?

Mohammed   This is a museum – we can make it safe – like my uncle said.

Ghalia   Don't you care what happens to these things? They belong to the world.

Mohammed   Of course I care – but if no one sees them, they may as well not exist.

Then/Now

Salim *enters.*

Salim   Did you call?

Gertrude   Just – a dream –

Layla *enters and returns to work.*

Then **Salim** *wraps things for storage, once he has finished. Now* **Layla** *unpacks them and inspects them, then logs them. A sort of unproductive factory assembly line.*

Layla *photographs the items she unwraps with a digital camera.*

She continues with her work. After she takes each picture she looks at the screen on the camera to check the image – but every time she does so she has to put on her glasses.

Gertrude   I must have fallen asleep.

Salim   It is hot and you are –

Gertrude   A woman? Old? Whatever it is – don't say it.

Salim   Working hard.

Gertrude   Oh. Yes.

Salim   May I ask what your dream was?

Gertrude   It was – like a mirage. Heat haze. It's so hot – like I'm beside a blazing fire . . .

Salim   Shall I fetch you some ice water?

Gertrude   No. No, I'm quite well now.

Mohammed *enters.*

Mohammed   You OK?

Layla   Fine.

They work.

Gertrude   Or perhaps I'm not . . . I imagined I saw her coronation (*indicating cabinet*).

Salim   Who? The goddess?

Gertrude   Ridiculous isn't it?

Salim   No.

Gertrude   Don't tell me you believe in ghosts and jinns? I thought you a sensible man, Salim.

Salim I believe in the power of the human mind – perhaps it was a sign about who should run this museum. Be the one in charge here. A woman? YES! You.

Gertrude But it wasn't my face I saw. I only saw the head that wears the crown.

Beat.

Salim (*of statue*) She is beautiful.

Layla (*to* **Mohammed**) Stop looking at me – get on with your work. I mean it.

Salim I too have dreamt of her.

Gertrude You're a young man, Salim – you should be dreaming of women of flesh and blood not cold stone.

Salim You misunderstand. It doesn't matter.

Layla The Director wants everything done double quick because of this opening. She's a tyrant.

Mohammed *still watches her taking pictures without and then putting on her glasses to inspect them on the screen. He laughs at her.*

Mohammed You don't need glasses to take the picture but you do to see the image?

Layla Blame sanctions.

Mohammed You blame the Americans for everything.

Layla We didn't all have generators, you know. Studying by oil lamp wrecks your eyes.

Mohammed Generator or not, it was still a shitty way to grow up. I was here too.

Layla I know you were. Unlike some people.

Mohammed She can't help it – she was kicked out.

Layla That's her story. I mean would you have left – if you had the choice . . .

Mohammed Me? No, I was born in this city and I will die in this city.

Beat.

Gertrude I'm sorry. I've offended you – tell me.

Salim I am embarrassed.

Mohammed The glasses suit you.

She gives him a look.

Salim You think of me as a man.

Gertrude Well you are.

Salim I am a human. And now an Iraqi. In a country of religions. Many. Mine differentiates carefully between women and men. About what they can and cannot do.

What their place in the world is. But people like you. And her (*indicating the empty cabinet*) tell me things don't have to be this way.

Gertrude Is that your dream?

Salim Yes. I'm afraid I do want to marry. My cousin. I dream of bringing her here. To see the goddess, to see what a woman can be. That it's not new thinking. It's ancient. A legacy. And I will bring my daughter. And my granddaughter. They will all find inspiration. Through these things. And they will change the world.

Gertrude How? The only way to change things, my dear Salim, is to hide in plain sight. Fit in to the structures that exist.

Salim They won't see it like that. They'll remake the world anew. Inspired by their past. I feel it. And it makes everything alright. Any version of life is acceptable in this knowledge.

Gertrude Any version?

Salim Six years ago I learned about war. Tribes uniting. Putting religion aside and rising up . . . Only to be viciously, violently pushed down again. Thousands killed. Property destroyed. Towns annihilated. From the land and sky. Showers of bombs . . . And yet these things survive. They live on. They must continue to exist.

Beat.

Salim We should build a basement. Secure. With locks. To keep them safe. Or . . . get special strong glass for the display cabinets . . . I have a cousin – in Najaf – who can help . . . I will ask him.

He begins to wrap things for storage. **Gertrude** *is impressed.*

Gertrude I want you to stay on here after the opening. Help me with my work in the museum. Will you do that, Salim? Will you stay?

Beat.

Layla This is so boring. Inside. So stuffy.

Mohammed This is important work.

Layla You've never been on a dig . . . *Ya Allah* when will I be on site again?

Mohammed You never know, if we work hard enough on this the Minister for Tourism might send us to the North East mountains in gratitude, think of it – you and me and all the treasures we might discover there together.

Layla Would your uncle do that? Find funding for a dig?

Mohammed Would your father allow you to go on a dig? With me?

Layla If you'd asked me that two years ago the answer would have been no way, but these days he doesn't say much. Doesn't do much . . . He's not really there.

Mohammed Then we could go. You and me. Under all those stars. We'd feel so small we'd have to hold on to each other – sanctuary – to make sure we were real.

Alive.

Beat.

Mohammed What? No acerbic retort?

Layla Sounds alright. The Director would never allow it though. Safety first.

Mohammed Her safety concerns are about artefacts, not human beings. I'd make sure we had an armed guard.

Layla As long as it's not that one. She's so irritating.

Mohammed I like it when you are rude to Americans. You get a bulging vein in your head like Julia Roberts.

Layla The Americans want to be involved in everything.

Mohammed I used to think they meant well.

Layla Like everyone else. I predicted that once the cowboys came in Baghdad would become a shooting alley. The wild east. No one believed me.

Mohammed *They* didn't loot the museum.

Layla No. But they didn't stop it either – did they?

Mohammed No, they didn't. They didn't stop it.

Layla They watched.

Mohammed Yes.

Layla And now they are here to help us clean up. Really?

Then

Woolley *enters and regards the crown.*

Gertrude You're here – alone?

Woolley Hello – where did you find that?

Gertrude How did you get in?

Woolley Abu Zaman – but he's gone – patrolling the corridors again.

Gertrude He does that . . . But it's not patrolling . . . It's as though he's lost something. Like he's retracing his steps . . .

Beat.

Woolley (*of the crown*) You know, this is very like some we've come across at the Royal Cemetery in Ur.

Gertrude Don't say it like that. I didn't steal it. Someone found it and brought it here.

Beat.

Gertrude You can't have it.

Woolley You're welcome to it. I'm sick to death of getting out gold headdresses. There are many more interesting things coming out of what I'm calling The Great Death Pit.

Gertrude Sounds *charmant*.

Woolley It is INCREDIBLE, Gerty. The burial pit covers an unusually wide area – the grave itself has not yet been opened and all our discoveries have been in the wider area of the pit. But what discoveries! Apparently after the body was laid in and a certain amount of earth put back, the general offerings were laid in a shaft above the grave. With the offerings were put the bodies of a large number of people who must have been sacrificed in order that they might accompany the king /

Gertrude / Or queen /

Woolley / To the next world. The first object was a harp elaborately inlaid.

Gertrude How many?

Woolley Harps – just one.

Gertrude No, bodies – humans, sacrificed.

Woolley Oh we can't be sure yet. The women's bodies were laid in parallel rows except for one which was crouched up by the harp, the rest were all wearing identical headdresses.

Gertrude But how many have you taken out so far?

Woolley Seventy-four.

Gertrude Seventy-four dead women, all laid out in rows.

Woolley Not all women – six were men. Don't look like that. Imagine it – down the sloping passage comes a procession of people, the members of the court, soldiers, men-servants, and women, the latter in all their finery of brightly coloured garments and headdresses of lapis-lazuli and silver and gold, and with them musicians bearing harps or lyres, cymbals, and sistra; they take up their positions in the farther part of the pit. Each woman brought a little cup of clay or stone or metal, the only equipment required for the rite that was to follow. Each drinks from the cup; either they brought the potion with them or they found it prepared for them on the spot – and they composed themselves for death. Then someone came down and killed the animals and perhaps arranged the drugged women, and there's evidence to suggest that when that was done the whole pit was set alight before earth was flung from above on them, and the filling-in of the grave shaft began.

Gertrude 'Composed themselves for death'.

Woolley They went willingly to a less nebulous and miserable existence – the evidence is there.

Gertrude What about the men – where were they? Laid out like dolls in a toy box too?

Woolley No. By the door.

Gertrude Guarding it. Locking them in.

Woolley That's very dramatic.

Gertrude Did they hold poisoned cups too or weapons?

Woolley Daggers now you come to mention it.

Gertrude All these women are laid out neatly and you presume that means a neat – a willing death. But I disagree, death is not neat or easy. They were forced to drink that poison – daggers held over them. Then they were burned. Incinerated. Out of existence.

Woolley Not entirely – their remains are still there. Probably just part of the ritual.

Gertrude The point is they had no choice. That's not suicide, it's murder.

Woolley What's got into you? You are so maudlin these days.

Gertrude Sixty-eight nameless, forgotten, dead, burnt women that's what.

Beat.

Woolley I'm sorry I find you in such a humour but you did call me here, you know. And I traipsed – on foot because of the flooding – through rain and mud, backstreets and hawkers who followed me and pestered me trying to flog month-old papers. It's not safe out there at the moment – you can feel something is in the air, building. But I came because you asked. So here I am – what do you want of me?

Gertrude You're right. I'm not entirely myself. I'm sorry . . . I wanted to ask if you'd help me plan this place . . .

Woolley The question is: What's in it for me?

Gertrude Nothing – except preserving the past, firing national pride and creating a lasting legacy that entrusts the riches of the past to a future Iraqi nation . . .

Then/Now/Later

Abu Zaman* (with chorus)

A noise.	ضجيج
It starts far away – this noise.	الضجيجُ يأتي مِنْ بعيد..
It could be natural.	يُمكِنْ أنْ يكون عادياً
Nature.	طبيعة
Rain.	مطر..
Thunder.	رعد..

The pounding of animals' feet – a stampede.	خُطواتُ حَيواناتٍ هارِبة..
But it isn't that.	لكنَّها ليستْ كذلكَ. ليستْ كذلكَ..
And it's not so far now. No. It's getting closer.	ليستْ بعيدةً الان، انها تقتربُ أكثر..
It gets closer and it sounds less like nature.	كُلَّما اقتَرَبَتْ قلَّ تشابُهُها بالطبيعةِ..
Less natural.	حَقّاً إنَّها لا تُشبِهُها..
And there's a buzzing to it.	فيها طنين..
Like bees.	يُشبِهُ طَنينَ النَّحلْ..
Like drums.	أو الطُبول..
Like drones.	أزيز
But it is human.	لكنها أصواتُ بشر..
It is voices.	إنَّها أصواتٌ
Many.	كثيرةٌ
Raised.	مرتفعةٌ
Shouting.	تصرُخ
And as it gets closer it gets louder.	وكُلَّما تقتَرِب، تُصبِحُ أعلى
The sound surrounds.	الصوتُ يُطوِّق
The sounds surround.	الأصواتُ تُحيطُ
And then hover.	ثُمَّ تحوم
Now the beating starts. The pounding.	الان بدأ يَدُقّ.. يخفِق..
Not a heart.	إنَّهُ ليسَ بقلب..:
A thud. A thump.	إنَّما رطمَة.. دويٌّ..
Singular at first.	صوتٌ واحدٌ في البداية
Then more. More.	
More.	ثُمَّ أصواتٌ كثيرة.. كثيرة.. كثيرة..:
More.	
Thuds. Bangs.	دَويٌ.. انفجارات...:
Heavy weight against	جسمٌ ثقيلٌ بُزاحِمُ:
Thick walls. Doors.	جدرانٌ سميكة. الأبواب
Now a shattering. Tinkling. Glass.	الآن تحطيم .. طنين .. زُجاج..

Sharp.	حادٌ: ..
More thuds.	دَويٌّ آخر..
The voices raise.	الأصواتُ تَرتَفِع:
Unite.	
In a wave.	تَّوَحد. تُصبِح موجة:
A swell.	تَّضَخَم:
A squall.	عاصفة:
A typhoon.	إعصارٌ:
Of will.	مِنَ الإرادةِ:
Pushing. Until.	تَدافعٌ حتى:
The flood.	الفيضان:
Dams collapse.	السدودُ تَنهار..
A tidal wave.	موجةٌ عارمةٌ:
Of intent.	مِنَ النَوايا:
Of destruction.	مِنَ الدمار:
Overwhelms.	يقهر:
Overwhelms.	يقهر:
Engulfs.	يبتلع
Drowns.	يُغرِق
Sinks us all.	يُغرِقُنا جَمعاً
What will be left when the waters subside?	وماالذي سَيبقى بَعدَ أنْ تَهمدَ المياه؟

Interval.

Then

Gertrude *is working on an article, she looks up and speaks to the audience.* **Salim** *is there but doesn't hear her.*

Gertrude I know how her civilisation fell. Through greed and mismanagement – the hubris of men. Have we learned anything?

Beat.

Gertrude I have such hope for our British Mandate here – but when I raise my eyes across the border to Syria and see how the French Mandate is playing out there. It's scandalous. It can only lead to war and bloodshed.

Beat.

Gertrude So then I must ask – what if disaster calls here too. It's always pounding on the doors – trying to get in. I see what could happen. And sound the alarm . . . But what if I'm ignored . . . What will happen to everyday people if the walls come down on their heads. The wonderful people here will hate me. Will blame me. And I will be to blame. But I won't bury my head in the sand. They may not heed my warnings but I can't stop. I will tell the truth – stand and scream at the rising waters though I feel powerless to stop them . . .

Beat.

Salim Did you say something?

Gertrude Would you do something for me? It's a bit – unorthodox.

Salim Of course.

Gertrude I've written something – and I can't decide if the tone is right. Would you read it out for me – and then forget everything you read.

Salim I'll – try my best. Though your handwriting is . . .

Gertrude Thank you – from here . . .

She shows him where on the paper and he reads out for her. She listens and watches his reactions closely as he reads.

Salim The Mesopotamian lands cannot fail to expand economically with great rapidity, and economic development will go hand in hand with the increase of political importance. We confidently anticipate that Baghdad will in a few decades replace Damascus as the capital city of the Arab world (*he looks very proud of this prospect*) and our task is not only to fit it for the part which it will play, but also to establish lasting amity . . .

He looks at **Gertrude** *questioningly as he doesn't understand what amity is.*

Gertrude Amity – friendship – *sadaqa*.

Salim Ah. *Sah*. (*He continues reading.*) . . . to establish lasting amity and confidence between ourselves and the Arab race, whatever modifications the future may bring to their political status. But if the French turn Syria into a French province, following the lines of their policy in North Africa and in their colonies elsewhere, it is inevitable that they will meet with armed opposition which, if successful, will bring their authority to an abrupt close, and if unsuccessful, will develop into a long period of guerrilla warfare.

Beat.

He looks worried.

Salim I hope you're wrong.

Gertrude I fear not.

Beat.

Salim You are like someone who sees the future. *Fatahit al fahl* [fortune teller]

Gertrude*   / What's the point in seeing the future if no one will listen to you?/

Abu Zaman*   / What's the point in seeing the future if no one will listen to you? /

لم وىنمـ ية لامستقبل ذاامل تمع لايك حاد؟

Salim They might.

Gertrude I don't know – I'm beginning to feel it's all mapped out. Like the picture's been taken and it is impossible to alter . . .

Now

Ghalia *sits on her computer while* **Layla** *logs items.*

Layla This would be much quicker if you helped with the items we actually have, rather than chasing the ones on the internet.

Ghalia *looks up surprised.*

Ghalia You're right.

She moves and sits next to **Layla** *and starts helping with the sorting of items.*

Beat.

Ghalia I wasn't actually looking at stolen artefacts online. I was looking at photographs of my grandson. Winston, my son just sent me some, they were playing in the park near his house in London. He looks so happy. Big toothy smile.

Layla Winston. Good English name. How old?

Ghalia Winston *Ahmed* is four.

Layla Boys are nice at that age. It's later you have to worry.

Ghalia My son turned out alright.

Layla He had you for a mother.

Beat. while this uneasy compliment lands.

Ghalia What about your parents?

Layla I come here for sanctuary – as a place not to think about the outside.

Ghalia I'm sure they are glad you work here and that you have a good career. I never used to worry until I had my son but when he was born all that changed. I became a worrier. When you're a mother yourself you will understand

Beat.

Layla What makes you think I want to have a child like you?

Ghalia Do you?

Layla   I don't know. Maybe I want to run a museum.

Ghalia   You can do both you know. Like me.

Beat.

Layla   Your never talk about your husband – is he dead?

Ghalia   To me.

Layla   I suppose we all have things we don't talk about.

She gets up.

Ghalia   Where are you going?

Layla   To get the camera.

Beat.

Layla   You know while your son is in the park taking pictures of Winston, Iraqi parents can't allow their kids to go out and play because there are no parks any more – there are no swings and roundabouts, slides and climbing frames, only snipers and mines, kidnapping and death. And not just for the children either – so don't tell me I'll learn about worry when I have a child. I am Iraqi. I can teach the world about worrying.

She goes.

Ghalia *sighs.*

Then

Woolley *enters triumphantly brandishing a newspaper* (*the same one* **Gertrude** *indicated previously*).

Woolley   Have you seen the latest *Illustrated London News*?

Gertrude   I don't take that paper. A rag.

Woolley   Well let me bring you up to date.

Gertrude   I'm busy writing my speech for the opening and no one will accept 'white ants ate it' as an excuse.

Woolley (*ignoring her*)   The headline reads: 'Heroic Archaeologist's Military Mind Saves the Day'. It continues – 'Regular readers will be familiar with our reports of the on-going archaeological dig in Mesopotamia which is unearthing rare artefacts to rival treasures discovered in the Valley of the Kings. Missives from none other than the chief archaeologist, Professor Leonard Woolley' – yours truly – 'have brought to light a dastardly plot to plunder the site by local Arab tribesmen. The good professor and his team were working into the small hours when they were set upon by two dozen men with rifles' – it was actually more like six but who's counting. 'The armed bandits made off with a large amount of Turkish coinage and a number of precious metal artefacts including gold jewellery. The quick-thinking professor used his local acumen –'

Gertrude Your foreman Hamoudi?

Woolley 'to track down the culprits. On doing so he took the ingenious action of offering the men security positions on his dig. The bewildered natives agreed and Professor Woolley was able to retrieve all the purloined items as well as gaining a mean security detail'. That's British military thinking for you!'

Gertrude You didn't get any of it back did you?

Woolley No. But they are rather good guardsmen. Oh don't yawn at my prowess.

Gertrude It's tedious I'm far more interested in the writing on the cuneiform tablets you found at Kish – any joy getting them translated?

Woolley As a matter of fact, yes, but they have a less happy ending.

Gertrude Tell me.

Woolley They detail the rulers of Kish from 1800 BC.

Gertrude Fascinating.

Woolley And then go on to say that a flood came down from on high devastating everything. After that the place became reborn as Uruk.

Gertrude Uruk – our Iraq – but we haven't had our flood yet have we?

Woolley It's lashing down out there at the moment.

Gertrude I mean it – nothing was swept away before we came in – you shouldn't start afresh until the slate is clean.

Woolley There was the civil war. The tribal uprising.

Gertrude But we dashed that – stopped it in its tracks by bombing and gassing the tribes into submission . . .

Woolley Many more would have died if we hadn't

Gertrude But we had no flood – we just broke the dam, steamrolled in, without invitation – have we made a fatal error – were we premature?

Woolley Disaster was coming – we stepped in and did what was required.

Gertrude War. Making war was required? We're getting rather good at it aren't we? You know – after the war in Europe many people said to me over and over again that it was a shock and a surprise to them to see Europe relapse into barbarism. I had no reply – what else can you call the war? How can we, who have managed our own affairs so badly, claim to teach others to manage theirs better?

Woolley We must go through it. And come out the other side.

Gertrude Yes – perhaps you are right – it may be that the world has now to sink back into dark ages of chaos, out of which it will evolve into something, perhaps no better than what it had.

Now

York You guys all want me to go but I still like it here.

Layla Iraq?

York Hell no! In this here museum, some folks would find it creepy but not me.

Layla Creepy?

York You know what I'm saying . . . the way Abu Zaman haunts the corridors – I see him when I secure the entrances every morning – he stops – suddenly and stares into space. Like he sees something that's not there.

Layla He's remembering artefacts that were taken. Where they stood. His own stocktake of the missing. Destroyed.

York It's not that. It's . . . something else.

Beat.

York Anyway it doesn't bother me. Anything's better than the base.

Beat.

York I had to strangle a dog over there to get the fellas to leave me alone.

Layla Is that some kind of euphemism?

York *looks at her blankly.*

York A what?

Layla Some American saying – you didn't really strangle a dog?

York I had to, you know what men are like. And put a whole battalion together and they're worse than a pack of starving wolves. Well I don't need to tell you – men are the same the world over.

Beat.

York The dog was just a stray – kept coming round for scraps and Private Armstrong took a liking to him. Treated the dog better than they treat some of the civilians, spoke to it nicer than they spoke to me.

Layla You killed it because they were nice to it?

York No, I had nothing against it, poor thing, but Armstrong that's another story – he's a no good son of a bitch if you'll excuse the expression, and he kept pinching me – every morning at breakfast in the mess I'd make sure I avoided his table, but wherever I sat – however much I tried to avoid him, every day I'd get pinched and they'd all laugh and whistle, the whole pack of them. Then this one morning he didn't just pinch – he crossed the line, put his hand – well you get the picture. So I said to him, you do that again you'll be sorry, and he was all like what you going to do, missy? And I just saw red, so I walked out of the mess, went to where I knew that old stray would be waiting for the morning scraps, squeezed him by the throat till he stopped yelping and then left the dog by the door for everyone to see.

Beat.

York They all call me a crazy bitch now, but Armstrong doesn't pinch me no more.

Pause.

York So a euphemism is something that doesn't mean exactly what it says?

Layla Yes, it's indirect. 'He passed away' rather than 'he died'.

York Amazing, your English is real good – you know more than me.

Layla We used to have the highest rates of English literacy in the Arab world.

Beat.

York Your brother passed away didn't he?

Layla Did Mohammed tell you that?

York He's into you, you know.

Layla He's my brother's friend. Was my brother's friend. And he didn't pass away, it wasn't peaceful – it was a shower of bombs.

York My brother died too. Now I'm the only one left, Mom was so mad when I joined the army.

Beat.

York Do you have any other brothers or sisters?

Layla No. It's just me.

York A lot of pressure to stay alive ain't it? Don't want to die and leave your folks childless, they'd never forgive us.

Layla Avoiding death in America is very different from avoiding death in Iraq. You chose to come here.

York Where I'm from there isn't much of a choice. I'd have liked to go to college like you. Wasn't an option.

Beat.

York We're the same age I think, I can imagine if we were at the same high school we might have been friends . . .

Layla *looks at her quizzically.*

York I've done a bad thing. I need to tell someone about it.

Layla The map? You've told me – remember? Or was it a story I once heard . . . did I dream it?

Then

Salim *and* **Gertrude** *sit and work at one table.* **Ghalia** *and* **Mohammed** *work at another.* **Ghalia** *is frustratedly sorting seals – she can't seem to get the order right.*

Salim Are you alright, Miss Bell?

Gertrude Perfectly well, thank you, Salim.

Salim You are breathing like you're underwater – coming up for air –

Gertrude Am I really? I didn't notice.

Salim Yes, Miss Bell, is there something I can help you with?

Gertrude Not unless you can read cuneiform I'm afraid, I'm trying to decipher what's on this tablet, I think it's some kind of a document of ownership, but I can't be sure.

Beat.

Gertrude Really, the Honorary Director of the Museum of Antiquities ought to be able to read cuneiform! Or have the support she needs – not be abandoned by everyone. Left to rot.

Beat.

Salim Honorary Director?

Gertrude I'm just keeping the seat warm.

Salim But who else could do that job?

Gertrude An Iraqi, I would hope.

Salim Why?

Gertrude Because this is Iraq.

Salim But it is ruled by Great Britain, so an English director would be better.

Gertrude It is ruled by an Arab monarch.

Salim Under Britain's mandate for twenty-five years.

Gertrude You don't think that's good for Iraq? There'd be chaos if we left now.

Salim You are right.

Gertrude After that we will give you independence.

Salim Independence is never given it is always taken.

Pause.

Gertrude (*of the cuneiform*) This is bloody annoying.

Salim Bloody?

Gertrude It's emphatic.

Salim Covered in blood.

Gertrude It's basically the same as 'very'.

Salim So when the English are emphatic they cover everything in blood.

Gertrude *gives him a look.*

Salim Perhaps you could ask Abu Zaman? About the cuneiform?

Abu Zaman *appears in the doorway.*

Abu Zaman I am here.

Gertrude So you are. I do wish you'd stop appearing out of thin air like that. And looking so grumpy – I told you I'm not happy about the opening either – I had to pretend I was all for it, but it's not my choice.

Abu Zaman It will be hard to keep things safe.

Gertrude I know that, what can I do? No one listens to me anymore.

Beat.

Abu Zaman May I see that tablet?

She hands it to him, grudgingly.

Abu Zaman It's a document listing all a farmer's assets – and what taxes he owes.

Gertrude A balance sheet! I knew it! Imagine if everyone in the West knew, bureaucracy, documentation, administration started here, in what they consider to be a barbaric land, that would show them in Kensington and Chelsea.

Abu Zaman If I can have twenty minutes with it, then I can write you a translation.

Gertrude Thank you.

Abu Zaman *Bil Khidme.*

Salim What is it like in your Kensington and Chelsea? Does it rain all day long. Is there green grass on all the rooftops?

Gertrude It certainly rains.

Salim Do you miss it?

Gertrude England? Grey London skies? No.

Salim Your family, your home?

Gertrude Home . . . It's complicated. Isn't it. And when you don't see a place every day you notice the little changes. The paint coming off the walls. Tarnished cutlery. Slates off the roof. If you were there every day you wouldn't notice, because it's gradual, this eroding. But in my memory it is all as it was – all perfect. And they're all there. Even the ones that are dead.

Salim Your brother? He died?

Gertrude (*nods curtly*) So it's rather disconcerting to go back and find things different.

Beat.

Gertrude Not the routine. That stays the same: callers at eleven, lunch at twelve, dinner at seven, then cards and inane chat in the library. But everything else is wrinkled, fraying, old. People who were indispensable are missing. Gone. The cabinet's empty. Like an unloved exhibit. Tatty. Unrecognisable. And yet they move around inside it like nothing has changed – like nothing will ever change. But it's all changed – do you see? And it's sickening . . . shocking . . . disturbing. A bit like catching yourself in the mirror and realising how you actually look – what people see – you know?

Pause.

Suddenly she seems to wake up, realise what she has been saying and feels exposed.

Gertrude Goodness, I don't have time to be chatting. I've got to finish writing my address for the opening ceremony. Please get on with the labels, Salim.

Salim All will be well, Miss Bell.

Ghalia This is a disaster.

Mohammed *Ya wash ya wash!*

Gertrude You Arabs – you're always so optimistic. / I have two weeks in which to make this place presentable for the opening, we have no glass for the cabinets – yes, I know – your cousin in Najaf, but that remains to be seen – we've intermittent electricity, not enough fans, and the security arrangements are insufficient. It's a disaster.

Gertrude *sets to writing her opening speech.*

Ghalia / I have two weeks in which to make this place presentable for the opening, we have no glass for the cabinets – yes, I know – your cousin in Najaf, but that remains to be seen – we've intermittent electricity, no air conditioning, and the security arrangements are insufficient. It's a disaster. /

Mohammed You need to be more Iraqi about things.

Ghalia I am Iraqi! And I came back to Iraq thinking I could make a difference, but we aren't making any progress. Every day I learn about something else that has been destroyed or stolen – everyone's trying to blame it on the Kuwaitis – revenge – that would be understandable but it wasn't them, it was Iraqis. And this place is for them, for us – to remind us of our humanity, our shared culture. How can we trust them? But if we don't open this museum to the public what is the point of it? How can we move forward? And now all the academics are being murdered. You know this morning when I came into work my driver stopped at traffic lights, a man knocked on the window and for a moment I was sure I wouldn't get here. I'd never see the mask of Warka again. Hold a seal between my fingers. Kiss my grandson. I was going to be shot in the head because I'm a woman who doesn't cover, because they think I'm pro-America or because I work here. And as the man raised his hand he had a copy of the paper, that's all he was doing selling a month-old paper. And my life flashed before my eyes. So forgive me if I'm a little 'irritable', but I imagined myself back on digs in the desert, discovering new things, not stuck in this airless box with you, fearing for my life. It makes me long for a grey London sky. There I said it. I'd rather be – (*She stops herself.*)

There's a camera flash . . .

Then

Gertrude *reads over what she has written so far – the first part is her rehearsing but by the end we have melted into the actual opening.*

Gertrude A hundred years ago the first photograph was taken. That was when we humans became able to capture moments. Things. Preserving them. Holding them forever in time and space. I've always enjoyed taking photographs on my travels. As a reminder. A way of stopping time. Until I discovered archaeology. You all know I love to travel. Especially in this part of the world. But with archaeology I discovered time travel. The ability to travel back to the distant past. Find out the truth about how things were then, in order to better understand how they function now. And with that knowledge I truly believe we can overcome divides and create nations, what was broken can be healed – united. This is the true power of archaeology.

There is a round of applause as we are now –

Then/Now/Later

Dignitaries from 1926 and modern day mill about the space. There is the necessary mingling. We are at the museum opening.

There are three ribbons, three pairs of scissors, three important people.

Each important person cuts their ribbon.

Important People I officially open this museum.

Abu Zaman* (*with chorus made up of* **Nasiya, Ghalia, Layla**) Again. مرة أخرى

People clap, then walk about the space looking at the items on display.

A Museum in Baghdad

Off-centre is the crown in a raised glass box with an open top.

Abu Zaman *stands close to it.*

Gertrude   Why are you standing here?

Abu Zaman   I'm just watching.

Gertrude   You're like a bundle of nerves! Anyone would think you know disaster is coming.

Abu Zaman   If it is I want to be ready – I'm here to try and prevent anything bad happening . . . to the artefacts . . . the people . . .

Gertrude   Well you can do that from the corner of the room. Go on. There are some wealthy Americans here who might donate – I don't want you putting them off.

Abu Zaman *reluctantly begins to move to the corner of the room but continues to watch proceedings nervously.*

Ghalia   Where's the Minister?

Salim   Where's the King?

Abu Zaman   I haven't seen him.

Ghalia   It's disgraceful he's not here.

Gertrude   He'll be here.

Ghalia/Gertrude   He's the one who was so excited to have it all on show.

Abu Zaman   The Prime Minister's here.

Salim (*to* **Gertrude**)   Are you very proud? You should be.

Ghalia *approaches* **Layla** *and* **Mohammed**.

Ghalia   You're drinking champagne.

Layla   I thought I should try it. Who knows when I'll get another chance?

Mohammed   Do you like it?

Layla   It's fizzy.

Ghalia   But your hijab?

Layla   Plenty of Muslims drink.

Ghalia   Not Muslims who wear hijabs.

Layla   I feel safer wearing a hijab. I was going to suggest you put one on. It might make you feel more . . . at ease.

Gertrude (*to* **Woolley**)   Now what do you make of it?

Woolley   Compelling speech. But these are hardly the 'people of Iraq' you keep talking about, dignitaries and military personnel and such.

Gertrude Heathens to a man. They've barely looked at the goddess and she won't be here for long thanks to you.

Woolley I'm only borrowing her. Don't look so glum – you've done sterling work.

Gertrude I'm not finished yet.

Ghalia (*to* **Mohammed**) Have you seen the Minister?

Layla No.

Ghalia I can't believe he's not here.

Layla The Prime Minister's here though.

Mohammed My uncle's probably just on Baghdad time.

Ghalia After the fuss he made about this opening.

Layla Relax. Try one of these –

Ghalia I wanted to try and convince him to put everything in storage until the time is right.

Beat.

Ghalia Mohammed!

Mohammed All right, all right, I'll go call him.

Woolley Well, you did it.

Gertrude I told you I would.

Woolley It's wonderful – wonderful ancient history – but you need to look to the future now, Gertie. Make plans . . .

Gertrude I've still a lot to do here.

Woolley Here? You intend to stay on? We're not getting any younger, you and I . . .

Gertrude Are you going to be giving up on digs then? Take a desk job at the BM? No. I didn't think so.

Beat.

Abu Zaman It's all on display – the crown, the goddess, I didn't think you'd allow it.

Gertrude/Ghalia They assure me it's safe . . .

Abu Zaman (*to* **Ghalia**) We know otherwise – I told you what I saw. The looting. . . showers of bombs, bodies. And there's worse. What's to come. What will happen next.

Ghalia I've tried –

Abu Zaman What's the point of knowing the future if no one will listen to you?

Beat.

Woolley   The King isn't here.

Gertrude   He'll be here. Baghdad time.

Woolley   I'll never forget the first lecture I gave in this country. You and he in the front row – you whispering madly, translating every word. You seemed so close then . . .

Gertrude   We're close now.

Woolley   Really? Then where is he?

Gertrude   He'll be here.

Ghalia   I didn't come back to be a guard dog.

Abu Zaman   That's my job.

An Iraqi woman – **Nasiya** *– who could be from any time is stood close to the glass box with the crown in it.*

Ghalia   Who is she? She's standing very close to the crown . . .

Abu Zaman   Shall I talk to her?

Ghalia   No – it's OK, I will.

She approaches the woman.

Abu Zaman *gets out his coin and fidgets with it anxiously.*

Woolley   Do think seriously about what you should do next, Gertie. You've lots of options – perhaps you've done your bit here.

Gertrude   'Here' the Museum?

Woolley   'Here' Iraq – perhaps it's time to go home.

Gertrude   And where exactly is that?

Woolley   Not this ferocious, dangerous place where even the weather kills . . .

Beat.

Gertrude   Do you know who I am? I've charted deserts, negotiated with Sheiks, crowned a King and made a country.

Woolley   I know all this.

Gertrude   Then don't talk to me of ferocious weather. This is my place.

Ghalia (*to the woman, indicating the space, the antiquities*)   Which is your favourite?

Beat.

No answer.

Gertrude You've always resented my position here, haven't you? My power to decide what stays and what goes.

Ghalia I know you shouldn't be here, but I won't say anything if you are enjoying the exhibits. After all it is all yours.

Nasiya What do you mean?

Woolley I've always respected your decisions, but it's time now. Your family need you at home – they're all mourning.

Gertrude Who's put you up to this? My father?

Woolley We're just worried.

Gertrude Who? The BM? The Foreign office? The King? What are you all afraid of? That I'm a woman alone?

Woolley You're not a woman – you're more than that.

Gertrude There's nothing more than that.

Beat.

Ghalia All of this – it belongs to you, every Iraqi. It's our heritage.

Woolley You're working so hard – you've barely even mentioned your brother's death, never mind shedding a tear!

Gertrude My health, my family, well that's none of your damn business. You wouldn't bring it up if I were a man – would you?

Beat.

Nasiya You are Iraqi?

Ghalia Yes.

Nasiya Your accent sounds Lebanese.

Ghalia I spent some time in Paris . . . France.

Nasiya I know where Paris is. You are very pale. Where do you call home?

Ghalia Here, Baghdad.

Nasiya Really?

Ghalia Really. I came back to make a difference, to change the future for these things. I'm doing what is right. Being where I'm needed.

Gertrude This is about my responsibility. Doing what is right. Being where I'm needed. I've started a job and I must finish it. I owe it to the people of Iraq.

Woolley Stop talking about the people of Iraq – what do you know of the everyday people – how they live?

Gertrude Plenty. I've a young man working here – Salim – he tells me.

Woolley Does he tell you the people don't want us here? They want us to give them back what's theirs and let them fight it out.

Nasiya You say this place belongs to Iraqis. If that is true why are the ordinary people being kept outside?

Ghalia Only for today, once it's finished all Iraqis can come.

Nasiya We have never been welcome in this place, it's barely been open in the last twenty-five years. You know what they used to call it – Saddam's gift shop. Not for us. Next it will only be open to tourists and students. You don't trust us after the looting but how can you blame us? You weren't here then were you? Well? No. Let me tell you how it was:

Abu Zaman *tosses his coin.*

Nasiya There was no food to eat, no water, nowhere was safe. They turned us into savages, the British.

Gertrude That's not true.

Abu Zaman *tosses his coin.*

Nasiya There was no food to eat, no water, electricity. They turned us into savages, the Americans.

Gertrude They need us.

Abu Zaman *tosses his coin.*

Nasiya There was no food to eat, no water. They beat us – murdered us, the State.

Gertrude They want us here.

Nasiya At least under Saddam we could dress how we wanted, listen to the music we liked, worship our own way without fear of what others might do. Now look at us – we are killing each other . . . they've made us animals, and while you are all in here enjoying the culture we are howling at the gates for food like dogs.

Abu Zaman *and* **Mohammed** *have noticed this increasingly volatile woman and have approached her*

Nasiya Look – your guards are here. I'm going – I'm going. You are all hypocrites.

She goes towards the door but as **Mohammed** *and* **Abu Zaman** *check* **Ghalia** *is OK, they don't see* **Nasiya** *slip around the back of the room, finding a stool picking it up and approaching the glass cabinet with the crown in it.*

Woolley Gertrude, the King of this made-up land's not even here. He's not coming – he never was. He pretends he's our man but he's secretly garnering the Arabs against us.

Gertrude That's not true. I'd know. I'd have heard about these things –

Woolley You're not listening anymore. Or no one's telling you. But you need to hear me now.

Gertrude NO!

Woolley It's over, Gertrude. We're going home. All of us. It's finished. DO YOU HEAR ME?

Gertrude *sinks down onto a stool deflated and broken at the same moment as* **Nasiya** *rises on the stool.*

Woolley LISTEN!

Nasiya We can't live like this anymore. (*She climbs on the stool puts her hand into the open top of the cabinet with the crown in it. She has it out in a flash holding it over her head.*) RAEESE AL WIZARA, PRIME MINISTER WHY ARE YOU LETTING THE IRAQI PEOPLE ROT! WHY? AREN'T WE SUFFERING ENOUGH!

Ghalia *shouts in horror.* **Nasiya** *holds the crown aloft – it's hard to tell if she will put it on or smash it.*

Ghalia She'll damage it.

Mohammed Ow fi tej. [*Put the crown down.*]

Nasiya This is all vanity can't you see? People are starving while you worry about dead things – these things aren't alive – they're dust –

She holds the crown in front of her and crushes it between her hands, then throws it to the floor. As she does so, **Abu Zaman** *and* **Mohammed** *rush towards her to stop her but it is too late.*

Nasiya – but I am real – flesh, blood – I'm ALIVE – HELP ME!

They take her gently by the arms and lead her out. Everyone watches.

York *picks up the remains of the crown.*

York Can we fix it?

Layla It's too late.

Ghalia/Gertrude How could I let this happen?

Then/Now/Later

Under this speech the action of **Mohammed**'*s kidnap is repeated. It begins from the word PUNISHMENT. Again he is older and toys with his lanyard and he is smoking a cigarette*

He spots the coin on the floor and looks at it. He is about to bend to pick it up when a group of masked men come in and run to him.

The masked men grab **Mohammed** *violently and cover his head with a pillowcase, they bind his hands behind his back they walk him forward and he stands in the middle of the stage awaiting his fate.*

Abu Zaman Then, Now and Later *(in English and Arabic, with chorus)*

'I was born in this city and I will die in this city'	"وُلِدْتُ في هَذِهِ المدينةِ وَسَأموتُ في هَذِهِ المدينة"
He said.	قال
He was right.	كان على حقّ
'Don't worry – As long as you are fine, it doesn't matter Family is what matters'	"لا تَقْلَقي- طَالما أنَّكِ بخيرٍ، لا يُهِم. المهمُّ العائلة".
He said.	قال
'They'll do nothing yet'	"لن يفعلوا شيئاً"
He said.	قال
He was wrong. The director of the museum, Wrong.	كان على خطأ.
'Punishment'	"عِقاب"
They said.	قالوا
'Director of Idolatry'	"زَعيمُ الوَثنيين"
They said.	قالوا
'Apostate'	"مُرتَد"
They said.	قالوا
He knew what they would do if he said.	كان يعلمُ ما سَيَفْعلونَ إنْ تَكَلَّم.
If he told the secrets of this place.	إنْ أخْبَرَهم بأسْرارِ هَذا المكان
If he told the places of secrets.	إنْ أخْبَرَهم بأسْرارِ هَذا المكان
Of sanctuary.	أماكنِ اللجوء.
Of hiding.	أماكنِ الاختباء.
So he didn't.	إذا لم يَفعَل
He didn't say.	لم يَتَحدث
And they	وهُم
In this Holy month	في هذا الشهر المقدس
Removed his head from his body.	أزالوا رأسَهُ عَن جَسَدِه
Unholy.	إثْم

Removed his body and hung it from a pillar.	غُلِق جَسَدُهُ على عَمود
An ancient pillar.	عمودٍ عَتيق
But his head was smiling	٥لكِنَّ رَأسَهُ كان يَبتَسِم
Was happy.	كان سعيداً
Because he didn't breathe the secrets	لأنّهُ لم يُفشي الأسرار
And his wish came true.	وتَحقَّقَت أُمنِيَّتُه
'I was born in this city I will die in this city.'	"وُلِدتُ في هذهِ المدينةِ وساموتُ في هذه المدينة"
And he's there still.	ولا زالَ هُناك..
Like the palm trees	مِثلُ أشجارُ النَّخيل
rooted in the ground	مُتَجذِّرٌ في الأرض
rooted to the secrets	مُتَجذِّرٌ في الأسرار
rooted to us.	مُتَجذِّرٌ بِنا

Now

Inside the museum **Ghalia** *turns to* **York**.

Ghalia   Where the bloody hell were you?

York (*she has a broom and is sweeping again*)   You can't blame us.

Ghalia   Yes I can – how did she get in?

York   Everyone knew the opening was happening – it was public knowledge.

Layla   At least it was just the crown. She could have destroyed something more precious.

Ghalia   The statue?

Layla   NO – a human – living – person – you – me, him!

Mohammed   As long as you are fine it doesn't matter. Family is what matters.

Layla   We aren't family.

Mohammed   We will be.

Layla   Everywhere violence – Iraqis killing Iraqis – and yet the military is in here.

York   Sectarianism is an unfortunate outcome to all this – but it's Saddam's legacy, you can't blame the US military.

Layla   Iraqis weren't killing each other before you came here.

York   Saddam was an Iraqi and he killed a lot of his own people. It's my understanding that's why she (*indicating* **Ghalia**) was living in England.

Ghalia   Who told you that? (*No answer.*) Well I've more right and reason to be here than you.

Pause.

Ghalia   I'm tired.

York   If you don't mind me saying you look terrible.

Ghalia   I barely got a wink of sleep. I kept thinking I heard the place being broken into again – by an angry mob, looted . . . But WE were in the cases, Layla, Mohammed and I. And we couldn't escape. I should have known it was pointless to try and sleep without my pills.

York   Prozac? I'm on that too.

Ghalia   Temazepam.

Beat.

Mohammed (*of* **York** *sweeping*)   Don't you mind doing that?

York   Not really. It's kind of therapeutic. Abu Zaman asked me.

Mohammed   Not what you were trained for though, is it?

York   Beats patrolling the streets waiting for a car to blow up in your face. Or to be kidnapped . . .

Beat.

Mohammed   I'm going for a smoke.

Layla   You should quit.

Mohammed   I will. Just not today.

He goes.

York   Did something happen – between you guys? (*No answer.*) He likes you, you know.

Layla   I know.

York   Do you like him?

No answer.

York   You pretend, but you're not so tough. You like him too. I can see it all now. You two – marriage, kids, the whole nine yards. He'll be the Director of the Museum. You'll be his right-hand woman.

Layla   The Professor is the Director of the Museum.

Ghalia What a job. Like having a target on your head. Mohammed's welcome to it.

Layla He has no experience.

Ghalia Not yet – but he's ambitious. Layla, will you get Abu Zaman for me please?

Layla *exits.*

York She going into hiding? (*Indicating the empty case.*)

Ghalia What?

York The statue. Into the basements?

Ghalia Until it's safe enough for her to be on display.

York That's a shame.

Ghalia Can no one hear me? Until we can secure this place it should not be open at all. I don't even know why I'm here.

Beat.

York Have you got a dustpan and brush?

Salim *enters.*

Salim Miss Bell, I just saw them – taking her away . . .

No answer.

Salim Why are they moving the statue?

Gertrude Why do you think?

Beat.

Gertrude She's going to London.

Salim The British Museum?

Gertrude That's correct.

Salim But you said that things that are found here belong to us Arabs, us Iraqis, you wrote the laws to protect our artefacts.

Gertrude Yes, I did.

Salim But you are sending her to the British Museum.

Gertrude Yes.

Salim Will she come back?

No answer.

Salim You said –

Gertrude Maybe she's not Iraqi at all – when she was carved there was no Iraq was there? So maybe it doesn't matter where she is.

Salim What is found in Iraq stays in Iraq you said!

Beat.

Gertrude When do you think we will be able to open this museum to the public, Salim?

Salim You already had the opening.

Gertrude Yes, yes, but I mean to normal people? Next week, next month? Next year? In ten years? 1936? One hundred? 2026? Will it ever be the right time – safe enough? Have I been premature in creating this place?

Salim No.

Gertrude Who will protect all this? Would you? Lie across the door if there was a braying mob trying to get in? Risk your life?

Beat.

Gertrude What would you risk your life for? The statue? The museum? Well?

Salim My cousin. I'd put myself in front of her. To save her. And you?

Gertrude I'm too old. Powerless now.

Salim That's an excuse!

Beat.

Gertrude You are angry with me.

Salim Yes. We need you.

Gertrude This is where I belong. I won't go back to England. Call the car.

Salim *exits.*

Gertrude *folds a letter she has written and puts it into an envelope.*

Abu Zaman *enters.*

Abu Zaman You wanted me?

Gertrude/Ghalia I want you to take this letter.

Abu Zaman You are leaving?

Gertrude I can't change anything.

Abu Zaman What did you say?

Ghalia I can't change anything. I've tried. I'm powerless.

Gertrude/Ghalia What will you do?

Abu Zaman Stay here until things are safe – until a caretaker is no longer needed. Maybe it is all inevitable.

Ghalia What if it is?

Nasiya It is.

Abu Zaman *Maktouba.*

Nasiya It is written.

Now

Layla You've packed the statue away?

Ghalia I said it to the Minister, I said it to Mohammed and I've said it to you, it is not safe here. Not safe for the artefacts, and now I know it's not safe for us either.

Layla Because of that woman? Oh, it could have been worse.

Ghalia I used to find your coldness – your pragmatism disturbing, but now I understand.

Layla What do you understand?

Ghalia That you have to be like this to live here. You've been made like this to survive.

Layla That's rather patronising.

Ghalia Is it? I don't mean it to be. I admire you enormously, Layla. You have more courage than me.

Layla No, just less options.

Ghalia I don't think so, you're a bright woman.

Beat.

Layla You might have been wasting your time, you know.

Beat.

Layla Putting her away. The Minister will decide whether we store her or put her on display.

Ghalia I know.

Layla You've packed up your computer.

Ghalia I'm going. Home, to my family.

Layla To England. Just like that?

Ghalia No, not just like that. I've tried but I can't work in this environment.

Layla What happened to 'This is our country and we have to protect it'?

Ghalia I came thinking about the artefacts, I'm leaving thinking about the people.

Layla You are afraid?

Ghalia Yes. Yes, as a matter of fact I am.

Beat.

Layla We all are.

Beat.

Layla I suppose everyone who can leave will leave eventually, one way or another. The British Empire did, eventually the Americans will, and whoever – whatever – comes next – whatever fresh hell awaits us here, once they've done their worst they too will leave, that will also pass. So you might as well go too.

Ghalia You are angry with me.

Layla Yes. We need you.

Ghalia I can't, I've picked a battle I cannot win. Maybe Mohammed's right, may be I'm not enough of an Iraqi to be able to withstand this place. It killed Gertrude Bell, I don't want it to kill me.

Layla No, Gertrude Bell chose to die here, and you are choosing to leave.

Ghalia And what do you choose, Layla? You have options too . . .

Layla No, I don't – I don't have the privilege of choice. That's reserved for other people, not Iraqis. None of us will have a choice until everyone goes, until then we are like dust, sand in the wind pushed here and there by the whims of the West.

Ghalia Aren't you afraid of what will happen when the Americans go?

Layla Of course, but we must go through that.

Beat.

Ghalia You are the future of this place, you'll do well.

Ghalia *exits taking her computer bag with her.* **Layla** *goes and kicks the pile of dirt that* **Sam** *has swept up in frustration.*

Pause.

York *enters with a dustpan and brush.*

York I just saw the Director leaving, it's early, is she okay?

Layla She's gone. For good.

York Gone where?

Layla Back to her family. To England.

York Lucky her. Oh shoot all the dust has been messed up.

Layla Well, you better start sweeping again.

York It's like a never-ending task . . . sweeping up sand in the desert.

Layla When will you go back to America?

York I don't know, no date yet, a few more months at least.

Layla A country full of people who we don't want here and who don't want to be here.

York I know – funny ain't it? You know what I think?

Layla No, and I don't want to know. It's time to go home.

Beat.

Gertrude *notices* **Abu Zaman** *cleaning his coin.*

Gertrude Why are you still here?

Abu Zaman Sometimes I sleep here.

Layla Come on – you can finish sweeping tomorrow.

They leave – **Layla** *turns out the lights.*

Gertrude I should go back to the house. But I can't face it. Another sleepless night.

Abu Zaman Bad dreams?

Gertrude No, too many things to . . . It feels like time is running out. Sand through the hour glass.

Abu Zaman Time doesn't run out, it keeps going.

Gertrude I'd like to sleep. And see what to do – a sleep where she comes and guides me. Wake up refreshed, knowing what to do.

Beat.

Abu Zaman Sleep here. It might help. Sometimes I feel like they talk to me.

Gertrude Alright. Yes. I'm not afraid. You can go.

Beat.

Abu Zaman It's time.

He goes, but not before putting his coin on the floor.

Gertrude *moves behind the glass cabinet. She looks through it trying to see what to do – trying to see the future.*

There is a building soundscape of the looting of the museum it should mirror **Abu Zaman**'s *description from earlier. An approaching noise that swells, doors being* *broken down then glass smashing, items being sawed, objects being dragged, feet running, voices, pandemonium.*

It should be loud, deafening, the audience should expect people to storm the theatre.

In distress and horror **Gertrude** *climbs inside the empty glass cabinet.*

At the same time:

Sand begins to fall.

It covers the stage.

It covers everything.

Still it comes.

It covers the box until we can no longer see **Gertrude**.

We just see sand now.

When the sand stops so does the noise.

Later

Abu Zaman *enters. He sees the sand and makes for where* **Gertrude** *was. He runs to that place and begins to dig with his hands.*

Abu Zaman   Here, here! Over here! Come!

A group of people from Later come in – **Layla** *is there – but she hangs back reluctant about what they will find.*

Abu Zaman   *Ahforo ihnana besorra* – quickly – here!

They all begin to help and dig.

Black out.

Playwright's Outro

The premiere of *A Museum in Baghdad* was at the Swan Theatre in Stratford-upon-Avon in 2019 and early 2020. I cannot quite describe the feeling of sitting in that theatre as the lights went down – a mix of terror and joy and disbelief. In my twenties I would visit Stratford every weekend, watching the plays and falling in love with the town and in particular the Swan. It's such a beautiful and exposing space, the thrust stage pushes out into the audience meaning there's nowhere for the actors or play to hide and the atmosphere becomes electric. Watching my own play and remembering myself first experiencing the Swan fifteen years earlier was quite a heady experience – I felt I was straddling time as the play does. *A Museum in Baghdad* was due to transfer to the Kiln. Unfortunately that London transfer was cancelled because of the COVID-19 lockdown. But the text of the play printed here is the version I had redrafted for that production and as such has never been performed or seen before. I do hope that one day this updated version will find life in front of an audience.

Last of the Pearl Fishers

In *Last of the Pearl Fishers*, Lillian becomes obsessed with her maid's disappearance. Resolving to find her, her search throughout Dubai proves more of a challenge than she bargained for.

Ten characters, 6 females and 4 males.

Last of the Pearl Fishers was commissioned by BBC Radio 4 and produced by Nandita Ghose. It was first broadcast on BBC Radio 4 on 8 January 2015. It had the following cast:

Lillian   Pippa Nixon
Celeste   Renee Montemayor
Ben   Ian Conningham
Mary   Tina Chiang
Amit   Paul Bazely
Marianne   Liz Sutherland
Jennifer   Elaine Claxon
Siobhan   Hannah Genesius

Playwright's Intro

I grew up in the UAE and one of the things that I have always found difficult to reconcile is the treatment of the migrant workers in the Middle East, by both Arab and Western ex-pat employers alike. Returning there as an adult, I was shocked to learn how literally the value of life differs there when I was told that in the case of a car accident, if you were to hit and kill someone with your car the amount of money you would pay as recompense would depend on the ethnicity and religion of the person you hit. Over the years I had heard many stories about 'house girls' (maids) going missing and was interested and rather horrified how often the inconvenience to the employer was at the forefront of said employer's mind as opposed to the welfare of the missing woman. Trying to understand this mindset was one of the spurs to writing *Last of the Pearl Fishers*.

Scene One

The Summers' kitchen.
SFX: Crystal glasses in a sink being rinsed in soapy water. They are being washed with care but not so much care that we don't hear them clinking on occasion.

We can also hear the tinny sound of music through cheap earphones – it is Bruno Mars' 'Just the Way You Are'. The person washing up, **Celeste**, *is singing along. She has a nice voice but the tone is slightly off because of the headphones, and her singing fragmented for the same reason.*

Lillian   Celeste?

No answer – **Celeste** *can't hear her.*

Lillian   Celeste, where's my green swimsuit? Celeste!

Celeste   Oh – ma'am!

She has taken the earphones out. **Lillian** *puts one in her ear.*

Lillian   Bruno Mars? Again?

Celeste (*giggling*)   I like him – he's Filipino you know, like me.

Lillian   Did you try the James Blunt I put on there for you?

Celeste   It's a bit – what's the word, ma'am? Stern? Serious?

The distant sound of the landline ringing in another room.

Lillian   I'll find some English music for you – it's my mission. Now do you know where my cossie is?

Celeste   It's in your bag – I've packed for you.

Lillian   You didn't need to do that.

Celeste   Of course, it's my job.

We can hear the music through the headphone, low and tinny. It has gone to the next song, 'Runaway Baby'.

Lillian   Oh, I like this one.

Ben (*shouting from next door*)   It's for you, Celeste!

Celeste   Oh – but – I didn't give anyone the number.

Lillian   A secret admirer?

Celeste *walks into next room.*

Scene Two

*The Summers' house, **Lillian** and **Ben**'s hallway outside **Celeste**'s bedroom. Night time.*

*We can hear **Celeste**'s muffled sobs coming from the other side of her bedroom door.*

Lillian (*in hushed tones*)   Ben – what are you doing here?

Ben   I couldn't sleep – she's crying.

Lillian   Of course she's crying. You weren't going in?

Ben   I didn't know what to do. How could you sleep with that?

Lillian   I'm awake now – what were you thinking? You'd scare her – barging into her room in the middle of the night –

Ben   I didn't.

Lillian   It's not appropriate.

Ben   I didn't go in – I just thought about it.

Lillian   How long for?

Ben   What?

Lillian   How long did you think about it for?

Ben   I don't know – a minute – not long.

Lillian   Go back to bed. Go on. I'll see if she's OK.

Ben *walks back to their bedroom and* **Lillian** *gently knocks on* **Celeste**'s *door.* **Celeste** *stops crying.* **Lillian** *opens the door a little.*

Celeste   Oh, it's you . . .

Lillian   Look at you – your beautiful face – all red and blotchy – your hair.

Celeste   I've been crying.

Lillian   I know.

Celeste   Did I disturb you. Sorry.

Lillian   You silly little thing – what is it – why are you looking at me like that?

Celeste *begins to cry noisily again.*

Lillian   What? Tell me? Oh love, come here.

Lillian *goes to her and rocks her and shushes her gently, the bed creaks a little as she rocks her in her arms.*

Lillian   It's OK, I'm here. I'll help. I'll do anything I can.

Celeste   Anything?

Lillian   Of course.

Celeste *cries again.*

Celeste   I want to see him – I want to see my boy again. I need to go back.

Lillian   Of course you do. I'll make sure you can. I promise.

Scene Three

Mrs Heighsmith's sitting room.
A room filled with air conditioning on high setting, so there's a constant high-pitched whirring metallic noise over the scene.

Three women sitting on comfortable plush sofas drinking coffee from mugs, there is a plate of biscuits on the table.

Siobhan   How absolutely awful. Awful.

Jennifer   More tea, Siobhan?

Lillian   She's devastated.

Siobhan   I can't imagine what I'd do if anything happened to Patrick. Even now. And he's fully grown, not a baby. Awful.

Jennifer   Six is not a baby – you said the child was six, Lillian?

Lillian   Yes. Just ran into the road after a ball.

Jennifer   Her only child?

Lillian   No. She has a girl too – they were twins.

Jennifer   Well then.

Lillian   They're not interchangeable, Jennifer.

Jennifer   I never said they were.

Siobhan (*teasing*)   Anyone'd think you were the one without kids, not Lillian, for all the sympathy you've shown.

Jennifer   You know I'm not sentimental.

Siobhan   But it's so sad. Like a novel. How long will Celeste be gone for?

Lillian   Gone?

Siobhan   The funeral?

Lillian   I don't know when it is – it all happened so suddenly. Last night. I gave the poor thing a brandy, put her to bed. I could hear her sobbing into the early hours. Ended up going in to her.

Jennifer Her room?

Siobhan God love her – it's desperate. At least she's her faith.

Lillian I should probably book her flight home.

Jennifer Book it? You're not – she is paying for her own flight, isn't she?

Lillian Well –

Jennifer I don't want to interfere, Lillian – but you've only been here a year.

Lillian Thirteen months.

Jennifer And I'm an old veteran of the Gulf – raised three children here,

Siobhan Practically a camel.

Jennifer and paying for this woman's flight home would be a mistake.

Lillian Why?

Jennifer There are lines. Rules. Ways to do things. Allow her to go by all means. Even give her holiday pay if you must. But paying for the flight itself would be breaking a code.

Lillian Code?

Jennifer Talk to Ben about it. He knows how it works. As I say I haven't lived in this country for eighteen years without learning a thing or two about dealing with House Girls.

Siobhan How many have you got through, Jenny – was it twelve or thirteen?

Scene Four

Outside, street, day.
SFX: The opening of a door and we can hear the hiss of heat and an almost generator-like whirr of the humidity outside. There's also the clatter and beep of slow-moving traffic and creaking hot car metal.

Lillian *and* **Siobhan** *step out onto the pavement.*

Lillian I don't think I'll ever get used to this heat. Humidity. It's like being slowly suffocated.

Siobhan Don't mind Jenny – what she says about Celeste. You talk to Ben. Do what you both think is right.

Lillian I'd love the chance. He's always working. I just don't want to overstep any line. Celeste and I are . . . friends – well as much as you can be with someone you pay.

Siobhan I know what you mean.

Lillian Ben will want to know what Jennifer thinks – it's all Jon and Jenny this, Jon and Jenny that.

Siobhan Well Jon is his boss.

Lillian Everything's just so different since we came here. Come on, I need to get in from this heat, the car's there.

Siobhan How are you going to cope in the desert this weekend?

Lillian I don't want to go at all. Wadi bashing – sounds like something students should do.

Siobhan It'll be lovely, driving over the dunes, swimming in the water. Romantic.

Lillian Not with half Ben's office coming too . . . Doesn't seem great timing does it? Poor Celeste . . .

Siobhan Don't worry, I'll ask Mary to check in on her, it's just the weekend.

Lillian That's kind of you.

Siobhan We live across the hall, for goodness sake. What else are neighbours for? Now, have you everything you need for your trip?

Lillian I think so.

Siobhan Surely there must be something you want from the mall? Don't make that face, we can't all be culture vultures and gallery curators like you!

Lillian Not any more. Used to be.

Siobhan Come on, shopping! It's the exercise here! The national sport. And look – if we time it right we'll catch the rain.

Lillian Rain?

Siobhan Didn't you know? It actually rains inside the mall now – at set times . . . janitors come and sweep up the water. It's amazing.

Lillian What magic money can make.

Scene Five

Lillian's *room*
Lillian *is in her room pushing clothes into a bag and zipping it.* **Celeste** *comes in.*

Celeste Did I forget to put something in?

Lillian No, it was – fine, I just like to pack my own bag.

Celeste I hope you have a nice time.

Lillian I'm dreading it.

Celeste I wanted to speak to you about when I could go – to Manila, the funeral will be next week.

Lillian Good. You should go. Of course. Go. For as long as you like.

Celeste I wanted to ask about the flight?

Lillian You'll need to book that yourself – feel free to use the computer.

Celeste But –

Lillian The password's the same – right – I better head off, wish me luck, I feel like I'm going to need it.

Scene Six

*The Summers' hallway/***Celeste***'s room.*
The sound of keys in a front door.

Ben Home sweet home,

Ben *and* **Lillian** *enter the flat with their bags.*

Ben Come here.

He tries to embrace **Lillian**.

Lillian Ben! Celeste.

Ben She might be out.

Lillian She can't be – look her keys are on the hook –

(*Calling out to* **Celeste**.) We're back! (*To* **Ben** *who is still grabbing at her*.) What's got into you?

Ben You were amazing – this weekend. Like your old self. A laugh.

Lillian Shall I get you a drink to cool you down?

Ben Or we could warm you up?

Lillian Good idea, I'll put the kettle on –

Ben Let the girl do it. It's her job.

Lillian I'm perfectly capable of making a cup of tea. Celeste! Want a cuppa?

Ben She's been doing nothing all weekend.

Lillian Maybe she's asleep.

Lillian *walks to the door of* **Celeste***'s room and knocks.*

Ben Lily, leave her alone.

Lillian I can't make tea and not offer . . . Celeste? Would you like a cup of –

She opens the door.

Ben.

Ben (*from the hall*)   What?

Lillian Come here . . . COME QUICK.

Lillian *starts to rummage frantically through* **Celeste**'s *wardrobe knocking clothes from hangers to the floor and pushing around pairs of shoes.* **Ben** *rushes to* **Celeste**'s *door sensing panic in his wife's voice.*

Ben What? What is it?

He pushes the door open as wide as it will go, it creaks a little.

There's nothing there.

Lillian I know –

Ben Lillian! – I expected her to be hanging from the curtain rail.

Lillian She's gone.

Ben Church?

Lillian She goes on Saturdays.

Ben Maybe she's in Abela getting supplies then. Lily – what are you doing?

Lillian *continues to clatter though* **Celeste**'s *belongings, hangers clank and swing in her wake.*

Ben They're her things, STOP!

Lillian She can't go out without keys can she – or shoes – they're all here.

Ben What?

Lillian She can't have gone barefoot.

Ben How do you know all her shoes are there?

Lillian Because I bought them. And look – her purse. And the iPod I gave her – she's never without it. Oh – oh, no . . .

Ben Calm down, Lily – she'll just have gone to the shop or – or –

Lillian Where is she? Ben? She was so upset . . . that night . . . where is she?

Scene Seven

The Summers' bedroom, late at night.
Lillian *cannot sleep.*

208 Last of the Pearl Fishers

The sound of air conditioning punctuated by **Ben**'s *gentle snoring and sleep sounds. In the background James Blunt's 'Same Mistake' plays* (**Lillian** *is listening to it on her headphones as she tries to sleep*).

Lillian (*interior voice*) Did she like the room? I decorated it. With my own hands.

Ben (*voice in* **Lillian**'s *head echoey memory*) It's not a nursery*.

Lillian 'It's not a nursery'* (*at the same time as voice above*), you said, and then looked immediately sorry. Thoughtless. To say that to me, after everything we went through trying . . . And then watching everyone else have kids, as easy as popping to the shops. I couldn't stand it anymore. Crumbled. Agreed to come here. But swore I'd never have a maid. Then. Everyone has one. And you made a persuasive argument. The way things are here. Giving a job to a person who needs it. Better with us than someone who'd be cruel. She'll have an easy life. And I was persuadable. Sick of an almost silent apartment, listening to the AC. You always at work. Busy. So, I really wanted it to be nice for her. Coming to live in someone else's house. So far away from her own family. Her babies for goodness sake.

Ben (*voice in* **Lillian**'s *head echoey memory*) Economics, they're modern pearl fishers.*

Lillian 'Economics, they're modern pearl fishers'* (*at the same time as voice above*), you said. People have always come here to make money. Pearls. Oil. Money breeds money. And so it's normal to have people working for you, everybody has house girls here. Maids. Call it what it is. But I thought we were – friends. Friends don't just leave, disappear without a word. Oh, where are you Celeste, what happened?

Scene Eight

The Summers' kitchen, the following morning.
Ben *stirs milk into* **Lillian**'s *mug of tea.*

Ben You barely slept.

Lillian I was worried. Going over things.

Ben What's wrong?

Lillian The milk. Always tastes odd here. Fake. Not like home.

Ben But it's OK? (*Pleased with himself.*) I remembered how to make it.

Lillian It's a cup of tea, Ben. Can we please talk about Celeste?

Ben I don't want you getting all worked up again.

Lillian I won't – I'm worried. She's a child.

Ben She's twenty-five.

Lillian Twenty-four. Anything could have happened to her.

Ben She might come back.

Lillian She's no shoes, no wallet, I can't even work out what she's wearing – all her clothes seem to be there. It's so strange.

Ben I suppose we just have to report her missing, yes? And pay the sodding fine.

Lillian Fine?

Ben You know we're her guardians – legally. That's how it works here.

Lillian Like her parents.

Ben No. Her sponsors. So if she's run off she's broken the law. And so we've broken the law. And we get fined.

Lillian That's absurd.

Ben When in Rome.

Lillian Dubai. What if she's done something stupid, Ben?

Ben Like what?

Lillian Hurt herself . . .

Ben Hey, hey – we've been over this –

Lillian Why did we listen to those people – you should have heard Jennifer's reaction to the child's death.

Ben Love, we pay her well – she gets a day off – you buy her shoes – apparently. She would have had the money to go to the funeral if she wanted.

Lillian How much is a flight to the Philippines anyway?

Ben Stop this. You were close – she'd have asked if she needed help.

Lillian I might have said something . . .

Ben What? What have you done? Did you give her the money?

Lillian No.

Ben Lily! We agreed we shouldn't give her money for the flight.

Lillian I didn't – how could I without your permission? Here you're in charge of every bloody thing.

Ben What is it?

Lillian I promised her I'd help her. And I didn't.

SFX: A knock on the door.

Lillian Celeste!

She rushes to the door, unlocks the bolty sounding deadlock and opens it.

Lillian   Oh. It's you, Mary.

Ben *has followed her to the door.*

Ben   Hello, Mary.

Mary   Sir told me Celeste's gone.

Ben   What do you know about it?

Mary   Me, sir? Nothing. Ma'am asked me to come and see if you needed any help.

Lillian   Siobhan's so thoughtful.

Ben   We're fine thank you, Mary.

Lillian   Wait a minute. Let's talk to her. She might know something. Do you want to come in – the kettle's just boiled.

Ben   Mary has work to do.

Lillian   This will only take a minute. You and Celeste are friends aren't you – maybe you can help us find her?

Mary   I don't know anything, ma'am.

Lillian   Did you notice anything unusual in her behaviour in the last while?

Mary   No, ma'am. Just . . . she was sad about Matthew.

Ben   Matthew?

Lillian   Her son.

Ben   Oh. Yes. Obviously.

Lillian   That's all? Please if there's anything else tell us, we are very worried about Celeste, we want to find her.

Mary   I can't tell more than that, ma'am. It's all I know.

Lillian   Was there anyone she might go and stay with here? Any other friends?

Mary   She was a private person, ma'am, didn't really tell me about anything. I've been praying for her.

Ben   We should let Mary get back to her work.

Lillian   Thank you, Mary.

SFX: **Ben** *shuts the heavy door – it clunks firmly into place.*

Ben   She was obviously uncomfortable there, Columbo.

Lillian   Should you have given her a tip?

Ben   What? No – why? She didn't tell us anything.

Lillian   She came over.

Ben They live next door. No. I'm sure that wouldn't have been appropriate. No. (*Beat.*) Well, better call the police I suppose. Hand in her passport.

Lillian You have to give them her passport?

Ben Of course.

Lillian I always thought it was strange we held it.

Ben Clearly for the best. At least we know she's still in the country.

Lillian What good's that to us. She could be anywhere – she could be hurt . . . or worse. I feel so guilty.

Ben Don't – don't get worked up again – we came here so you could avoid stress.

Lillian Did we?

Ben (*ignoring her*) I'll take the passport in on the way to work.

Lillian Do you have to go now?

Ben Just for a few hours . . .

Lillian What will they do if they find her – alive.

Ben Deport her of course. And that'll be it. She won't be allowed back.

Lillian Ever?

Ben If she's run, she's a criminal here.

Lillian Let's give it forty-eight hours. Like in the UK. Just in case she turns up.

Ben Doesn't seem likely. She was obviously a bit – you know . . .

Lillian Perhaps. But perhaps it's a misunderstanding.

Beat.

Lillian (*aping **Jenny** to convince him*) No point in paying a fine needlessly and losing a perfectly good house girl.

Ben True. Alright. Forty-eight hours.

Scene Nine

Celeste*'s room.*
Lillian *is in* **Celeste***'s room and is looking for something.* **Lillian***'s voice in this scene is interior monologue.*

Lillian Where is it, where is it, where is it? I can't believe Ben didn't think of it.

She lifts the mattress off the bed (it's heavy).

Lillian Aha. Mobile. What have you got to tell me?

SFX: She's handling the mobile and she turns it on, it beeps.

Lillian   No SIM? What do you mean no SIM?

She opens the back of the phone with a click to check and fiddles with it – there is no sim inside – she sighs.

Lillian   No SIM.

She sits back on the bed – the mattress moves under her weight – she leans her head on the wall, then taps it on the wall a little, surveying the small room.

Lillian   I gave you the spare room, Celeste – the spare room. Not the utility room or a cupboard like some people. And I decorated as I would have liked it. Those curtains are from Liberty. Matching cushions . . . How could you do this to me? Leave me not knowing . . . It's so – cruel.

Lillian *gets up off the bed and agitatedly hunts around the room for clues. Hangers clang against each other and the wardrobe door swings shut noisily.*

She sits on the floor and places the objects she has found in front of her.

Lillian   Phone. Missal. iPod. Dried flowers. That's it. Is that all you had Celeste? (*Beat.*) The photos . . .

Another cursory rummage around, this time much more carefully and quietly, she stops.

Lillian   You took the pictures of your babies with you. Does that mean you're alive? That you chose to leave everything except those pictures? Chose to go. Leave me. Yes. I think it does . . . I think it does . . . The missal.

She picks up the missal and leaves the room, swinging the door shut behind her. she picks up the car keys from the hall table and goes to the front door.

Scene Ten

The interior of a modern Catholic church in Dubai.
SFX: We hear a woman singing 'Lamb of God' in Tagalog, 'Cordero ng Dius'. Footsteps as **Lillian** *walks down the aisle and knocks on a side door by the altar. An Italian* **Priest** *comes to the door and opens it.*

Priest   Can I help you? Come, sit down. I have five minutes before 'From Our Own Correspondent' on the World Service. I never miss it. (*Shouting.*) Joyce – please stop Lamb of Godding!

Lillian   Don't stop her on my account, it's beautiful.

Priest   Not on a loop, again and again – it's gonna drive me over the edge. Basta! So?

Lillian   Yes. Um. I wanted to ask if you knew Celeste Matapang.

Priest I have lots of lollipops – (*She looks confused.*) It's what I call my parishioners.

Lillian I think she used to help with the collection – I've a picture on my phone – here, look.

Priest Ah yes. Nice child. Bright. Brilliant with numbers. Used to get her to count up for me.

Lillian Has she been to see you this week?

Priest No – why?

Lillian I thought she might have talked to you? Her son died. I'd have thought she'd have come here for comfort.

Priest Must have found comfort somewhere else.

Lillian Now she's missing . . .

Priest You know these girls have a hard life. They can be like slaves. Beaten. Worked like dogs.

Lillian I can assure you she had a perfectly nice life. I'm her –

Priest Owner.

Lillian Guardian. Sponsor.

Priest Ah, my English!

SFX: The alarm on the **Priest**'s *mobile phone goes off.*

Priest Aha – 'From Our Own Correspondent'. Do you want to listen with me? They have fascinating stories from everywhere – last week there was one from my home – Sicilia – a man with a voice like honey described about a boat filled with dead people – they were trying to escape poverty – war – in Africa and they died on the ship . . . they were so desperate they risked everything. Poor souls. They called Italy the door to Europe. I suppose here we are in the door to the West. So close, yet so far.

Scene Eleven

Interior of **Lillian**'s *car.*
Lillian *slams the car door, then bangs her hands against the steering wheel in frustration.*

Lillian Owner! How dare he! (*She growls in frustration.*) Oh Celeste, how could you put me in this position? Where are you?

She sighs then rummages in her bag and pulls out **Celeste**'s *iPod.*

Lillian Bit of Bruno Mars for inspiration . . .

She takes the iPod out of its case to hook it up to her car stereo and we hear the rustle of a scrap of paper which she finds at the back of the iPod case.

Lillian   Paper? What's this? Shopping list? – love letter? – suicide note? – ransom demand?

She unfolds the paper.

Lillian   WiFi code. Useless!

She crumples it up and throws it on the floor.

Beat.

Lillian   Hang on – let me see.

She leans down to retrieve the paper, then uncrumples it again and reads out.

Lillian   WIFI code – Oasis internet café – Al Hamdan road – Bingo.

SFX: *Car starting and the sound of Bruno Mars' 'Runaway Baby' blaring through the car's speakers and the car drives off.*

Scene Twelve

Internet café.
Lillian *enters the internet café, the door closes and the traffic noise quiets behind glass doors.*
SFX: *Café noises, air conditioning, cups clinking, chatter.* **Lillian** *pulls back a chair and sits at a table.*

Waiter   What would you like, Madam?

Lillian   Cappuccino, please, and also can you tell me if you know this girl. (*Showing picture on her phone.*)

Waiter   I'll send Marianne over.

Lillian   Does she know her?

Waiter   They're related.

Lillian   Oh. Right.

Lillian *drums her fingers on the table impatiently as she waits.*

Marianne   Yes?

Lillian   Hello – I'm looking for –

Marianne   Celeste? What's she done?

Lillian   You're related?

Marianne   I'm her husband's cousin.

Lillian Oh, I'm so sorry about what happened to him.

Marianne What happened to him?

Lillian He drowned.

Marianne Is that what she told you?

Lillian Isn't it the truth?

Marianne He's working as a chef in Manila.

Lillian Oh.

Marianne She always makes things up. I'm sorry – I'm busy.

Lillian Please, I need your help – I'm trying to find Celeste – she's disappeared.

Marianne Ah! Run away.

Lillian We don't know that.

Marianne Wouldn't be the first time.

Lillian Sit down – tell me.

Marianne I can't –

Lillian Please – she might be in trouble . . .

Marianne I'm working.

Lillian First her boy dies, then she goes missing – don't you care?

Marianne Listen, that girl can look after herself . . . she married my cousin – everyone wanted her, everyone chased her, she loved that I can tell you, but she chose him – he was so happy. Idiot. Then she got pregnant.

Lillian With the twins.

Marianne Yes. But the dates were – they didn't seem quite right. So he asked questions and she got angry and then just decided to go – planned it with her family, left the babies with her sister and came here. First my cousin knew was when he went home for the weekend to visit them.

Lillian Really?

Marianne She sent money though. Said that's why she did it. Came here. For the money. Wanted her children to have chances she didn't have. And like a donkey my cousin believed her.

Lillian You didn't?

Marianne I think coming here was to avoid questions at home.

Lillian But she came to this café? – she didn't avoid you?

Marianne Coincidence. When she first arrived she came here to use the computer – she saw me and got scared but I gave her a free latte and wifi code. I felt sorry for her.

Lillian   After she'd treated your cousin like that?

Marianne   She's a house girl. A maid. And she's smart you know. Math. Then she would come and download music to her iPod and I'd get her to help me on the till. But she stopped coming. After Matthew. I presumed she was praying, you know they wouldn't let her go home for the funeral.

Lillian   She said that?

Marianne   Yes. The last time I saw her, she came here she was very upset. I gave her coffee and told her to go anyway. Quit. Demand her passport. These bloody people think they own us. That's why I work here. No money but at least I can do what I like. I'm no maid.

Lillian   You must have a sponsor.

Marianne   Yes. But he's a nice Pakistani man who is married to a Filipina. He lets us come and go as we wish. Pays us nothing. But never mind I'd rather be poor and free. As free as you can be when you are a Filipina in the Middle East. I told Celeste to leave those awful people and come and work here. But she said she needed money.

Waiter (*shouting from counter*)   Marianne – we're busy – it's not break time.

Marianne   Work, work, work – it's what the world thinks we Filipinas were made for. But I'm no slave. Listen, if Celeste wanted you to know where she was you'd know.

Waiter   MARIANNE!

Marianne   I said I'm coming!

Scene Thirteen

The Summers' kitchen.
Lillian *is chopping food for dinner.* **Ben** *hovers around.*

Lillian   So apparently he's not dead at all.

Ben   No?

Lillian   No. He's a chef in Manila. And she left without him knowing.

Ben   Got form then.

Lillian   Sit down will you – you're making me nervous.

Ben *sits down.*

Ben   Sorry. Not used to being in here. Are you sure you don't want me to get a takeaway?

Lillian   I like cooking. It's fine. I always cooked before Celeste.

Lillian *turns on the electric hob and pours oil into a pan, she adds the onions and begins to cook.*

Lillian What were you saying?

Ben Celeste – she's got form. Ran away before. It seems likely she's done a bunk again.

Lillian *is stirring the onions on the hob with a spatula.*

Lillian But why? What makes my blood boil is that she would lie and then just go without a word. She didn't worry how I'd feel, I did everything I could to make her part of the family.

Ben Too much some would say.

Lillian Let me guess, Jenny and Jon –

Ben Don't get cross, they just said space and formality with servants works better in their experience.

Lillian Don't use that word.

Ben Servant? Why?

Lillian I don't like it –

Ben So that's it – the trail's gone cold . . .

Lillian It's so strange . . . who was this person that was living in my house? I thought I knew her.

Ben She had more of a life than we realised. Now maybe you understand why they all lock them in.

Lillian Listen I stand by that decision – what if there was a fire? What then? She burns like the rest of our possessions.

Ben Calm down. You're not on the hormones anymore – what's got into you?

Lillian I just – I feel hurt. I did so much for her. Looked after her. Treated her like –

Ben An equal?

Lillian You know what I mean. But she had something else going on and she didn't tell me about it. Who else was there in her life? Who else did she see? It was just her, me and you.

Ben Well there's – Amit.

Lillian The gardener?

Ben He's the only other person.

Lillian Amit. The dried flowers in her room . . . I never – Bloody Amit.

Ben Just a thought, love –

Lillian Was it him?

Ben I suppose it's worth asking him /

Lillian AMIT!

She rushes out of the room.

Scene Fourteen

The Summers' garden.
SFX: The sound of cicadas, distant traffic noise, sprinklers, and gardening shears being used by **Amit**. *He is up a ladder, pruning a hedge.*

A moment of calm. Then we hear a French window being flung open and **Lillian** *storming out.*

Lillian AMIT!

Amit Good morning, ma'am.

Lillian Get down from there!

Amit I am just finishing the hedge – neat and tidy, ma'am.

Lillian Get down now. NOW!

She grabs the ladder and shakes it hard, he screams out and holds on for dear life.

Amit *is shocked. She has never behaved like this before.*

Amit Ma'am! Ma'am! I'll fall!

Lillian GOOD.

Amit *falls to the ground with a thud.* **Lillian** *stands over him wielding the shears.*

Amit *whimpers in pain – gulps for breath, shocked and winded.*

Lillian Where is she?

Amit Who, ma'am?

Lillian Where is she? Celeste! Don't look at me like that – did you do something to her? Did you rape her – she's twenty years your junior you filthy bastard.

Amit Please, ma'am – the shears – they're hurting me.

Lillian Good. Tell me.

Amit I don't know.

Lillian Liar – did you hurt her? Did you? Tell me!

Amit *begins to cry.*

Amit Please, ma'am, please don't send me back there – I can't go back into the desert – to that holding room. Hundreds of men – on top of each other – worse than a prison. The smell. The heat. If you report me to the police I'll be deported, but I have no money saved – no one will pay my flight and they'll put me back in that place – with all those other men – in vans every day to work on construction sites for no money and die without anybody caring. That is what happens to us here. Please, please don't send me back there. I have a family. I'll never survive it. Kill me. Cut my throat now. I'd rather die than go back there. I'm not an animal.

Lillian *takes a step back in the grass, then throws down the shears with a metallic thud onto the cement patio.*

Lillian   Amit – I'm sorry – I just. I need to know what happened to her. You must tell me everything.

Amit   You shook the ladder, you watched me fall, you held a blade to my neck.

Lillian   I'm sorry.

Amit   And I have done nothing wrong. Nothing.

Lillian   But you were close. She used to bring you lunch.

Amit   She is the same age as my daughter – I haven't seen her for ten years. She reminded me . . . And when she cried because her boy died I comforted her.

Lillian   Comforted?

Amit   Held her hand. Talked to her. That is all.

Lillian *is going inside. She's ashamed of her actions, we stay with* **Amit** *so her voice is getting distant.*

Lillian   I'm sorry, Amit. Let's not talk of this again. I just – I need to know what happened. How she could do this to me?

Scene Fifteen

Mrs Heighsmith's sitting room, as before, cold and air-conditioned. Three women back on comfortable plush sofas drinking coffee from expensive mugs.
SFX: Back in the cold air-conditioned room.

Siobhan   Isn't it horrible to think there were things going on in your house you didn't know about – I mean she could have been stealing from you or wearing your clothes or anything.

Lillian   I know.

Jennifer   That is why there need to be rules. Boundaries. We never let Lola eat with us. Her room is – utilitarian. She gets several hours off for Mass on a Saturday and the driver takes her there and brings her back and that is all. Boundaries. Like children.

Lillian   We got on.

Jennifer You didn't pay for her flight in the end did you? Because if you open that door what's next? You'd be making her cups of tea and doing the housework yourself before you knew it. Give these people an inch and they'll take a mile. You have checked none of your jewellery is missing?

Lillian She's not like that.

Jennifer This ghastly episode must have taught you something. Formality is everything.

Siobhan You were born in the wrong age, Jenny. More Downton than Dubai.

Jennifer No. I'm perfectly suited to my time and place. I understand the rules. Whatever you say you do too, Siobhan . . . And now so do you, Lillian. So you must report it to the police, pay the fine and get another one.

Lillian Another one?

Siobhan Come on, Jenny!

Jennifer Sorry, sorry, sorry, I'm just cross that Lillian's been put through this with her first house girl. I don't want it to put her off the place. I was really hoping she'd stay a while. Set up a gallery like we've talked about. We need a bit more culture in our set.

Lillian The British Museum is going to Abu Dhabi.

Jennifer But we're in Dubai. Now do you want to borrow Lola – poor thing you're going to have to wait three months until you can get another one, you know, another house girl – it's the law.

Lillian We managed before – I don't think I want to –

Jennifer Lily – we can't have you cooking and cleaning, it's not on.

Siobhan I've said Mary will help with anything she needs for now. What do you think happened to her, Jenny?

Jennifer What happens to any of these girls – they vanish. Working for someone else illegally no doubt. Let's hope she's dead.

Lillian Jennifer! How can you!

Jennifer I'm being hyperbolic, I suppose. But wouldn't you rather that than have been betrayed by someone in your service? How dare she do this to you, Lillian. You who are so kind and thoughtful. You don't deserve it.

Siobhan It's true, you don't –

Lillian Thank you.

Siobhan I always felt there was something aloof about her – ungrateful.

Jennifer Now, you must hand that passport in and put all this behind you. Would you like me to come with you?

Lillian No. It's OK. You're right. I'll do it.

Jennifer Good. LOLA! Where are those biscuits?

Scene Sixteen

The interior of **Lillian***'s car.*
Lillian *slams the door. Sighs. She takes out her phone and dials a number:*

Lillian Hello, it's me. I'm sorry I've been such a grump. I had coffee with Jenny and Siobhan and that's sort of helped . . . they were really nice. Then I spoke to the agency and they gave me a family contact in the Philippines, but it rang out. So that's that. I've just this minute handed her passport in and reported it like I said I would, so the good news – because we have her passport we don't get fined. The bad news is we lose the deposit we paid for her visa – 2,000 dirhams – but three-hundred-odd quid out of pocket's not too bad, is it? If she'd have had her passport we'd have lost that and been fined another 5,000 dirhams – a grand would be harder to stomach I suppose. So. You were right. Just as well we kept it under lock and key. Now, I'm going to forget about it all and I've changed my mind about the drinks thing at the Embassy tonight, I'll see you there at seven . . . OK. Bye.

She hangs up, puts the phone down. Sighs. She starts the car engine.

Scene Seventeen

Exterior of the Summers' flat. Night time.
SFX: *High heels clacking along a marble floor.* **Lillian** *puts her key into the front door lock, she's a little drunk. The noise of another door opening up the hall.*

Lillian Who's there?

No reply.

Lillian Who is it? Mary? – You scared me.

Mary Excuse me. Are you OK? Where's sir? It's late.

Lillian Had to go on to another do – I was too . . .

Mary Let me help you with the key.

She does so.

Lillian Did you like her?

Mary Who?

Lillian Celeste.

Mary She was my friend.

Lillian   But was that just because of the situation? Living in the same building? Both house girls? Under different circumstances, at home, would you have been friends?

Mary   Oh I doubt it, ma'am. She didn't like me very much.

Lillian   Why would you say that?

Mary   I'm quite a straight person. You know. Doesn't take much to make me happy.

Lillian   But Celeste wasn't like that?

Mary   She always had a goal. And when she achieved it she wasn't happy. She just started to want something else. Like she was born in London or something – not a village two hours from Manila.

Lillian   Can you spare five minutes –

Mary   I –

Lillian   I want to see if you'd like any of Celeste's things . . . come on, come inside.

Scene Eighteen

Celeste's *room.*
SFX: **Mary** *is already in* **Celeste**'s *room opening drawers looking through* **Celeste**'s *things.*

Mary   So many lovely clothes.

Lillian   How did you know this was Celeste's room? I didn't realise you'd ever been inside our place before.

Mary   Oh, I. Just once.

Lillian   Where was I?

Mary   I can't remember – may I have these shoes?

Lillian   Anything you like.

Mary   Look at this jacket.

Lillian   Put it on – it'll suit you.

Mary   Wow – it fits perfectly – are you sure Celeste won't come back for it?

Lillian   She can't come back now. We've handed over her passport. I did it today.

Mary   Then I hope they don't find her.

Lillian   Why?

Mary   They'll question her before they deport her, and questioning here I've heard they use more than words.

Lillian Why would they question her?

Mary To find out who helped her. Get her to name people. I like this – I didn't know we were the same size.

Lillian It's yours. You were saying outside. She always wanted more. Like what?

Mary She wanted to come here – make money, she did. She wanted a kind ma'am and sir – she got you, look at this room, it's perfect. Like a magazine. The clothes. She told me you bought them. So kind. She talked about going back to college and becoming an accountant.

Lillian She never mentioned –

Mary I think she wanted to get married first.

Lillian She was married.

Mary Only to a Filipino man

Lillian She wanted someone else? Was there someone else?

Beat.

Mary I – I don't know.

Lillian You can have the iPod if you like.

Mary Really?

Lillian Here –

Mary Thank you – I've always wanted one – I've only got a Discman . . . you are kind. . . I came here the night before she left.

Lillian When we were in the desert?

Mary Yes. She text me. Late. Ma'am and sir were asleep. And she was behaving strangely. I think she had something to drink. Alcohol. She told me that she was going away. That she had had enough of being a maid. I said you don't even have children to look after, Mr and Mrs Summers are clean people, kind, don't be stupid, but she said what kind of a world was it where she couldn't even keep her own passport. Other people come and go as they please she said. I tried to tell her she just needed to work hard, save money and pray and in a few years she would go home and build a house and be with her husband. And she laughed in my face. Called me stupid. Said something really bad – about God not existing . . . because of Matthew I think and then she cried. I'd never seen her cry before. It made her look normal. Ugly. And then she asked me a favour. That was why she wanted to see me. Not to say goodbye. She wanted something. She always wanted something.

Lillian I'm getting a different picture of Celeste . . . What did she want?

Mary She asked me to look after this until she came back.

She takes the missing sim card out of her bra.

Lillian The sim card!

Mary Don't be cross, ma'am – here you can have it.

Scene Nineteen

Celeste's *room.*
Lillian *holds* **Celeste**'s *phone – she dials the number noisily (it's an old-fashioned mobile) – she is shaking, nearly crying. The number connects and a ring tone is heard.*

Man's Voice (*muffled*) Allo?

Lillian Who is this? Hello? Where's Celeste? Where is she?

The **Man** *hangs up. With shaky hands and heavy breathing* **Lillian** *dials again.*

Lillian Answer you bastard – answer.

This time the phone doesn't ring but goes to an automatic message (in Arabic and English) 'Sorry. This number is currently unavailable'.

Scene Twenty

Mrs Heighsmith's sitting room.
SFX: Back in the cold air-conditioned room.

Lillian The texts were positively blue. Sexually explicit.

Jennifer Disgusting.

Siobhan Maybe she was inspired by *Fifty Shades*.

Jennifer Siobhan – this isn't a joke. And was there any indication who this man was?

Lillian No – none.

Siobhan Did you try and call the number?

Lillian Of course. He answered.

Siobhan Mother of God – what did you say?

Lillian Not much. He hung up.

Jennifer So that's that. Done now. You need to move on, focus on finding investors for your gallery – forget this whole thing. We need you here and we'll appreciate your efforts much more than those spoiled Londoners. Now, I've a list of suggestions – a few dinners, cocktails receptions and you'll be well on your way.

Lillian Thanks, Jenny, I really appreciate it.

Jennifer No thanks required – you're one of us.

Siobhan It is strange though to think we will never know what happened to her. Such a pretty girl.

Jennifer Was she? I didn't notice.

Scene Twenty-One

Abela supermarket.
Inside an Abela supermarket. A few months later.
SFX: Supermarket noises, announcements, distant music, trolleys being manoeuvred around, people talking.

Lillian What else?

Mary The trolley is full of food – you could feed my village for a week – your guests won't starve.

Lillian How much salad does Siobhan get when she's entertaining?

Mary She always has caterers, ma'am. I think your gardener will be eating like a king for weeks with the leftovers.

Lillian Good. Keep up, Mary.

Mary (*sotto voce*) Mam – there's a woman over there following us.

Lillian Which one?

Mary In the abaya.

Lillian You'll have to be more specific.

Mary The lady with her face covered and the gold trim scarf. She's been watching us since we came in. Moving when we move.

Lillian Odd. Shall I say something?

Mary She's making me nervous, ma'am. Could she be from the police?

Lillian Do they have women police here?

Mary I'm only supposed to work for my employer – I could get into trouble, you could get into trouble.

Lillian Don't be silly. This is all above board. Siobhan lent you to me – I mean – she knows you're here. Don't look so scared. Go up to the meat counter, I'll talk to her – go on.

Mary *moves away with the trolley,* **Lillian** *goes to the* **Woman**.

Lillian Excuse me, I just need to reach the Earl Grey – thank you.

Woman I want it back.

Lillian Sorry?

Woman It's mine. I want it.

Lillian Celeste? Is that you under all that black?

Woman I need my passport.

Lillian What happened – where are you staying, are you safe?

Woman You must return it.

Lillian Take that thing off, I want to see your face.

Woman I can't – my husband doesn't like it.

Lillian Your husband is in Manila. Alive and well. You lied.

Woman Just give me my passport – he'll pay you the deposit and more, we want to get away from here. And until I get it back I'm a prisoner in this country.

Lillian Well I'm sorry, but we've given it to the authorities.

Woman Why – why would you do that?

Lillian What choice did we have – you leave without so much as a – a /

Woman He loves me.

Lillian This person. Why didn't you tell me about him – couldn't you trust me? Wasn't I kind? I've been beside myself – I thought we were friends.

Woman Would a friend wait on you? Cook and clean for you? Would you take your friend's passport away? Take their freedom?

Lillian It's the rules here! You ungrateful girl, you could have had had employers who beat you – treated you like an animal. I gave you Liberty curtains.

Woman But you didn't give me the chance to go to my baby's funeral.

Lillian You could have gone.

Woman With what? I had no money. Everything to pay his debts in Manila. Friends? How could we ever be friends? We're not equals. You don't think I'm your equal.

Lillian How dare you. I was different – you'll learn.

Woman Don't you see, it doesn't matter if you throw me in a cell or put me in a guest bedroom with an en-suite. If you have my passport locked up it's all the same.

Lillian And you want it back to give to this man.

Woman Until I leave this country I cannot be in control of my destiny.

Lillian Let them deport you, then you can go home.

Woman I can't go back there. I thought here I would be able to lift myself out of the injustice of my birth. Several thousand miles too far east. Here, I thought I'd have a chance. But I was wrong. All my gifts. Unappreciated. I don't want to die without anyone looking at me and seeing who I am – who I really am.

Lillian And you think this man will do that? Naïve girl.

Woman He'll take me to Europe. If you give me my passport back. And once I'm there /

Lillian Well you've misjudged things – I'm afraid you're stuck.

Woman Yes, I misjudged things. You. Now I look closely I see you're just like all the rest of them.

Mary has tentatively made her way over to see what is going on.

Mary Celeste – is that you? I'm so embarrassed I'm wearing your clothes – but ma'am said I could have them. She says we have the same figure. That I look like you when I wear them. That made me happy. She's so kind. Everyone knows you are much prettier than me. Do you mind?

Woman None of it was mine.

She has turned on her heel and walked away.

Mary Oh – was she cross?

Lillian Not with you, Mary, don't worry,

Mary Are you sure?

Lillian Don't look so concerned, you silly little thing.

Mary I couldn't hear her voice properly. Her face was covered. Was it really her?

Lillian I think so, it sounded like her. I can't be sure. No I don't know if it was her. I can't remember her any more really. Come on – let's . . . go to the clothes section – I promised you a new blouse.

Playwright's Outro

When Chris and I were conceiving this anthology, the idea of including a radio play hadn't occurred to me at all. But when Chris suggested it, I really liked the idea. It's rare you see radio plays in print these days – though in the past writers like Harold Pinter would include radio plays in their published texts. I am passionate about writing for radio. The BBC Radio Drama Department was the biggest commissioner of new writing in the world when I first wrote for them and they were the first people to give me a proper paid commission – for that I will always be grateful. I'm fascinated by the history of BBC Radio Drama and have spent much time researching its beginnings pre-Second World War under the leadership of Val Gielgud (the brother of renowned actor Sir John Gielgud). I have loved my experiences working with the in-house team at the BBC, particularly Mary Peate, who has always championed my work. The speed at which decisions have to be made means the writer is at the heart of the process. And having the chance to watch Foley artists and sound technicians weave their magic is a real privilege.

Hakawatis: The Women of the Arabian Nights

**With contributions from Hanan al-Shaykh,
Suhayla El-Bushra and Sara Shaarawi**

Translations by Hassan Abdulrazzak

What if Scheherazade wasn't the legendary storyteller of fable? A reimagining of *1001 Nights*, putting five women with a shared predicament at the centre of the action.

Five characters, all of them female.

Hakawatis was commissioned by the Globe Theatre, London. The characters are as follows:

Fatah *the young*
Akila *the writer*
Zuya *the warrior*
Wadiha *the dancer*
Naha *the wise*

Playwright's Intro

People often ask where I get my ideas. Normally, they come when I am angry or feeling frustrated and impotent about the world. But that's not the whole story here. *Hakawatis* is the first play I have ever written that is partially inspired by a space. That space is the Sam Wannamaker Playhouse at Shakespeare's Globe in London. Along with The Swan at the RSC in Stratford-upon-Avon and the Lyceum in Edinburgh, it is one of my favourite theatre venues in the UK. For those who don't know it, it's an indoor theatre in the Jacobean style, modelled on the Blackfriars Theatre of Shakespeare's day, based on a set of blueprints for a late seventeenth-century playhouse drawn up by John Webb, Inigo Jones's former assistant. It has a wooden interior and a magnificent ceiling mural. And all of its beauty is magnified by the fact productions there are candlelit.

Production Note

A note on storytelling: Stories can be told direct to the audience as monologues or in a more innovative way at the director's discretion, except for places where the form of the storytelling is specified.

*The Fisherman and the Jinn story should be improvised live every night by the women. They do not need to learn the story word for word as written down – rather, this is an exercise in group storytelling.

**Wadiha's story could be told solely by Akila or by a mix of the women, either way it should be read from papers.

One Night

The woman all hold candles to light their faces.

All It hurts. What they do to you.

Fatah It's planned to make you feel safe – beautiful – like everything's going to be OK. But then:

All Rip

Cut

Pluck

Burn

Rip

Cut

Pluck

Burn/

Rip

Cut

Pluck

Burn

Rip

Cut

Pluck

Burn.

Fatah / Hands everywhere, on your body. Touching, pulling, pushing, testing, changing. Changing. Changing. Everything.

*The hand-held candles are blown out and a door slams – all the women suddenly turn to **Fatah** as if she has just entered the room. She is surprised – shocked – afraid, as they inspect her.*

Wadiha I thought we were the only ones left.

Zuya Where did they find you little one?

Naha How old are you anyway?

Fatah My name's Fatah. And I'm sixteen.

Naha HA! An old woman.

Wadiha She's ready anyway.

Fatah Ready for what?

Akila Shaved to within an inch of her life.

Zuya (*lifting her skirt*) Did they caramel your –

Fatah Hey!

Wadiha Doubt she had anything to wax yet anyway.

Akila Where did they find her? He'll make mincemeat of her.

Naha He'll make kibbeh of all of us.

Zuya Not me. I'll kill him first.

Akila (*to* **Naha**) Not you – you're too old – more of a Mansaf.

Naha HEY!

Akila (*to* **Naha**) Think yourself lucky he only wants fresh meat.

Fatah Who?

Zuya The man who is the reason you are here. The reason we are all here.

Fatah My fiancé?

Wadiha Is that what they told you?

Naha Adorable.

Akila Kelbs. Sending her here without all the facts.

Fatah What facts?

Zuya They gave her a proper little send off. Look at her – plucked and waxed and creamed and painted. Ready for battle. For the inevitable.

Naha No one is ever ready for that.

Fatah Don't make fun of me. I know what to expect.

Akila How do you?

Naha Did your mother tell you?

Fatah NO. She just said to open my flower and his insect would fly in. And that it might sting.

The women laugh in derision.

Fatah But I know that's not what happens. I've talked to my friends. My cousins. I've seen pictures – in books.

Akila In books? What books?

Fatah Books from Europe.

Zuya HA! They don't know about such things there.

Fatah Babies are born in Europe too.

Naha Teach us little one. What are we to expect?

Wadiha As if YOU don't know. You can't have got to your age without experiencing –

Naha Let her speak.

They all listen with interest.

Fatah Well . . .

Zuya She knows nothing, she is a child!

Fatah I DO!

Wadiha Then tell us. We won't laugh.

Fatah Well . . . First come lips. pressing lips.

Akila Pilgrims.

Fatah Kisses. Tongues. Wet. Then hands.

Akila Profane.

Fatah Caresses. Moving down.

Akila Unworthy.

Fatah Down. Under. In. Between.

Zuya And are you vertical or horizontal at this point?

Wadiha Shush, ZUYA, I'm enjoying this.

Fatah On the bed. Pressed together. Into each other. Then he frees himself.

Naha His manhood.

Wadiha His snake.

Akila His column.

Naha His weapon.

Zuya His cock. His penis.

Fatah And gently pushes it /

Zuya / gently?!?!

Fatah In between your legs.

Beat.

Zuya And

Akila then

Wadiha what?

Fatah He releases himself.

Naha Just like that.

Fatah See – I do know.

Naha Just like that?

Fatah No, not just like that – he moves in and out. Gently.

Zuya He's very gentle this one.

Fatah And the movement makes a tide – a

Zuya Yes,

Fatah swelling tide

Wadiha yes,

Fatah that rises

Naha yes,

Fatah and rises

Akila yes,

Fatah and grows.

Zuya yes,

Fatah From my core

Wadiha yes,

Fatah To my toes

Naha yes,

Fatah Through my body

Akila yes,

Fatah Electric.

All YES!

Fatah And then,

Zuya Then,

Wadiha then . . .

Naha then,

Fatah it's over.

Naha Not quite . . .

All eyes are on **Naha**.

Naha Then he gets off. Rolls off. Breath heavy. Somewhere else. Other. Not here. Not with you. He gets up slowly – like a man drunk. Unsteady. And he straightens. Perhaps he wipes himself. Pulls on something to cover him. Perhaps he doesn't bother. But he definitely goes to the table – goes and picks up a blade. It shines. Like the moon. Like a diamond in the night. Sparkles. Reflects your eyes. And he raises it over you. Like the crescent over the minaret. And holds for a moment. Before it all comes crashing down . . . everything ends. And you spill – everywhere.

Beat.

Naha Another set of silk sheets are ruined.

Beat.

Fatah Are you saying he's going to kill me?

Wadiha All of us.

Zuya Not me.

Akila He won't stop until he's killed

Naha all of us.

Fatah NOBODY TOLD ME IT WOULD BE LIKE THIS. I WASN'T WARNED. IT'S NOT FAIR.

Naha Don't be scared – death comes to all of us.

Zuya Some of us sooner than others.

Naha Will you STOP going on about my age. I'll outlive all of you sharmutas.

Wadiha That just depends what order we go in.

Fatah BUT – Are you all to marry him? The King? Not just me?

Zuya Think you were special did you?

Wadiha We're all that's left. He's been marrying women, girls – whatever – taking them to bed – and then killing them . . . for weeks.

Akila Months.

Zuya Years. So many dead – gone before us . . .

All the women look to the audience with sadness and remembrance – they see them as the souls of the women who have gone before.

Pause.

Fatah And we're the only women left????

Naha Exactly.

Fatah What about my *teta* – and my aunties?

Naha Too old – for this task. It's just the young ones.

Zuya Young-ish.

Naha *shoots her a look.*

Akila How have you not heard?

Fatah (*fearful*) Who will be next?

Wadiha I don't know.

Akila Maybe we should draw straws.

Zuya I'll go first. And before he can touch me I'll pick up his sword and slice him into pieces – feed him to the dogs.

Wadiha And then his guards will come in and arrest you and you'll be executed. Great plan.

Zuya You have a better idea?

Wadiha I do, as a matter of fact. I will hypnotise him.

Naha With what?

Wadiha My hips.

Akila Haven't you heard of her – she's a famous dancer.

Fatah Really?

Akila That's her story anyway. But she refuses to show us.

Wadiha There are always men watching. Peeking. And this dance is not for them. It's meant to lubricate the joints for childbirth. Not fulfil some Orientalist's fantasy.

Zuya The King's a man.

Wadiha Yes, and when I dance for him he will be my husband – so it will be OK.

Naha Without us seeing it we can't be sure if this dance is up to the task of subduing a barbaric murderer.

Wadiha Well what are YOU going to do?

Naha My lovemaking will be so intoxicating – he will want his days and nights to be a marathon of pulsating undulating passion, on a sea of me.

Akila Are you joking? You get out of breath standing up from the toilet.

Naha What's your plan? Use your pen to write away the problems of the world – are you going to write him into submission?

Akila Well it's working for Scheherazade isn't it?

Fatah Scheherazade?

Akila The current wife. She was in here with us until yesterday when she got the call for her 'wedding'.

Fatah   Is she dead?

Akila   Not yet.

Zuya   She'll be fine. Got a battle plan.

Fatah   What plan?

Akila   To tell him stories.

Fatah   Bore him to sleep?

Wadiha   NO, entertain him with such enthralling never-ending stories that he'll keep her alive to hear what comes next.

Fatah   Well that sounds OK.

Akila   OK? It's GREAT.

Fatah   As long as . . .

Akila   What?

Fatah   Well – as long as . . .

Zuya   Yes?

Fatah   As long as she's a good storyteller.

Naha   That's a fair point. Is she?

Zuya   I don't know – is she?

Akila   I've got to be honest. She's good at *telling* stories – weaving a yarn – but the *ideas* bit . . . she's not really – the best . . .

Fatah   WE'RE ALL GOING TO DIE!

Zuya   Calm down!

Fatah   LET ME OUT OF HERE, I'M SIXTEEN, I HAVE MY WHOLE LIFE AHEAD OF ME!

Naha   SHHHH! Calm little one – calm. She can't be that bad. She's lasted one night . . . she's already winning.

Zuya   For now.

Naha *shoots her a look.*

Fatah   What's she like, Scheherazade?

Zuya   A warrior – tall and dark.* [*The actress should use adjectives that describe herself.*]

Wadiha   She moves well – and her hair is like long.* [*The actress should use adjectives that describe herself.*]

Akila Hard to describe, the colour – it's blackish.* [*The actress should use adjectives that describe herself.*]

Naha Sometimes close to the candle she's older and you see her lines, sometimes away from the light she's young . . .

Fatah She sounds like hundreds of other women. Like any woman.

Akila She is any woman. Every woman. And she is THE woman. The only one.

Wadiha The only one for now.

Naha She's a survivor. She will get through it. I believe.

Fatah (*rising fear*) But if she doesn't . . .

Naha If she doesn't – well you'll be alright . . . look at you, you're so lovely. How could anyone hurt you?

Beat.

Zuya You know who she reminds me of?

Akila Scheherazade?

Zuya No, this one (*indicating* **Fatah**). She's very like his first wife.

Wadiha The one who?

Signifies fucking.

Wadiha With the servant?

Zuya The one who's the reason we are in this shit in the first place.

Fatah (*terror*) I don't look like her do I? Then he'll definitely kill me.

Naha Don't worry – you just need to come up with a back-up plan like Scheherazade.

Akila What can you do?

Fatah I make a nice maqloobeh.

Akila Cooking won't save you now.

Fatah Then what?

Zuya Got any good jokes?

Akila Can you sing?

Fatah *sings. It should be in the Western scale and sound nice and sweet to Western ears.*

Fatah (*sings*)
  To-morrow is Saint Valentine's day,
  All in the morning betime,
  And I a maid at your window,

> *To be your Valentine.*
> *Then up he rose, and donn'd his clothes,*
> *And dupp'd the chamber-door;*
> *Let in the maid, that out a maid*
> *Never departed more.*

Naha What the hell was that? You sound like one of them. Occidentals. All throat. No heart or stomach.

Naha *sings a full Arabic scale, then morphs into a traditional Arabic love song. Perhaps 'Ataba.*

Naha
> *betaali l-leyl shaddoo 'aa reHalhom*
> *Hebaaby jarraH eqleaby raHeelhom*
> *wa kam maktoob min eedy raH elhom*
> *wa la maktoob raddoo lee jawaab*
> *[At the end of the night, they prepared for departure*
> *My loved ones whose departure wounded my heart.*
> *How many letters, from my hand, went to them*
> *And no letter from them to reply to mine]*

Naha That's what the King wants. As well as – you know.

Fatah This is a nightmare. When I left my house this evening I was excited. All day getting ready – my teta and my aunts so attentive – I've never seen so many lotions and potions and smelled so many smells and felt so many feelings. And they whisper things in my ears.

The women gather round her, becoming her family.

Zuya (*whispered*) Don't be afraid.

Naha We all go through this.

Wadiha Try and enjoy it.

Akila Close your eyes.

Zuya Look right at him.

Naha Be silent.

Wadiha Make lots of noise – they like that.

Naha Act surprised.

Akila Shy.

Wadiha But aroused.

Zuya Even if you aren't.

Wadiha Touch him.

Naha Don't touch him.

Akila Climb on top – they like that.

Zuya Be in control.

Wadiha Arch your back.

Akila Lie flat – like a corpse.

Naha Don't move a muscle – they like that.

Akila Follow his lead.

Zuya Don't show it hurts and

Wadiha never

Naha ever

Akila cry –

Wadiha they don't like that.

They all step away.

Fatah And then as if by magic I was at the gates. Of the palace. Dressed like a Princess. Shining like a jewel. Smelling like a rose. Waiting to be plucked.

Zuya You'll be plucked alright.

Akila We're all plucked.

Fatah I was ready for anything that could happen. He could be ugly. Or handsome. Beat me. Or stroke me. Eat food off my naked body. Maybe even make me shit on him . . . But of all the things I was expecting – waiting in a room for my inevitable execution was not one of them.

Zuya It's not inevitable. We must not give up. Scheherazade may not fail.

Akila Scheherazade MUST NOT fail. For all our sakes.

Fatah Well we better start praying that her stories are good then.

Wadiha Full of sex.

Akila And suspense.

Zuya And battles.

Naha And intrigue.

Akila *Is* that what makes a good story? Sex, suspense, battles and intrigue.

Zuya You tell us, Akila – you're the writer.

Akila You have to know your audience. What does the King like?

Naha All those things surely – he's a man.

Wadiha And dancing.

Akila They say stories need a beginning, middle and an end, but these stories are different . . . these stories must keep going . . . be threaded very carefully. They must be like a reflection within a reflection within a reflection.

Naha Why?

Akila So they go on forever. Keep him guessing. Turning the pages.

Fatah Like water turning down the plug hole, round and round.

Akila Exactly, Fatah. That's right. And a good story needs a hook. A hook to catch the attention of a big King Fish. And if we can come up with a suitable hook, then we ladies we will land that fish and change our destiny – the destiny of all women.

Fatah How?

Akila We'll teach that King a thing or two.

Fatah Men don't like being taught things. Especially by woman.

Akila They don't need to know they're being taught . . . Never underestimate the power of a good story.

Wadiha Like the Jinn and the Fisherman.

Naha Everyone knows that one.

Akila Really? OK then. Yulla. Tell it. All of us. Together.

She lights her a candle and hands it to **Naha** – *this is the candle of the Hakawati and every time someone tells a story, they are given one to signify they are the sun for this moment. So as this story is told the candle is passed from teller to teller.*

The Women* (*see the note on storytelling at the top of the script*) OK. So . . . there was a poor fisherman whose family were starving. The less he caught the hungrier they became and the more maggoty his net until one day he was ready to give up. He decided he would put out his net three times and if he hadn't caught some fish by the third he would drown himself and his family.

So praying to himself he goes to the shore and puts out his net for the first time. He feels something heavy and gets excited, so hauls it in – only to find a dead stinking donkey. He curses his luck, throws the beast back in and casts his nets a second time.

Hours pass and suddenly he feels something – a tug – he hauls the net in again and finds . . . an old chest . . . It could hold riches aplenty – may hold his future. He fumbles excitedly with the rusty latch and eventually gets it open to discover . . .

NOTHING, it is empty. So now the Fisherman's fuming. He decides to cast his net one last time. Almost immediately he feels something – not so heavy or big but something in them. When he yanks them in he finds a copper lantern. Dirty but definitely metal – he could sell it at the market and get something to eat. He opens the lantern to see if there's anything inside – no nothing. Then he cleans it on his shirt a little. Suddenly clouds of black smoke fly out of the spout and a Jinn appears before him – huge – eyes of fire, a mouth like the opening of hell – the man's so terrified he pisses himself.

The Jinn laughs and says YOU HAVE ONE WISH – but before the Fisherman can get excited the Jinn adds, YOUR WISH IS TO CHOOSE HOW YOU DIE. The Fisherman is horrified and pleads with the Jinn – I FREED YOU – SURELY YOU SHOULD BE GRATEFUL, NOT KILLING ME.

The Jinn explains that he had been one of the rebellious jinns that tried to overthrow God. He was sealed in the lantern as punishment and thrown out to sea. He had been trapped for hundreds of years. At first he vowed he would make whoever found him rich beyond his wildest dreams. Then after millennia waiting he got impatient and cross and vowed to vent his fury on whoever released him – killing them instantly.

As the Fisherman listened he realised this was one crazy Jinn and there was no reasoning with him. He'd need to outfox him. So the Fisherman smiles at the Jinn – YOU EXPECT ME TO BELIEVE THAT YOU – YOU HUGE HUNK OF JINN SQUEEZED INTO THAT TEENY TINY LAMP? I'M NOT AN IDIOT. THIS IS A TRICK.

The Jinn insists he has been living there but the Fisherman just shakes his head in disbelief. FINE says the Jinn. I'LL PROVE IT TO YOU and just like that he transforms himself into a whisp of smoke and flies back into the lamp which the Fisherman corks in a flash.

Wadiha When the Jinn realises he has been tricked, he begs and begs the Fisherman to release him. But the Fisherman says no.

The last line of the story must always be told by **Wadiha** *who blows out the candle to signify the end of the story.*

Beat.

Zuya We can't just end it there.

Wadiha Why?

Akila She's right – it's too finished. Final.

Wadiha What would you add, oh great writer?

Akila Well . . . I'd say the Fisherman said, 'No do you think I'm stupid. Don't you know the story of the King and Sage? Let me tell you.'

Fatah She's wrapped a story in a story – I understand now.

Akila The Jinn didn't, so the Fisherman went on: once there was a King who had a terrible disease – limbs falling off, the works. No one could save him – he tried all the lotions and potions, ointments and pills. Then a Sage came and without even touching him cured him. It was a miracle. Everyone was happy and the King showered gifts and blessings on the Sage promoting him to high office. But the King's advisor did not like this – he became jealous and warned the King about the Sage – if he can cure you without touching you, he could kill you without touching you too – he's a sorcerer and they are dangerous. The King became worried and decided to put the Sage to death. The Sage begged for his life (much as I begged for my life the

Fisherman reminded the Jinn, and like you the King ignored the Sage's pleas), so the Sage said: 'When you have cut my head from my body take this book and turn to page six – if you read the words written there, my eyes will open and I will sing to you.'

Naha   That's a bit tame. isn't it? A song.

Akila   What would you have him do – open his mouth and suck his cock?

Naha   Good idea – that'd be much more interesting.

Akila   Fine. The Sage said, 'When you have cut my head from my body take this book and turn to page six - if you read the words written there my mouth will open and I will suck your cock.' The King was delighted –

Naha   You bet he was.

Akila   So he took the book and called the Executioner who removed the Sage's head from his body. Next the King excitedly turned to page six of the book ready to read the incantation and receive his cock sucking – but there was nothing written there – he licked his finger to break up the stiff pages and turned them over – there was nothing written in the book at all. The King was confused but before an answer to this riddle could form, he dropped down dead. The Sage had poisoned the pages. 'So you see, Jinn,' said the Fisherman, 'if you had let me live I would have let you live but you would surely have killed me so I must do away with you.'

Fatah   Then what happens?

Naha   How about he pleasures himself?

Akila   You're obsessed.

Wadiha   He has to free him –

Akila   Yes – so the Jinn begs and promises the Fisherman to bewitch his net so the fish jump into it . . .

Naha   Great, so he lets him out of the lamp.

Zuya   And the Jinn strikes him dead.

Akila   NO, we want to show people in power can learn – change. That's the moral. He doesn't kill him . . .

Naha   He takes him to a spot high up and tells him to cast his nets.

Akila   That's right and they immediately fill with fish. And the Fisherman worries he will have to waste them – he could never sell so many.

Fatah   But then they turn into beautiful jewels and diamonds – sparkling

Zuya   and the Fisherman is rich and happy and the Jinn flies off into another story. Perfect!

Fatah   But how do we link it?

Zuya   Let Scheherazade figure it out – she's gotta do SOMETHING, we can't do it all.

Naha How about it ends saying, 'The Fisherman was lucky but not as lucky as his brother the Porter . . .'

Akila That's a great hook . . . I'll write those down – you all come up with ideas for the Porter's story . . .

They take pens and paper and begin to write, except **Naha** *who goes to each corner of the room and spits, chanting 'baraka, baraka, baraka' as she does so.*

Zuya What is she doing?

Akila Cleansing the room from the jinni.

Zuya *Majnouna!*

Naha DON'T call me mad – you should be thanking me for saving you all from the bad spirits.

She continues her task.

Fatah Hold on – how are we going to get these stories to her? To Scheherazade?

Wadiha You leave that to me.

Fatah But how?

Akila Just write, little one. Come on – write . . . ALL OF YOU.

They set to action.

Akila We need lots of stories. Lots and lots. Don't worry how we get the stories to her – just hope that he likes them – pray she tells them well – that she lasts another night . . . or it'll be us next . . .

They all set to writing ferociously as though their life depends on it, as it does. Music signifies the passing of time. Perhaps there is a tally on the wall or the floor in chalk to denote how many nights have passed.

Five Nights

Naha I'm tired.

Akila Think about Scheherazade – think about how tired she must be. Telling him stories all night long, then all day coming up with new ones . . . well, reading ours and learning them . . .

Naha She's not just telling stories either . . .

Fatah What's he like, the King?

Akila What do you think he's like?

Fatah Oh I don't know . . .

Zuya Tall.

Naha Dark.

Wadiha Handsome.

Akila Like all Arab men.

Zuya Or hairy.

Wadiha Spitty.

Naha Plotting.

Zuya Evil.

Wadiha Religious.

Akila Like all Arab men.

Fatah I prefer the first version.

Akila Fine, stick with that.

Fatah But I want to know what he's really like. What will it BE like with him? Will I like it?

Zuya IF you end up in his bedroom and IF you end up in his bed, under his weight, all you'll be thinking about is the fact that dessert is your red, red blood splashed all over the room.

Fatah *runs to the door in fear trying to open it but it is locked fast.*

Fatah I. NEED. MY. BLOOD. I. WANT. TO. LIVE.

Naha *goes to her and stops her.*

Naha Then put your imagination into something useful, *ya binti*. Put it into a story. You haven't shared even one yet,

Fatah I have got one – I just don't want to /

Akila *gets a candle – lights it and hands it to her.*

Akila *Yulla*, don't be shy.

Fatah But what if it's not good enough?

Zuya Be brave. The writer has to be fearless – the Hakawati is a warrior – *yulla*.

Fatah *slowly, fearfully takes a deep breath and haltingly begins, but grows in confidence.*

Fatah There once was a very poor farmer who lived in a small house with his wife. They had one *dunum* at the back to grow vegetables and a small yard at the front with a lemon tree on either side.

Now the Farmer worked hard as most do getting up early and working till dusk. Every night he was so tired that as soon as his head hit the pillow he fell into a deep sleep. That is until one night when he has a strange dream. He describes it to his wife the next morning: 'In my dream,' he says, 'I had to go to Damascus Gate in Jerusalem – I didn't know why, just that something would happen there that was vitally important.' 'How strange,' says the wife, and the two think nothing more of it and go on with their day. But the next night the Farmer has the same dream, and the night after, and the night after that, until his wife tells him that this is obviously a sign – he should go to the gate, and see what happens.

So the next day he packs some bread, zaatar and water and trudges the long road to Jerusalem. It takes him two whole days to get there, and when he does he goes and waits by the gate. He waits and waits all day but nothing happens. So he goes and finds somewhere to sleep for the night under a tree, and the next day he goes back to his spot by the gate, again nothing happens that day. On the third day when he takes up post once more, he's approached by a shopkeeper from across the road. The woman says to him: 'I've been watching you these three days just stood here by the gate – do you mind me asking you what you are doing – I'm curious.' The Farmer tells the Shopkeeper his story and at the end the woman is laughing loudly at him, 'You are a stupid man,' she says, 'you've wasted three working days to come here and do nothing, that'll teach you to follow your dreams. Where would we be if we all did that – for example, I keep having a dream about treasure buried in the yard of a house between two lemon trees.' Before the woman had finished speaking, the Farmer had scurried away leaving the Shopkeeper puzzled and scratching her head, "What a strange man," she thought.

Beat.

Fatah *blows out the candle.*

Fatah   I'd love to see Al Quds – Damascus Gate . . . I've never even left this city . . .

Beat.

Fatah   My *teta* used to tell me that story.

Wadiha   It means follow your dreams . . .

Fatah   If only I was allowed to go there.

Akila   Shhh, don't spoil the mood . . . the afterglow of the story – it's nice.

Naha   What is this – nursery time?

Akila   Respect the Hakawati.

Naha   I thought we were going to excite, arouse, so far it's all been Mother bloody Goose. They're sweet stories and everything but don't you think we need something a bit more. You know. X-rated.

Wadiha   Go on then – what's your brilliant X-rated story – oh great Hakawati.

Naha   I can't just pull one out of my ass.

Wadiha   Then don't be a critic. If you don't write the stories, you don't get to criticise. That's how it should always be.

Akila It doesn't work like that. Everyone has an opinion. Whether you want it or not. And the problem with telling stories is every hmar thinks he can do it. If you cook something they don't like they're polite and they nod. They know the effort that goes into making food. But stories. They think it's no work at all. That anyone can do it. So they refuse to keep their fat mouths shut. 'I didn't believe it', 'He would never do that', 'She should have left him – that would be a better ending'. Did I ask for their opinion? NO. Do they share it with me? Of course.

Beat. while she fumes.

Naha Well now there's only one person whose opinion matters. THE KING. And, Wadiha – I think YOU have a story for him don't you?

Wadiha Well . . .

Naha Oh, you do – one that will tickle his turban and caress his kaftan . . .

Akila *hands her a lit candle, but* **Wadiha** *looks stubbornly at* **Naha***.*

Wadiha I don't know if I'm ready to tell it. Out loud.

Akila Then I will tell it for you –

She indicates for **Wadiha** *to give her the paper she has written the story on and takes the candle, then reads it out loud.***

Akila OK so gather near, my sisters, and let me tell you the truth about love and desire. This is about a woman. She loved a young man who loved her back since they were teenagers. Their love for each other was strong like a ball of steel. No matter how much you hit or threw the ball, it remained unchanged.

When her family wanted her to marry a relative, she went on hunger strike. And when the family of her beloved tried to force him into marrying his rich relative, he stayed in bed and stopped talking.

They both remained in that state until their families accepted their love and allowed them to marry.

They spent their honeymoon eating lamb and duck and pounced on each other until they fell asleep. They were stuck together like an orange and its navel. She was the soil that wants to be watered and watered and he was like the waterfall wanting to gush and gush without pause.

Naha Gushing. Wonderful.

Akila (*reading*) Days and months were spent like this, with both living in a perpetual honeymoon. But the seas were calling him and he obeyed. He wanted to travel to all corners of the world and mix with different people like the merchants he saw in the markets. They seemed so dignified and self-assured. Her ambitious husband, rode the boats that traversed the seas. Trading, selling, negotiating, returning laden with coins and jewels that he would spread beneath her feet. She would show gratitude for his gifts even though all she wanted to do was to take him in her arms and banish the loneliness she felt during his absence.

She woke up one morning when he was away with a lot of energy and headed to the market. She bought apples and grapes as she smiled at the sun and everything around her, even to the blond youth who, as soon as her smile reached him, started following her from alley to alley and shop to shop. Every time she turned, he was behind her.

Her heart fluttered and sang. She entered a women-only bathhouse and the steam of the hot water whispered in her pores 'You long for a man, you long for a man'. She left to find the young man waiting for her, and walked home in a hurry. She took out the key and opened the door. She left it open. The youth entered and every part of him was pleading and begging: his eyes, mouth, arms, abdomen, thighs. She let her body taste the forbidden wine of his lips instead of the vinegar that had settled in her soul during her husband's absence.

Twenty days were spent in this bliss. And every time she knelt to pray, she thanked God for sending her this soul mate. She became infatuated with the youth so much that when her husband returned from his travels she wished the waves had overwhelmed his boat and drowned him. She began to count the seconds until his next trip.

Her desire for the blond boy made her think of meeting him during the day when her husband would visit the market to sell or buy but she refrained from taking this crazy chance. God answered her prayers because a messenger arrived inviting her husband to a dinner at the house of Sindbad. Her heart danced and swayed with happiness because while he was gone she would meet the blond youth.

When her husband was about to leave she said she would accompany him in order to see Sindbad's famous palace from outside. In reality she wanted to make sure her husband was inside the palace so she could hurry to her blond youth and dissolve in his arms without worry.

One of the palace guards armed with a sword approached her and asked if she wanted to enter the palace. She thanked him, following her husband with her eyes as he walked through the palace's orchard. She was relieved when her husband disappeared from sight and she turned and almost flew like a butterfly.

Running away from the guard, to her house she saw the blond boy waiting for her, weeping. Indoors together she in turn cried until their bodies began to converse with frantic breaths and kisses.

Suddenly they heard a knock at the door which terrified them. 'My husband must have come back,' and in the blink of an eye she hid the youth in the basement. Then she opened the door only to find the Palace Guard in front of her. He entered and pounced on her as if she was freshly made dough and he was the oven giving her heat. She swelled and rose with desire and forgot about the entire world. They both let out mighty screams as they climaxed. His was like the roar of a lion and hers like the song of a blackbird. They remained thus until they heard yet another knock on the door.

Was this the knocking of the blond youth who heard their orgasm from the floor below? No. It was her husband whose cough she recognised. Her heart skipped a beat but her mind became alert. She whispered to the Guard to start shouting and swearing and threatening to throw her in jail, telling him to say 'Where is he? Where is he?' The Guard didn't understand why but when the woman knelt down and tossed her hair and began wailing he did as she had told him. He shouted and insulted her in his highest voice, making sure her husband had heard all this. Then, when he entered, the Guard put his sword back in his scabbard and left quickly, full of fake anger.

Her husband rushed to his wife and helped her up asking 'What happened?' As he hugged her to him. She told him how she was feeding the hungry cats outside the house as usual when a young man appeared, crying and begging her for help. 'Help me, madam, someone wants to kill me for no good reason. There is a palace guard who falsely accuses me of stealing. He wants to take me to prison.' She felt sorry for the youth and hid him in the basement. She added that the Guard kicked down the door and entered without permission, 'he took out his sword and questioned me about the youth. And every time I said he wasn't here, the Guard threatened and insulted me. Until God and his angels sent you to save me.'

'Don't worry. God finds a way,' murmured her husband as he hugged her. He praised her bravery and valour. He hurried down to the basement and released the youth who flew out of the house like a fiery arrow.

The woman was so relieved and overjoyed and her lungs clapped like two hands after holding her breath for so long. And when she went to bed she thought that what happened was truly a miracle: First, she saved herself. Second, she is still married and her husband loves her. Third, she succeeded in getting rid of the youth without him realising that the Guard broke into her house and her heart. This, my sisters is the story of the woman, as she told it to me word by word. She begged me not to file her story under the category of womanly deceit because desire is not deceitful. We are born with it and it grows to complete our hearts. Desire and love go hand in hand. What she did was not deceitful but good and blessed. She said:

'I saved myself from the vengeance of my husband who if he had known the truth, would have killed me.

And I saved the youth from my husband,

and I saved my husband from the sword of the palace Guard,

and I saved the Guard from scandal,

and in so doing I saved myself from deprivation and longing.'

Akila *blows out the candle.*

Fatah   It's beautiful.

Akila   Erotic.

Naha   She's a goer!

Akila   It's clever – the way it excuses her behaviour in the end.

Beat.

Zuya It's a bit. I dunno – read out.

Wadiha Because she read it out.

Akila Literary you mean, it's a bit literary.

Fatah But it's still sexy.

Naha I got wet with all that rising dough and ovens talk.

Fatah NAHA!

Naha What? It's true.

Akila But remember Scheherazade's not reading it – she's acting. Writer performer. She will improvise a bit.

Fatah She won't learn it by heart – say it the way Wadiha wrote it?

Naha She'll tell the story but it won't be exactly the same.

Fatah But in *my* story about Damascus Gate it's my words. I don't want her to paraphrase. I put them in that order for a reason . . .

Akila You can't be so precious, little writer. Actors will always take ownership of the words. It's fine if they're good. They make the writer look even better.

Fatah What if they're not good?

Akila Well Scheherazade can't be too bad, she's keeping him entertained.

Naha For now.

Beat.

Zuya I don't believe it. That story. All the affairs. That woman. It doesn't ring true.

Naha *and* **Wadiha** *share a look.*

Akila Does that matter? Why does it have to be true?

Zuya It doesn't, but we have to BELIEVE it's possible otherwise what's the point?

Naha And you didn't believe it?

Zuya Not really – and I'd like it more if I did.

Wadiha Believe it. It's true. All of it.

Zuya No way.

Wadiha I know.

Beat.

Wadiha It's my story.

Zuya What happened to your husband then?

Wadiha Drowned.

The woman all seem surprised

Fatah   And that guard in the story? Is HE one of the ones?

She indicates outside the room. **Wadiha** *nods.*

Fatah   So that's how we are getting the stories to Scheherazade!

Time passes. Music may signify this.

Fifty Nights

The women are all writing. **Fatah** *suddenly tears up the paper she's writing on.*

Zuya   What is it?

Fatah   Rubbish – it's all rubbish. I don't want to do this anymore. I want to go home.

She jumps up and rushes to the door trying to open it and get out.

Fatah   I can't breathe! I want air – light – I need to get out of this this this – coffin! LET ME OUT LET ME OUT LET ME OUT LET ME OUT LET ME OUT!

Zuya *goes to her and puts her hand over her mouth.*

Zuya   SHHHH.

Wadiha   We mustn't annoy them.

Naha   Be good girls.

Akila   Do as we're told.

Zuya   Not kick.

Wadiha   Scratch.

Akila   Punch.

Zuya   Bite.

Naha   Lie still.

Akila   Pretend that we are already dead.

Wadiha   They like that.

Fatah   Why? WHY DO THEY LIKE THAT? We're alive . . . WE'RE STILL ALIVE IN HERE.

She rushes from **Zuya** *and the others and bangs on the door, the others try to stop her, then suddenly a banging comes in response. It is the noise of a hundred swords bashing on the outside of the room in which the women are trapped. It is loud – overpowering – threatening, terrifying.*

Fatah *screams,* **Naha** *holds her – they all huddle together in fear until the noise abates.*

Fatah (*quietly*)   They'll forget about us and we will die. That – that woman won't remind anyone we are here – she needs us – needs our stories and we will be stuck here forever.

Naha   No, no, little one, don't let your mind go there. That's a bad place.

Akila   What we need is a good story – cheer us up. Come on, ZUYA. A strong story – about winning . . .

Zuya   I have one – about a fox but – no it's not quite right for now . . .

Akila   Wadiha?

Wadiha *shakes her head.*

Naha   OK, OK . . . Mashi. I have a good story. Something cheeky to take us away . . . so.

Akila *hands her a lit candle as she begins to talk. In* **Naha**'s *story the women should take on some of the speaking roles to dramatise it.*

Naha   This happened in a hammam in a small village outside of Fustat, so far away from here but wallah I have good sources that every word is true.

I heard it from my cousin Esraa' who heard from Um Mohammed who heard it from Nour, Salah Nasrallah's daughter who heard it from Um Soliman who swore that she heard it from Um Hakim who heard it from her daughter's friend, the hammam masseuse herself, so it must be true.

Zuya   Just get on with it.

Naha   OK, so . . . Marra there was this woman, Safiya, she was the local butcher's wife. Khalas she was at the age where her children were grown and married themselves, and her wedding bed was a bit . . . cold. Safiya was a woman of pride and always managed to get what she wanted, except for her husband's attention. It had been years since she felt that man's touch. She tried everything to seduce him, putting her hair up and lining her eyes, wearing revealing clothes to bed, a couples of times she even climbed on top of him only to find him fast asleep. It was useless. And so she gave up and accepted the life God had provided her.

But then . . .

One Thursday she goes to the hammam as usual, to bath and clean her hair and relax. She arrives, she washes herself and then decides to get a massage, she calls the girl over and the girl starts to massage her. She starts with the shoulders, and works her way down. After a few minutes Safiya is passed out, completely asleep, the girl tries to wake her but it's useless so she leaves.

Hours later, they're getting ready to close the hammam, almost no one is left. Safiya begins to feel something . . . down there. She wakes up to see this head in between her thighs, and she's wondering who could it be, she sits up against the edge to check that no one is there and closes her eyes, pressing herself against the head. Urging it on. Safiya has been waiting for this, waiting for this sensation, waiting for this hotness, for . . . this . . . moment . . . and FINALLY! She does everything in her power not to scream too loud and collapses back on the floor.

BOOM! As she hits the ground, CRACK, she feels something break under her.

She quickly recovers.

Stands up.

Looks down at the floor.

And . . .

It's a puppy! She had fallen on to the puppy that had given her the most intense pleasure she's ever felt, crushed it. Snapped its neck.

Safiya Oh no!

Naha Safiya then notices the tag.

Safiya Yeeeeeeh it's the King's puppy! *Ya lahwiiii!* He's going to kill me! Safiya what did you do? Keda you get yourself killed for an orgasm? What am I going to do? Wallah you deserve to die ya Safiya you fool!

Naha At this point Um Hassanein, the owner of the hammam, comes in to tell Safiya that it's time to leave.

Um Hassanein Closing time! *Yalla*, finish up, it's time to leave, I don't care if there's still soap in your – oh dear God above! What's this? Why is there a dead dog in here?

Safiya You're asking me? What kind of establishment are you running here? Letting in dogs . . . letting – letting people drag dead dogs in – I want my money back!

Um Hassanein How do I know this is not your dog?

Safiya My d – Well . . . I . . . Um Hassanein you know I don't own a dog!

Um Hassanein How do I know you didn't sneak one in anyway?

Safiya Because . . . It's the King's dog.

Um Hassanein THE KING'S DOG?

Safiya Yes

Um Hassanein Safiya! Did you kill the King's puppy??

Safiya I . . . Well . . . Yes.

Um Hassanein Safiya!

Safiya I didn't mean to! I – it just happened.

Um Hassanein Why are you killing puppies in my hammam?!

Safiya I didn't kill – it was by mistake!

Um Hassanein How? How did it happen?

Safiya I fell. You know how I told you that the steps here are too slippery, well I slipped and fell on top of it.

Um Hassanein He's going to kill you.

Safiya It's your hammam, he's going to kill us both.

Naha The women then take a moment to look at each other. They both think about the time someone picked flowers from the Royal garden without permission. It did not end well.

Safiya You need to help me, Um Hassanein, there must be a way to fix this.

Um Hassanein OK, come with me, I think I know a jinn that can help us.

Safiya Um Hassanein . . . remember last time?

Um Hassanein Don't worry, my dear, this is a different one, this one lives in the sewers.

Safiya The sewers??

Um Hassanein Trust me.

Naha So the women head towards the sewers to the jinn. They arrive at a hole in the ground, and Umm Hassanein pulls the cover away and yells

Um Hassanein JINNI! MAY YOU HELP ME OVER THE EARTH AND MAY IT BRING YOU PEACE UNDER IT.

Naha They wait for a bit. When they don't receive a response, Um Hassanein tries again.

Um Hassanein JINNI! JINNI! ARE YOU DEAF? I SAID MAY YOU HELP ME OVER THE EARTH –

Jinni OK! OK! I HEARD YOU THE FIRST TIME. I'M COMING!

Um Hassanein What's his problem?

Naha And out of the hole the jinn appears, unlike the jinn of the lamp or the fields, this jinn looks fragile and old. He moves slowly and has a large frown amidst a million wrinkles on his face. He reaches the top, he looks at the women, then glances at the bag containing the puppy. He raises his frown slightly.

Jinni How may I help you women?

Naha Um Hassanein pushes Safiya forward.

Safiya We . . . I mean . . . I – we were wondering if you could help us?

Jinni Yes ... Help you with what?

Safiya You see ... We were in the hammam ... And I was just having a massage, which is something I like to do before I clean my –

Um Hassanein Safiya killed the King's puppy.

Safiya I didn't kill it! I fell on it.

Jinni What kind of person kills a puppy?

Safiya It was an accident!

Jinni What do you want me to do about it?

Um Hassanein Fix it.

Jinni Fix what exactly?

Um Hassanein I don't know! The puppy, the situation, something has to be fixed. Make sure I don't lose my business and Safiya here doesn't lose her head.

Jinni Hmm ... This looks like it's going to be a hassle.

Um Hassanein Pffff ... Come on jinni, what do you want in exchange for this favour?

Naha The jinn thinks for a moment, then looks at the women and says

Jinni OK I can help you. If you suck my cock.

Um Hassanein Eeeehhhh!

Wadiha What is it with you and cock sucking?

Naha (*continuing regardless*) Umm Hassanein smacks the jinn on the back of head

Um Hassanein *Fi eih?* What's wrong with you? Give us something realistic to do! Suck your cock eih? What cock? Is this a joke?

Jinni Alright, alright, woman! No need for all this. It was worth a try.

Um Hassanein Worth a try? I'll tell you what's worth a try –

Safiya Um Hassanein!

Um Hassanein The things I have to deal with! At my age! Allah, what have I done to deserve this? *Ya rab* give me the strength –

Safiya Um Hassanein, please!

Jinni Yes control yourself, woman!

Um Hassanein What did you say to me, you dirty old –

Safiya Please! We don't have time for this.

Jinni Listen to your friend, do you want my help or not?

Um Hassanein Fine. I'm done. For now.

Safiya OK, jinni, tell us.

Jinni Alright. So. I will help you, in exchange though I want a moment from you.

Um Hassanein What?

Safiya You want . . .

Jinni A moment. I want a moment from you.

Um Hassanein Jinni, no funny business.

Jinni I'm being serious. Yaani, I ask you to suck my cock you say no, I ask for a moment you tell me no funny business. Wallahi, I should leave you both to die. He's going to turn you into dog food and feed you to his new puppy, I've been here a long time, I know how this man thinks. Mark my words –

Safiya OK, OK! Khalas! You'll have a moment, whatever that means. Now tell us what to do.

Jinni I can make a new puppy. In order to do this, I need you to bring me three things. Energy, warmth and curiosity.

Safiya Energy, warmth and curiosity.

Jinni Yes.

Safiya How are we supposed to do that?

Jinni You know how this goes, I've told you what I need, it's up to you to find it.

Naha The women look at each other. How are they supposed to bring energy, warmth and curiosity? It made little sense, and it's not like that they had a lot of time to think about it either! It was only a few hours before sunset.

And so feeling a bit discouraged, and very confused, they set off.

As they were walking through the village, each deep in thought, a man stopped them for directions. He was carrying a big bag on his back. He was wearing a foreign hat and several objects around his neck.

Man 1 I'm sorry, I'm looking for somewhere to eat and sleep.

Naha Safiya started to answer his question.

Safiya There's an inn –

Naha But Um Hassanein sniffed an opportunity . . .

Um Hassanein Where are you from?

Man 1 Oh, I am an explorer, I've come from the East. I've been travelling for so long, I've forgotten where I have begun this journey.

Um Hassanein So why do you keep moving?

Man 1 There is so much to see in the world! I can't stop until I have seen every bit of it, tasted every food, drunk from every river.

Um Hassanein That's very nice. How do you know where to go?

Man 1 I don't.

Um Hassanein And you've crossed the desert without knowing where you're going??

Man 1 Haha, no, I use this bit of technology.

Naha He points to one of the objects around his neck.

Man 1 This is a compass, it helps me orient myself and thus I can keep discovering new places, new people –

Um Hassanein Very interesting. The inn is around the corner from here, come, we'll walk you.

Naha The women begin to walk with the foreigner, Safiya senses that something is up and whispers.

Safiya Um Hassanein, what are you doing?

Um Hassanein That compass. We need that.

Safiya What?

Um Hassanein Curiosity. That's curiosity, how else would a foreigner end up in this part of the world?

Safiya You want to borrow the man's compass?

Um Hassanein Borrow, take, something like that.

Safiya Um Hassanein!

Um Hassanein Shhhh.

Safiya If we take it then the man will be lost!

Um Hassanein And if we don't then we'll be dead!

Safiya But he needs it to travel.

Um Hassanein He can just stay here, might do him good to stay put for a bit.

Safiya He's an explorer! He'll be out in the desert by tomorrow, how will be find his way?

Um Hassanein Let him use the stars, the old-fashioned way.

Naha At this point they arrive at the inn. They say goodbye to the man, but wait outside.

Um Hassanein Do you see him?

Safiya He's having dinner now.

Um Hassanein Is he wearing the compass?

Safiya No.

Um Hassanein OK, let's go!

Naha Quickly they climb through his room's window, grab the man's compass and continue their walk. As they are walking, full of excitement at finding something to take to the jinn, Safiya suddenly trips.

Safiya Hey!

Naha It's a man sleeping in the road.

Safiya Sorry! I didn't see you there!

Man 2 Watch where you're going, woman!

Um Hassanein OK, she said, sorry! Why are you sleeping in the middle of the road, why don't you go sleep in a chicken coop like everyone usually does? Stupid people.

Naha As Um Hassanein shouts at this man, she notices that he is sleeping under a blanket which is why they didn't notice him to begin with. Immediately she gets an idea.

Um Hassanein Safiya! The blanket.

Safiya What?

Um Hassanein His blanket! Warmth!

Safiya Um Hassanein what is wrong with you? This man has no home.

Um Hassanein How do you know that? He looks like Ali ibn Bakr's son, he's probably been kicked out.

Safiya The blanket keeps him warm!

Um Hassanein Who needs warmth in this weather?

Safiya He's sleeping in the street!

Um Hassanein He shouldn't be upsetting his father then.

Safiya We don't even know if it's Ali.

Um Hassanein *Yalla,* he's going back to sleep, not even using the blanket properly, he won't notice it's gone I promise you.

Naha Um Hassanein sneaks up behind the man who had already fallen fast asleep, only half covered. She grabs the edge of the blanket and slowly pulls it off him. The man stirs but doesn't wake up.

Um Hassanein Let's go before he wakes up again!

Naha And they walk off quickly.

Safiya   You're going to hell and you're taking me with you.

Um Hassanein   *Estakhfarallah!* Why are you being so dramatic Safiya? I'll bring him a new blanket tomorrow, I'll even go chat to his father.

Safiya   You don't know its Ali!

Um Hassanein   It might as well be. Like his father would know the difference!

Safiya   We're stealing now. Stealing!

Naha   As they stood there arguing, suddenly a boy runs between them screaming in joy, holding a kite. He lets go and the kite flies in the air. The boy continues running, looking up, eyes sparkling with excitement.

Without even thinking about it, Safiya then grabs the kite's string and snaps it.

Safiya   RUN!

Naha   Before the boy could even process what happened, the women run back towards the jinn's sewer holding the compass, the blanket and the flying kite.

They arrive a few minutes before sunset.

Um Hassanein   JINNI! WE'RE HERE! JINNI WE GOT THE THREE THINGS! JINNI WHERE ARE YOU? MAY YOU HELP ME OVER THE EARTH –

Jinni   ALRIGHT! STOP SHOUTING! YOU DON'T HAVE TO SAY THAT EVERY TIME!

Um Hassanein   But isn't that the way to summon you?

Jinni   I prefer not to use the term 'summon'.

Um Hassanein   So what 'term' do you use?

Jinni   I prefer –

Safiya   It doesn't matter! We're here, we have the three things.

Um Hassanein   Warmth.

Naha   Um Hassanein hands over the blanket.

Um Hassanein   Curiosity.

Naha   She hands over the compass.

Safiya   And energy.

Naha   Safiya hands over the kite. The jinn looks at the objects. The woman can't tell if he looks impressed or disgusted under all those wrinkles.

Jinni   Very well. Give me a minute.

Naha   The jinn then disappears into the sewer. A couple of minutes pass and he emerges holding a tiny, fluffy bundle.

Jinni Have a look, does it look like the one you killed?

Safiya Jinni! What's this? His mouth is huge! Have you ever seen a puppy with teeth bigger than its paws?

Jinni You're right. I thought it looked a bit strange. One second, I'll be right back.

Naha The jinn disappears for a minute, by now the sun has set and the guards can be heard looking for the puppy. The jinn appears again.

Jinni What about now?

Naha Safiya looks at the dog, and relief floods her.

Safiya Yes! It's identical! Oh Jinni thank you!

Um Hassanein *Alhamdulillah!* Thank you God, for getting us out of this mess!

Jinni I got you out of this mess.

Um Hassanein Yes! Thank you, Jinni, for not being full of shit.

Jinni I can keep this puppy, you know? I've always wanted –

Um Hassanein No! Sorry, Jinni. Thank you, thank you for everything, thank you for saving us, thank you for being so gracious, so kind, thank you for your wisdom, without you we would not be here right now, without you –

Jinni Yes, yes, now it's time for you to pay me back.

Um Hassanein Yes of,course, anything!

Safiya Except for . . . well you know.

Jinni We had a deal. I want a moment from you.

Safiya Yes, yes. How do I give you a moment?

Jinni You humans always find ways to connect, even for just a moment. That's all I ask for, I want you to give me one of those moments.

Naha The women look at one another, they're both at a loss at what to do. The guards' calls are getting louder. Safiya thinks about the moments she's had that have stayed with her, the day her daughter smiled for the first time, the gifts a boy used to leave by her window, the time she swam in the Nile in the middle of the night, the first time she heard a song sung by her grandmother . . . (**Safiya** *begins to hum a tune.*)

That's it, she thought. I can give him that moment. And so Safiya stands in front of the jinn and sings him the song, a lullaby. (*The humming becomes singing.*) She couldn't remember the words perfectly, she wasn't entirely sure of the melody but the more she sang, the stronger the memory became and the memory filled her, and filled that space between her and the jinn. Soon she forgot that this was a deal, that it wasn't her grandmother singing, that it was her voice. At the end of the song, the jinn thanked her, handed the puppy to her and quietly went back into his sewer.

Um Hassanein Well done, Safiya. I really thought we were done for. *Yalla alhamdulillah.* God has protected us and I have a feeling he will continue to do so.

Safiya *Yalla*, let's go home. It's been a long day.

Naha And so the women head home in silence. Um Hassanein's mind full of thoughts about how she needed to cleanse her hammam from bad spirits, she was going to need to strike a bargain though, because the local exorcist is always trying to rip people off (the bastard). And Safiya's mind, trying to push out those gnawing thoughts, those quiet thoughts that the puppy maybe didn't look quite as identical as she thought, something deep inside is telling there was something about the eyes, maybe it was the light but it looked like maybe, just maybe, this dog had one blue eye and one green . . . No, she must have imagined it . . .

Beat – she blows out the candle.

Naha Now that's a story . . .

Fatah The dog – licked her – is that even – ?

Wadiha I liked it.

Zuya Me too.

Fatah And the jinni was so – ergh.

Naha It made you forget though, didn't it?

Akila For those few minutes you forgot you were stuck in here. You were transported. All your worries gone.

Fatah It's true.

Naha So let's keep magicking, ladies. It's our only hope. The only way out of here. OK, beauty? No more attempted escapes, ah? We need to keep the guards on side.

Fatah *nods but still looks longingly at the doors.*

Zuya *starts spitting in the corners of the room, chanting 'baraka baraka baraka'.*

Naha I thought you didn't believe in that.

Zuya It can't hurt. Besides it's a better way to cleanse the place than my bitch of a mother's.

Akila What did she do?

Zuya Spray us all with her piss.

Fatah Did it work?

Zuya I'm in here, aren't I? But we need all the help we can get . . .

Naha *gives her a look.*

Zuya (*to* **Naha**) We don't have an endless supply of stories, do we? And when we run out . . .

Naha gives her a look indicating **Fatah** – *she doesn't want her upset again.* **Zuya** *resumes her task. The others all set to writing. Music signifies the passing of time. Perhaps there is a tally on the wall or the floor in chalk to denote how many nights have passed.*

100 Nights

The women have all drifted off while working. **Wadiha** *is gone. Suddenly* **Fatah** *wakes up.*

Fatah   She's gone! Wake up – wake up everyone – we're doomed – Scheherazade has failed.

Zuya   How do you know?

Fatah   Wadiha has gone. She was next.

Naha *wails, crying out in fear in Arabic, she wasn't expecting this, she can't keep up a brave face –* **Fatah** *runs to comfort her, shocked at this reaction.*

Zuya   Stop it . . . Don't worry about Wadiha – her dancing will entrance him. For now.

Fatah   But what if it doesn't?

Zuya   Then I'll go next and kill the bastard.

Akila   You're all talk. You've never killed a man.

Zuya   Why was I in prison then?

Naha   You were in prison?

Zuya   You're surprised?

Naha   Not really.

Fatah   What happened?

Zuya   I don't tell that story.

Akila   Scheherazade has failed. The great Hakawati has overstretched herself – we are all going to die because she thought she was better than she is.

Zuya   Silly bitch – she gave us all false hope but deep down I knew she was useless – a waste of time – lazy – self-centred – vain – nothing special,

Naha   a false goddess,

Zuya   like the useless fucking *asfoura*.

Fatah   Sparrow?

Zuya   It's a stupid story my lying cow of a mother used to tell me.

Akila Tell it – it might calm us.

Zuya I don't want to.

Akila Tell it.

Zuya NO!

All TELL IT!

Fatah We need it . . . please . . .

Akila hands her the candle.

Zuya OH FINE! There was once a sparrow who thought very highly of himself – he thought his pathetic tweets were the dulcet tones of a nightingale – that his dun feathers could outshine a peacock. He didn't realise what a dull, scrawny, pathetic, useless thing he was. One day he witnessed something astonishing as he was perched on the branch of a tree near some grazing sheep – an eagle suddenly flew down and grabbed one of the animals with her talons and flew off with it. The sparrow was beside himself – What a feat! What a meal! How bold and outrageous. What daring!

He was also very turned on. He decided he wanted this amazing eagle for himself. For his wife. So he started following her around places. Watching her every move. And at last he found her nest. He waited till nightfall when she was asleep and then he flew down to try and make love to her. The eagle felt a strange movement in the nest and cocked an eye to see what was happening. And there was this little sparrow jiggling about.

'What are you doing?' she asked. 'Seducing you,' said the sparrow. 'Seducing me? I'm the queen of the birds and you are a scrawny little worm-eating embarrassment. Get lost before I crush you with my beak and feed you to my chicks.'

The sparrow was miffed. 'I'll show that eagle', he thought. 'I'll bring her a delicious sheep for her dinner, then she'll see my worth. Then she'll want me.'

So the next day, stupid sparrow headed to try and catch a sheep for the eagle's dinner. He flew up high over the flock as he'd seen her do, and chose the largest animal he could spot, then flew down, his little feet outstretched to grab it. Of course he'd gone for the biggest beast of all – the ram whose coat was matted and dirty and his little sparrow feet got tangled, so not only could he not lift the thing he was now enmeshed – trapped and unable to fly away. The shepherd witnessed all this and was bemused. He went to the sparrow and freed it only to place it in a cage and give it as a gift to his daughter. And that was it for the sparrow. Trapped in a cage of his own making because of his arrogance and lack of humility.

She blows out the candle.

Fatah Your *mother* told you that story???

Zuya Yup. To stop me going to school. Bitch. She said deep down she knew I was useless – a waste of time – lazy – self-centred – nothing special . . . but she didn't give me a chance to be anything. She'd already made up her mind . . .

Fatah How could she be so cruel?

Zuya I reminded her of my father . . .

There is a round of applause from **Wadiha** *who has returned and been listening to all this. She carries a tray of fruit and a letter.*

Fatah You're back!

Akila What happened?

Zuya We thought he had carved you up.

Naha That Scheherazade had overstretched herself . . .

Wadiha So did I. While you were all asleep one of the guards – not mine – a different one – he woke me and led me out of the room. I thought my time had come. That the sickle blade of death was hanging over my head. I was ready to do my final dance.

She starts to sway and move. Music rises. We think she is going to dance to an Arabic song. Anticipation builds – she sways more – but then she stops as suddenly as the music does.

Wadiha But no. The guard was calling to give me these.

She signifies what she is holding.

Fatah What is it?

Wadiha A platter – and a letter.

Zuya Who from?

Wadiha The woman herself.

Fatah Scheherazade?

Akila What does it say?

Naha Probably a thank you.

Wadiha See for yourself.

She hands the note to **Akila**, *the other women gather round and read over her shoulder. They are incredulous.*

Fatah I can't – believe it –

Akila Of all the nerve.

Naha Cheek. That's what it is.

Fatah 'Coarse and mundane at the same time, stories not fit for anyone's ears let alone a King –.'

Zuya Ungrateful little *sharmuta*.

Fatah 'Enjoy this – it'll be your last meal if you don't start weaving yarns that enchant and delight him – he's not just a cock.'

Akila *tears the paper into a hundred pieces and throws it up into the air like confetti. They all watch the finality of it.*

Akila We stop. Leave Scheherazade to it. Let's see how she gets on without our help.

Fatah But what will we do?

Naha While we wait? For the inevitable.

Fatah I need the stories . . . or I'll go . . . [mad]

Zuya Need?

Fatah Of course. It's my only escape.

Naha She's right – we must keep on. Doesn't the King like our stories?

Wadiha The guard says he hears him roaring with laughter – or groaning with ecstasy.

Naha That might not be the stories . . .

Zuya We should write back – tell her to f-[uck off].

Fatah No. We should respond with a story.

Zuya About what?

Akila No way. I'm not having anyone talk about my writing like that. Who does she think she is???

Zuya You did say everyone is a critic, aren't you used to it yet? You need thicker skin.

Akila How am I meant to get used it? We writers need gossamer thin skin to let the stories get inside us, but at the same time rhinoceros hide to repel the slings and arrows of these kelbs

Wadiha Wait, wait, listen – like I said the guard listens at the door every night. They all do – love the stories Scheherazade tells. He says the King does too.

Naha Then why write the letter?

Fatah I had a teacher once who always gave me bad grades. As an incentive. Maybe that's what this is.

Zuya Maybe she's having a bad day and wanted to take it out on us?

Akila Fuck the bitch. If she's so high and mighty let's see how she manages on her own.

Zuya She's the sparrow! High and mighty! What happened to gratitude – to sisterhood?

Wadiha Sisterhood. Ha. It's a myth. Haven't you heard the story of the Three Women?

Naha Wait – Akila, get the pen, Fatah, the candle.

Akila But I'm not.

Naha The pen! Candle! – Go on, Wadiha.

Fatah hands her the candle.

Wadiha Three single women lived in the countryside, so close they were like sisters.

Naha AKILA – WRITE, go on.

Reluctantly she transcribes.

Wadiha A good-looking bachelor lived nearby. He was a farmer, and owned a lot of land.

Zuya Sounds like a catch, where do I sign up?

Wadiha One day, out walking, the women sat down to rest in his field of courgettes, admiring their girth.

Naha Girth – *mabrouk!*

Wadiha 'What a fine man, with such natural bounty! Imagine the joy of being his wife,' they exclaimed. 'Why, if he asked for my hand,' said the loudest, 'I'd make him a loaf of bread out of a single grain.' 'If he asked to marry me,' said the oldest, 'I'd make him a bowl of soup out of one single bean.' The quietest of the three thought for a minute. 'If I were lucky enough to be his wife' she said, 'I'd give him a daughter so precious, she'd be born with a ruby in her gum and a golden birthmark on her forehead.'

Little did they know that the owner of the land was up a tree, picking apples, and heard every word. Delighted, he proposed to all three and they accepted, overjoyed – 'How wonderful that we shall live together and be like sisters!'

A year passed and the first wife had yet to produce a loaf out of a single grain. The second's bowl of soup, made from a solitary bean, was also not forthcoming, but the third did give birth to a baby girl. The other two delivered her for their friend, it was a long and arduous labour. As they wrenched her from her mother they were dazzled by a bright light, a shining gold birthmark on her forehead. They checked her mouth with dread. Sure enough there was a small ruby nestled in her gum.

'You know what this means for us?' they cried. 'We'll be thrown out on our ears while she and her precious baby get everything.' So they chopped off the baby's little finger, and shoved it, bleeding, into her mother's mouth, while she slept. They gave the child to a travelling merchant woman with strict instructions to bury her alive. Then they screamed as loud as they could in horror. The husband ran in. 'She ate her own child!' they cried, and pointed at the bloody finger in the mother's mouth as evidence. 'Is this true?' he asked. Broken hearted, but with no recollection of what had happened, the poor mother had to concur that it must be. She was banished to the edge of his land, and forced to wear a dog's hide, and herd the goats in the field for the rest of her days.

Meanwhile the old merchant woman took the girl back with her to the forest where she lived and brought her up as her own, for of course she couldn't bring herself to bury a baby alive. She named her Rabia, and the girl grew up, free and happy, wandering around the woods with her animal friends. But the woman was old, and after a mere ten years she found herself at the end of her life. As she lay on her deathbed she told the girl the truth about her mother, her missing finger, and the cruel trick her aunties had played.

Once the old woman had passed away young Rabia set off to find her real mother. She bought herself a fine headscarf in the hope of impressing her, and some beautiful robes to give to her as a present. She took with her on this journey a wolf, a sheep and a cat.

Off she went with her companions, and whomever she passed would cry, '*Ya Allah!* A wolf, a sheep and a cat, and yet they don't fight?' 'Glory be to God!' Rabia would cry back, 'They are animals but capable of loving each other, and yet there once was a mother who ate her own child!' And everyone would reply, 'Really? What a strange tale,' and Rabia would continue.

After some time Rabia arrived at her mother's village. There she met one of the farm hands, who exclaimed, '*Ya Allah!* A wolf, a sheep and a cat, and yet they don't fight?' 'Indeed they don't,' she replied. 'They are animals, but capable of loving each other, and yet there once was a mother who ate her own child!' 'Ah yes . . .' nodded the farm hand. 'I know the woman of whom you speak.'

Rabia begged him to show him where she lived. 'She's in that field right there!' said the farm hand. The girl looked, but all she could see was a dog chasing around after the goats. She looked again and realised, to her horror, that it was a woman, wearing a dog's hide, covered in dust and dirt, running around on all fours.

She went to speak to her. 'Is it true you ate your baby?' 'Apparently so,' nodded the woman with great sorrow, 'although I cannot remember such a horrific deed. I am now rightly condemned to living as a dog in this field.'

Rabia took her mother to the river, encouraged her to wash and gave her the clothes she had brought her. She was transformed. Then she took her mother to the farmer's house. Impressed by such a well-dressed and polite young woman, the farmer invited her in to dine with them. 'I would be delighted,' said Rabia, 'but I insist on bringing a guest.' 'By all means,' said the husband and was stunned to see his third wife, now out of her dog's hide, walking into his house. Neither he nor her two jealous friends wanted to dine with the dog-woman, but none of them could refuse this smart newcomer.

They sat and enjoyed a fine meal. Rabia was a charming dinner guest and kept them all entertained with various tales as they ate. Finally, as they finished their final course of cakes and tea, she told them her last story. The one about the woman whose friends were so jealous of her, they tricked her into believing she had eaten her own baby.

The mother gasped. The two wives nearly choked on their cakes. The husband cried, 'Impossible! Why I saw it with my own eyes – didn't I?' Rabia merely shrugged, and poured them all some more tea. They looked on, eyes wide, as they all noticed her missing finger at the same time.

Rabia looked up at them with a smile, displaying the ruby in her gum. 'Hot in here, isn't it?' she said, and took off her headscarf, dazzling them all with her golden birthmark. Her mother jumped to her feet, embracing her long-lost daughter, weeping tears of joy and gratitude.

The husband banished his two wives to the outer fields, forcing them to wear dog hides and herd goats until such time as they died of exhaustion. 'Come,' he said to his wife and child, 'at last we can be together as a family!'

'You must be joking,' said Rabia. 'After the way you've treated her?' 'She's right,' said the mother. 'You were quick to condemn and swift to punish. You've treated me cruelly for the last ten years. Enjoy your land and your dog-hide covered wives. Me and my girl are going off to start our lives together.'

And with that, the girl and her mother left, busking and dancing their way around the land with their entourage of animals, free as birds.

She blows out the candle.

Beat.

Fatah   I don't want us to wear dog hides.

Akila   Nor do I.

Fatah   I want to be free as birds . . .

Wadiha   Then we are agreed. This is our answer to Scheherazade – this story – we are all in this together. Because these stories are for us – all of us – not just her. Let's make a pact.

She puts her hand to her heart and they all touch it too.

Wadiha   While the hairs continue to grow on our head and we're above the ground not under it – we will write stories to save all our lives – we will stick together. Agreed?

All   Agreed

Fatah   But what if [she betrays us].

Wadiha   No – we can't doubt her – or ourselves. We must keep going . . . *yulla!*

They get back to work with urgency. Time passes.

500 Nights

They are all studiously working away at their stories. **Naha** *paces frustrated.*

Akila Do you HAVE to do that? It's distracting me.

Naha I'm stuck. I don't know what she wants. This – character . . . People always *want* things in stories don't they?

Akila Of course.

Naha How can I put myself in the mind of a young girl who WANTS to marry . . . it's just not me . . . FATAH maybe you can help?

Fatah Me? Naha, I spent my life trying to be a good girl. DO what was expected of me. What *they* wanted. I thought that was the right way to live . . . I never thought about what I wanted. I was so busy pleasing everyone else . . . And now what's going to happen to me . . . us . . . Imagine doing that to all those women, girls.

Zuya Killing us.

Fatah Yes.

Naha He fucks us first.

Wadiha Lucky us.

Fatah He must really hate us all. All women.

Zuya They all do – underneath it all. They don't trust us. You know what my husband once said to me? 'how am I supposed to trust an animal that bleeds every month but doesn't die?'

Akila We don't bleed anymore now though, do we?

Naha That's because we can't see the moon – the sky. He's turned everything upside down. Unnatural.

Fatah Does that mean there will be no more children. Ever. That we are the last?

Zuya Good. No more little bastard dictators running round killing everything.

Fatah No more little girls. I always wanted a daughter . . .

Zuya Why – why the hell would you want a daughter? When the world is the way it is. When we are treated like this. When she would have to endure all we've endured. Better never to have been born.

Beat.

Fatah (*to* **Zuya**) He really said that? About bleeding once a month and not dying?

Wadiha What a charmer . . . They're not all like that.

Zuya The King is. My husband was. But we will get our revenge . . . like the Fox and the Wolf.

Beat. as they look at her expectantly.

Wadiha (*handing her the Hakawatis' lit candle*) *Yulla,* tell it.

Zuya So the fox and the wolf lived together. But it was NOT an easy match. The wolf was physically stronger and that made him the boss of all things in his mind. He bullied all the other animals, was mean and didn't share – he was generally loathed by all but no one had the guts to say anything to him because of his size and vile nature. Then one day the fox gathered all her strength and went to the wolf and warned him – mend your ways. Be kinder. Think of others and most of all stop talking with your fists. In reply the wolf belted the fox, who was knocked clean out. She eventually came round and found herself apologising to the wolf – saying she shouldn't have provoked him. But with every word that came out of her mouth she hated him more and prayed and planned and connived to get her revenge. He would pay for what he had done.

Her opportunity came a few days later when, walking past a farm, she noticed a hole in the fence. She was starving and nearly darted straight through it to the hen house but something – a voice, the clever little voice in her head stopped her – 'Wait,' it said. 'Be cautious – nothing is ever this easy,' and so she carefully approached the fence on her guard and of course her instincts were quite right. There – by the gap in the fence – was a trap. The farmer had dug a hole and covered it with some leaves so he could catch whatever beasts came to steal his chickens. The fox grasped her chance and ran back to the den where the wolf was sleeping. She told him that there was a hole in the fence and that she'd already had a bellyful – surely he'd like a feed too? The greedy wolf didn't need to be asked twice. He bolted to the fence and just as he passed through it fell into the farmer's trap.

At first he was furious with the fox, shouting at her and ordering her to get him out. Then he wheedled – cried – asked for her to fetch his mother who would surely know what to do. He begged – bargained – offered the fox the den all to herself saying if she freed him he would disappear. The fox listened to all this smiling, then she threw her head back and called and screeched and wailed until the farmer and his family were alerted. They ran out to the trap and as they did the fox hid behind a tree watching them as they discovered the wolf, gathered fistfuls of rocks and then threw them at him one by one and they crushed into his loathsome body – breaking his bones, drawing blood from his flesh, stoning him to death.

She blows out the candle.

The women step away from her, a little shocked.

Pause.

Naha So much for a happy ending.

Zuya No one said anything about a happy ending.

Akila It's very – vivid.

Wadiha Violent.

Akila Men are violent.

Zuya Women can be violent too. Life is violent.

Naha You're a widow right?

Zuya How did you guess?

Naha (*backing away from* **Zuya**, *understanding that she has committed violence*) And your husband?

Zuya Got what he deserved. I don't tell that story.

Akila I think you already did.

Zuya What?

Akila Nothing.

Fatah Won't the King think the wolf is him and be angry?

Wadiha Don't worry – no one ever notices themselves in stories. Trust me.

Akila Fatah has a point – whether he recognises himself or not that story is an invitation to violence . . . No. We cannot send it. We cannot send this story to Scheherazade. Get rid of it.

Zuya Who made you the boss?

Akila I'm the writer.

Zuya We all are now. And that took me time. Effort.

Akila It's completely irresponsible. Foxes getting revenge on wolves. It's transparent. But if she was kind – forgave him. Helped him out.

Zuya NO, NO, NO. It's not your story to change.

Fatah You're trying to censor her.

Akila That's a big word for a little girl.

Naha Don't patronise her.

Akila This story will do too much damage. Change the ending or we are not sending it.

Wadiha You're as bad as them. Why can't we win? Why do we have to be veiled – demure – beaten – subdued – why? ITS OUR TURN TO WIN!

Zuya YES!

Akila Because we don't want to provoke a blood thirsty murderer into killing any more people. We are trying to subdue a lion.

Wadiha We are lionesses!

Zuya We will eat him alive! I'll eat you alive!

She approaches **Akila** *ferociously and stands eye to eye with her threateningly. Who will blink first?* **Akila** *doesn't move.*

Beat.

Zuya Fine – give me one of yours.

Akila What?

Zuya I'll change mine but I want to see one of yours – I want to see if I can improve it.

Akila No.

Fatah That's not fair. We are all equal here.

Wadiha It seems some of us are more equal than others.

Akila I'm a professional writer.

Zuya Either you want our stories or not?

Akila Of course I do –

Zuya Then we need to be fair. We all need to have a voice. I'll change mine if you let me change one of yours.

Akila I'm not comfortable with that.

Naha Course not – it's your baby . . .

Zuya Then I'm not comfortable with you censoring mine. You see this.

She pulls a hair from her head and burns it.

And this.

She takes a page of her writing and burns it.

Do you understand? It's the same. You erase my story you erase me.

Akila Of course I understand – but THIS IS NOT A GAME, we are not children – these stories are not for kids. THIS IS LIFE OR DEATH. Keep your story. Tell it when the time is right, but now is not that time.

Zuya But –

Akila Writers have a responsibility.

Zuya To the truth.

Akila There is power in words. Stories. They must be told in the right way and at the right time.

Zuya Who made you the arbiter – the censor?

Naha Leave it, ZUYA.

Zuya (*she swears roundly in Arabic*)   *Que summak sharmuta.*

Fatah We must stick together. Stay unified. Please . . . It's just a story

Zuya It's MY story. And you know what, you CAN'T HAVE IT. I *choose* not to send it, I choose to keep it.

Akila Thank you, ZUYA.

Zuya Fuck you, Akila.

An uneasy return to work. **Naha** *keeps a watch on* **Zuya** *in case she goes for* **Akila**. *Music signifies the passing of time. Perhaps there is a tally on the wall or the floor in chalk to denote how many nights have passed.*

1,000 Nights

All the women are sat staring into space. Pens down. They are stuck. Blocked. Fucked.

Fatah *suddenly draws in a breath as if inspiration has taken her. They all look at her expectantly, hopefully. She grabs a candle and moves to the centre of the stage – it seems as if she is about to tell a story.*

She breathes in and is about to speak but then slowly doubts herself, shakes her head and blows the candle out.

Everyone sighs disappointed.

Fatah *returns to her place, depressed.*

Pause.

Zuya There are no more left.

Wadiha We've used them all up

Naha I knew this would happen

Akila He was right.

Fatah Who?

Akila Some old white guy. He said there are only seven kinds of story.

Fatah Seven?

Akila Overcoming the Monster. Rags to Riches. The Quest. Voyage and Return. Rebirth. Comedy. Tragedy.

Beat.

Akila And we've told them all.

Wadiha Hundreds of times.

Zuya There's no more stories.

Akila If that's true, then what will I do? Writing is my job – there's nothing else for me!

Wadiha You'll have to become a wife. Be happy with that. Like everyone else.

276 Hakawatis: The Women of the Arabian Nights

Fatah I'm not going to marry. All this has made me sure.

Zuya You won't have a choice if / [Scheherazade fails]

Naha Shush!

Fatah When we get out of here.

Akila If –

Naha That's right – believe little one believe . . .

Fatah I'm going to travel the world. Explore places no one has ever discovered.

Akila We are never getting out of here. If the stories have run out, then Scheherazade must fail. And we will all die. And when he's finished with the women in his country he will move on – his blood lust won't abate. He will travel to the next country and the next – marrying women and slaughtering us like animals – until there are no females left.

Pause as misery sets in.

Zuya Bet you want my fox and wolf story now – but you can't have it.

Akila ZUYA!

Wadiha STOP it! Both of you!

Naha *gets up.*

Naha I don't care about this seven stories idea – we are chefs of words. We are magpies of literature, gatherers of meaning, magicians of text. And most of all we are thieves – we can whisk a story from right under your nose and deliver it back to you afresh . . . Like . . . like . . . like . . . (*eureka*) THE THIEF AND THE DONKEY.

The women are alerted to the story coming – they are incandescent with anticipation – they grab a candle for her and light it as she continues.

All Tell us – tell us, tell us our *HAKAWATI*.

Naha There was once a thief so brilliant that she could steal the eyelashes off your face. She was challenged by another of her kind – who was nowhere as talented – to steal a donkey from a man who was passing. 'I can do it,' the great thief replied, 'but I need your help.' So the two thieves followed the man and the donkey quietly until they came to a fork in the road. There the great thief approached and quietly unbridled the donkey as he was being led – handed him over to the lesser thief who led him to the left fork and put the harness over her own head continuing with the owner to the right. A few minutes later when the man turned around to check his donkey he was amazed to see a woman in his place. 'WHO ARE YOU?' he asked, and 'WHERE IS MY DONKEY?' 'I'm afraid', replied the thief, 'that I am your donkey. You see I have a terrible fondness for wine. And I overindulge. And one night I got so drunk that my father screamed and shouted at me when I got home – so I got a broom and beat him with it – I'm not proud of myself. He in return cursed me to heaven calling me a *H'mara, a Hayawani* and God was listening and turned me into a donkey. Next thing

I know I'm being bought by you at the market. But today – today my Father must have forgiven me and blessed me and so I've turned back into me.'

The man was shocked and apologised for how hard he'd worked the woman when she was a donkey and sent the brilliant thief on her way. The thief had proven her cunning and skill. Several days later she took the donkey to market where his previous owner spotted the beast. As the thief hid she heard the man berate the animal – 'YOUVE BEEN DRINKING AGAIN HAVENT YOU?? AND BEATING YOUR FATHER YOU DEVIL.' The donkey recognised his old master and began to bray, 'BEG AS MUCH AS YOU LIKE I'M NOT BUYING YOU AGAIN,' he replied.

The women all laugh so hard and gather round her to hug her.

Wadiha And not a cock sucking in sight, *mabrouk!*

Zuya When she said donkey I did get worried . . .

They laugh and laugh and blow her candle out with their laughter.

Music signifies the passing of time. Perhaps there is a tally on the wall or the floor in chalk to denote how many nights have passed.

1,001 Nights

The women are all sat around writing. Working hard as usual. Suddenly the doors open. No one moves, they are too engrossed.

Beat.

Then **Fatah** *looks up.*

Fatah The doors are open. EVERYONE – look!

They all look.

Fatah What does it mean?

Wadiha Someone's coming?

Fatah Has he had enough of Scheherazade? Enough of her stories? OH GOD, which of us will be next?

Zuya NO ONE IS TAKING ANY OF US. COME HERE.

They stand together ready for the onslaught.

Zuya We will be ready.

Tense pause.

Nothing happens.

Fatah What will happen?

Akila Why is no one coming?

Zuya I can't bear it – I'm going to find out.

Fatah Don't – ZUYA – you might get in trouble.

Zuya We are all threatened with death – what's worse than that?

She goes.

They all look anxious.

Wadiha Maybe now is the time. Maybe now I'll get to do my dance . . . My last dance.

Akila Can you remember how? We've been in here 1,001 nights. Locked in.

Wadiha Forget dancing? Never. It presses to my memory. It's in my blood, my bones, my soul.

Music starts and she gets up and slowly loosens her hair – she begins to do – not a belly dance but a traditional Saudi Arabian hair dance. The other women watch on mesmerised – then join in one by one . . . it's a slow tune at first but the tempo rises and it gets faster and faster, rising to a climax

As

Zuya *re-enters – out of breath.*

Zuya Stop!

The music and dancing stops suddenly.

Zuya It's over! She did it.

Naha She killed him?

Zuya NO she made him love her. Want to keep her. He fell for all the stories . . .

Beat.

Zuya WE did it. IT'S OVER! WE'RE FREE! FREE!

Cheers and ululations as the women realise it's over.

They all head for the door.

Akila Wait – wait – where are you going?

Naha Didn't you hear her? We are free to go! The stories worked.

Wadiha The King is keeping Scheherazade – for good – and ending his tyrannical revenge.

Fatah I can travel the world.

Zuya I can join the army.

Naha I'm going to buy a puppy . . .

Wadiha And I'm going to set up my own dance studio. Women only.

Fatah What about you, Akila? What will you do?

Akila I'll do what I've always done. Go where it's safe. Here (*tapping her head*) and here (*indicating the page*).

Wadiha Haven't you had enough of stories?

Akila Not yet. And you know why – because every time I tell a story the chaos of the world stops. The mindless violence and unforgiving randomness, the tortuous knife edge disappears. I am in control. Just for a few minutes. And everything makes sense. It's safe.

Fatah Sometimes stories can be scary. They can be bloody. Gruesome. They can get out of hand.

Akila That's the power of the *HAKAWATI* to decide what happens. How it ends.

Beat.

Wadiha Well, good luck.

They all go to leave except **Akila**.

Akila Wait. What about her?

Wadiha Who? Scheherazade?

Akila Yes. We can't leave her.

Zuya Why not?

Fatah How can we be free if she's still captive?

Naha He's her husband.

Wadiha He's a murderer. We need to save her.

Akila That's what we've been doing all this these nights.

Fatah We've been saving ourselves.

Akila And her – all of us . . . and we need to do it again. One last time. Come on. COME ON!

They run out the doors.

The End.

Playwright's Outro

Hakawatis was commissioned by Michelle Terry, Artistic Director of Shakespeare's Globe, and the play was workshopped at the theatre in 2019. At time of publishing the play had yet to be programmed because of COVID-19 closures. When we finished the last day of the aforementioned Globe workshop in 2019, the five actresses – all of whom have a connection to the Arab world – approached me, apologised and then started pulling hairs out of my head. I shouted at them to stop, and asked what they were doing. They threw my hairs onto the stage and told me it was a sort of spell. If we all left a bit of ourselves there, then that would guarantee we would all be back in that space and on that stage again. I hope those wonderful women are right.